Pascalian Meditations

PIERRE BOURDIEU

Translated by Richard Nice

Stanford University Press
Stanford, California

Stanford University Press
Stanford, California
© 1997 Editions du Seuil
This translation © 2000 Polity Press
First published in France as *Méditations pascaliennes*
    by Editions du Seuil
Originating publisher of English edition:
    Polity Press in association with Blackwell Publishers Ltd.
First published in the U.S.A. by Stanford University
    Press, 2000
Published with the assistance of the French
    Ministry of Culture
Printed in Great Britain
Cloth ISBN 0-8047-3331-7
Paper ISBN 0-8047-3332-5
LC 99-71220
This book is printed on acid-free paper.

Contents

Contents

Introduction

∿

If I have resolved to ask some questions that I would rather have left to philosophy, it is because it seemed to me that philosophy, for all its questioning, did not ask them; and because, especially with respect to the social sciences, it never ceased to raise questions that did not seem to me to be essential – while avoiding asking itself about the reasons and above all the (often not very philosophical) causes of its questioning. I wanted to push the critique (in the Kantian sense) of scholarly reason to a point that questionings usually leave untouched and to try to make explicit the presuppositions entailed by the situation of *skholè*, the free time, freed from the urgencies of the world, that allows a free and liberated relation to those urgencies and to the world. And it has been philosophers who, not content with engaging these presuppositions in their practice, like other professional thinkers, have brought them into the order of discourse, not so much to analyse them as to legitimate them.

   In order to justify an inquiry that hopes to open the way to truths that philosophy helps to make it hard to reach, I could have invoked thinkers who are close to being seen by philosophers as enemies of philosophy, because, like Wittgenstein, they make its prime task the dispelling of illusions, especially those that the philosophical tradition produces and reproduces. But, as will become clear, I had various reasons for placing these reflections under the aegis of Pascal. For a long time I had adopted the habit, when asked the (generally ill-intentioned) question of my relations with Marx, of replying that,

all in all, if I really had to affiliate myself, I would say I was more of
a Pascalian. I was thinking in particular of everything that concerns
symbolic power, the aspect through which the affinity appears most
clearly, and other, less often observed, facets of his work, such as the
refusal of the ambition of foundation. But, above all, I had always
been grateful to Pascal, as I understood him, for his concern, devoid
of all populist naivety, for 'ordinary people' and the 'sound opinions
of the people'; and also for his determination, inseparable from that
concern, always to seek the 'reason of effects', the *raison d'être* of the
seemingly most illogical or derisory human behaviours – such as
'spending a whole day in chasing a hare' – rather than condemning
or mocking them, like the 'half-learned' who are always ready to
'play the philosopher' and to seek to astonish with their uncommon
astonishments at the futility of common-sense opinions.

Being convinced that Pascal was right to say that 'true philosophy
makes light of philosophy', I have often regretted that academic pro-
prieties prevented me from taking this invitation literally: more than
once I have wanted to fight the symbolic violence that is often exercised, firstly on philosophers themselves, in the name of philosophy,
with the weapons most commonly used to counteract the effects of
that violence – irony, pastiche or parody. I envied the freedom of
writers (Thomas Bernhard on Heideggerian kitsch, or Elfriede Jelinek
on the fuliginous clouds of the German idealists), or of the artists who,
from Duchamp to Devautour, have, in their own artistic practice,
constantly subverted the belief in art and artists.

The vanity of attributing immense and immediate effects to philosophy, and to the utterances of intellectuals, seems to me to be the
example par excellence of what Schopenhauer called 'pedantic com-
edy', by which he meant the ridicule one incurs when performing an
action that is not included in one's concept, like a stage horse that
defecates on stage. Now, if there is one thing that our 'modern' or
'postmodern' philosophers have in common, beyond the conflicts that
divide them, it is this excessive confidence in the powers of language.
It is the typical illusion of the *lector*, who can regard an academic
commentary as a political act or the critique of texts as a feat of
resistance, and experience revolutions in the order of words as radical
revolutions in the order of things.

How can one avoid succumbing to this dream of omnipotence,
which tends to arouse fits of bedazzled identification with great
heroic roles? I think it is important above all to reflect not only on
the limits of thought and of the powers of thought, but also on the
conditions in which it is exercised, which lead so many thinkers to
overstep the limits of a social experience that is necessarily partial
and local, both geographically and socially, and restricted to a small

region, always the same, of the social universe, as is shown by the limited scope of the references invoked, often restricted to one discipline and one national tradition. Attentive observation of the course of the world should, however, incline them to more humility, because it is so clear that intellectual powers are most efficacious when they are exercised in the same direction as the immanent tendencies of the social world, at which time they indubitably redouble, through omission or compromise, the effects of the forces of the world, which are also expressed through them.

I am well aware that what I have to say here, which for a long time I wanted to leave at least partly in the implicit state of a practical sense of theoretical things, is rooted in the singular, and singularly limited, experiences of a particular existence; and that the events of the world, or the minor dramas of university life, can have a very profound effect on consciousnesses and unconsciouses. Does that imply that what I say is thereby particularized or relativized? The unceasing interest that the 'gentlemen of Port-Royal' showed in authority and obedience, and their determination to reveal its principles, has been related to the fact that, although very privileged, especially in cultural terms, they almost all belonged to the bourgeois aristocracy of the *robins* (*noblesse de robe*), a social category still very distinct, in the eyes of others and in itself, from the *noblesse d'épee* under whose insolence they chafed. Their special lucidity as regards aristocratic values and the symbolic foundations of authority, especially that of title, may well have owed something to the marginal position that inclined them to critical dispositions towards the temporal powers of Church or State, but this in no way invalidates the truths it reveals.

The vestiges of religious or political moralism that lurk behind a number of apparently epistemological questionings have to be repudiated. In the order of thought, there is, as Nietzsche pointed out, no immaculate conception; but nor is there any original sin – and the discovery that someone who has discovered the truth had an interest in doing so in no way diminishes his discovery. Those who like to believe in the miracle of 'pure' thought must bring themselves to accept that the love of truth or virtue, like any other kind of disposition, necessarily owes something to the conditions in which it was formed, in other words a social position and trajectory. I am even fairly convinced that, in thinking about the things of the intellectual life, where so many of our investments are placed, and where, as a consequence, the 'refusal to know' or even the 'hatred of truth' that Pascal refers to are particularly intense (if only in the inverted form of the perverse false lucidity of resentment), a degree of personal interest in unveiling (which may well be denounced as denunciation) is no bad thing.

But the extreme vulnerability of the historical sciences, which are in the front line of the danger of relativization that they introduce, does have some advantages. And I could invoke the particular vigilance towards the injunctions or seductions of intellectual trends and fashions that results from constantly taking them as one's object; and above all, the work of critique, verification and elaboration – in a word, sublimation – that I have brought to bear on the impulses, revolt or indignation that lie behind a given intuition or anticipation. When I uncompromisingly examined the world to which I belonged, I could not but be aware that I necessarily fell under the scrutiny of my own analyses, and that I was providing instruments that could be turned against me. The image of the 'biter bit' simply designates one very effective form of reflexivity as I understand it – as a collective enterprise.

Being aware that the privilege given to those who are in a position to 'play seriously', in Plato's phrase, because their estate (or, nowadays, the State) gives them the means to do so, could slant or limit my thinking, I have always asked of the most radically objectifying instruments of knowledge that I could use that they also serve as instruments of self-knowledge, and not least knowledge of myself as a 'knowing subject'. In this way I learned a lot from two research projects, carried out in very different social milieux – the village of my childhood and the Paris universities – which enabled me to explore some of the most obscure areas of my subjectivity as an objectivist observer.[1] In fact I am convinced that only an enterprise of objectification, divested of the particular indulgence and complacency normally asked for and granted to evocations of the intellectual adventure, makes it possible to discover, with a view to going beyond them, some limits of thought and especially those that arise from privilege.

I have always felt some impatience with 'puffed-up words' [*les mots d'enflure*], as Pascal puts it, and the grand affirmation of peremptory theses that often accompany major intellectual ambitions; and, partly no doubt in reaction against the taste for epistemological and theoretical preliminaries or the endless exegesis of canonical authors, I have never shunned what are regarded as the humblest tasks of the craft of ethnology or sociology – direct observation, interviews, coding or statistical analysis. Without succumbing to the initiatory cult of 'fieldwork' or the positivistic fetishism of 'data', I felt that, by virtue of their more modest and practical content, and because they took me out into the world, these activities, which are in any case no less intelligent than others, were one of the chances I had to escape from the scholastic confinement of the habitués of ministerial offices, libraries, lectures

[1] P. Bourdieu, 'Célibat et condition paysanne', *Études Rurales*, 5–6 (Apr.–Sept. 1962), pp. 32–136; *Homo Academicus*, tr. P. Collier (Cambridge: Polity Press, 1988).

and speeches that I encountered in my professional life. So I could have attached to almost every line the references to empirical investigations, some of them going back thirty years before the moment at which I now write, which made me feel I was authorized to put forward the general propositions that they presupposed or that they had enabled me to establish, without providing all the supporting evidence at each point and in a tone that may sometimes appear too abrupt.[2]

The sociologist has the peculiarity, in no way a privilege, of being the person whose task is to tell about the things of the social world, and, as far as possible, to tell them the way they are. In itself, that is normal, even trivial. What makes his (or her) situation paradoxical, sometimes impossible, is that he is surrounded by people who either actively ignore the social world and do not talk about it – and I would be the last to criticize artists, writers or scientists for being totally absorbed in their work – or worry about it and talk about it, sometimes a lot, but without knowing much about it (there are some of these even among recognized sociologists). It is indeed not uncommon that, when associated with ignorance, indifference or contempt, the obligation to speak that derives from suddenly acquired notoriety or the modes and models of the intellectual game inclines people to talk everywhere about the social world, but as if they were not talking about it, or as if one were talking of it to help to forget it and have it forgotten – in a word, while denying it.

So, when he simply does what he has to do, the sociologist breaks the enchanted circle of collective denial. By working towards the 'return of the repressed', by trying to know and make known what the world of knowledge does not want to know, especially about itself, he takes the risk of appearing as the one who 'gives the game away' – but to whom, except to those with whom, in so doing, he breaks ranks, and from whom he cannot expect recognition for his discoveries, his revelations or his confessions (which are necessarily a little perverse, it has to be said, because they are also valid, by proxy, for all his kind)?

I know fairly well what one can expect from working to combat the repression, so strong in the pure and perfect world of thought, of everything that touches on social reality. I know that I shall have to confront the virtuous indignation of those who reject the very principle of the effort to objectify – either because, in the name of the

---

[2] As regards both my own works and works by others which have been useful to me, I have limited myself here to the references that seemed indispensable to those who might themselves wish to extend the research; and I am well aware that the middle way I have chosen, after much hesitation, between a total absence of references and the long enumerations of the names of philosophers, ethnologists, sociologists, historians, economists, psychologists, etc. whom I could and perhaps should have invoked at each moment, is simply the least bad solution.

irreducibility of the 'subject' and its immersion in time, which condemns it to endless change and singularity, they identify every attempt
to convert it into an object of science with a kind of usurpation of a
divine attribute (Kierkegaard, more lucid on this point than a number
of his acolytes, talks, in his *Journal*, of 'blasphemy'); or because, being
convinced of their own exceptionality, they only see there a form of
'denunciation', inspired by 'hatred' of the object (philosophy, art or
literature) to which it is applied.

It is tempting (and 'profitable') to proceed as if a simple reminder
of the social conditions of 'creation' were the expression of a desire
to reduce the unique to the generic, the singular to the class; as if the
observation that the social world imposes constraints and limits on
the 'purest' thought, that of scientists, artists and writers, were the
effect of a bias towards denigration; as if determinism, for which
sociologists are so much reproached, were, like liberalism or socialism, or some aesthetic or political preference, a matter of belief or
even a sort of cause on which one took up a position, either for or
against; as if the commitment to science were, in the case of sociology, a prejudice, inspired by resentment, against all intellectual
'good causes', singularity and freedom, transgression and subversion,
difference and dissidence, the open and the plural, etc.

Faced with the pharisaical denunciations of my 'denunciations', I
have often regretted not having followed the example of Mallarmé,
who, refusing to 'perform, in public, the impious dismantling of the
fiction and consequently of the literary mechanism, to display the
principal part or nothing',[3] chose to save the fiction, and the collective belief in the game, by enunciating this seminal nothingness only
in the mode of denegation. But I could not be satisfied with the
answer he provided to the question whether one should utter publicly the constitutive mechanisms of social games that are as shrouded
in prestige and mystery as those of art, literature, science, law or
philosophy and charged with the values commonly held to be the
most universal and the most sacred. To opt to keep the secret, or to
unveil it only in a strictly veiled form, as Mallarmé does, is to pre-
judge that only a few great initiates are capable of the heroic lucidity
and willed generosity that are necessary in order to confront the
enigma of fiction and fetishism.

---

[3] S. Mallarmé, 'La musique et les lettres', in *Œuvres complètes*, ed. H. Mondor and
G. Jean-Aubry (Paris: Gallimard, Bibliothèque de la Pléiade, 1970), p. 647. I have
offered an analysis of this text, likely to provoke shudders in the pious celebrants of
the seraphic poet of absence, who have turned a blind eye to it, in *The Rules of Art:
Genesis and Structure of the Literary Field*, tr. Susan Emanuel (Cambridge: Polity
Press, 1996), pp. 274–7.

Conscious of all the expectations that I was forced to frustrate, all the unexamined dogmas of 'humanist' conviction and 'artistic' faith that I was obliged to defy, I have often cursed the fate (or the logic) that required me consciously to take up such a difficult cause, to engage, armed only with the weapons of rational discourse, in a struggle that was perhaps lost in advance against enormous social forces, such as the weight of habits of thought, cognitive interests and cultural beliefs bequeathed by several centuries of literary, artistic or philosophical worship.

This feeling was all the more paralysing because as I wrote on *skholè* and all these other things, I could not fail to feel the ricochet of my own words. I had never before felt with such intensity the strangeness of my project, a kind of *negative philosophy* that was liable to appear self-destructive. On other occasions, to try to still anxiety or worry, I have been able, sometimes explicitly, to assign myself the role of public scribe and try to convince myself – and also those I carried with me – of the certainty of being useful in saying things which are not said but deserve to be. But once these (so to speak) 'public service' functions were set aside, what remains by way of justifications?

I have never really felt justified in existing as an intellectual; and I have always tried – as I have tried again here – to exorcise everything in my thinking that might be linked to that status, such as philosophical intellectualism. I do not like the intellectual in myself, and what may sound, in my writing, like anti-intellectualism is chiefly directed against the intellectualism or intellectuality that remains in me, despite all my efforts, such as the difficulty, so typical of intellectuals, I have in accepting that my freedom has its limits.

To conclude these preliminary considerations, I would like to ask my readers, even the most well disposed of them, to suspend the preconceived or precautionary ideas they may have of my work and, more generally, of the social sciences, ideas which sometimes oblige me to return to questions that I believe I settled a long time ago, as I shall do again here, in clarifications which should not be confused with the doubling back and the revivals required by the sometimes imperceptible progress of research. I do indeed have the sense of having been rather ill-understood, partly, no doubt, because of the idea people often have of sociology, based on vague school memories or unfortunate encounters with the most salient members of the corporation, which can, alas, only reinforce the politico-journalistic image of the discipline. The diminished status of this pariah science inclines the poorly sighted to think that they surpass what surpasses them and the ill-intentioned to produce a deliberately reductive image without incurring the sanctions normally attached to excessively flagrant transgressions of the 'principle of charity'. These prejudices seem to me all the more unjust or inappropriate because part of my work has consisted in reversing a good number of modes of thought current in the analysis of the social world (starting with the vestiges of a Marxist vulgate which, beyond political affiliations, clouded the brains of more than one generation). The analyses and models that I put forward were thus often perceived through categories of thought which, like the obligatory alternatives of dualistic thought (mechanism/finalism, objectivism/ subjectivism, holism/individualism), were precisely rejected.

But I do not forget all that was due to myself, to my difficulty in explaining or my reluctance to explain; nor the fact that the obstacles to comprehension, perhaps especially when social things are in question, have less, as Wittgenstein observed, to do with the understanding than with the will. I am often surprised at the time it has taken me – and this is probably not over – really to understand some of the things I had been saying for a long time with the sense of knowing exactly what I was saying. And if I rework the same themes and return several times to the same objects and the same analyses, it is always, I think, in a spiralling movement which makes it possible to attain each time a higher level of explicitness and comprehension, and to discover unnoticed relationships and hidden properties. 'I cannot judge of my work, while doing it. I must do as the artists, stand at a distance; but not too far.'[4] I too have wanted to find the point from which the whole of my work might be seen in a single gaze, relieved of the confusions and obscurities that I could see there 'while doing it' and which one lingers on when looking from too close. Being inclined rather to leave things in the practical state, I had to convince myself that I would not be wasting my time and trouble in trying to make explicit the principles of the *modus operandi* that I have implemented in my work and also the idea of 'the human being' that, inevitably, I have engaged in my scientific choices. I do not know if I have succeeded, but I have in any case acquired the conviction that the social world would be better known, and scientific discourse about it would be better understood, if one were able to convince oneself that there are not many objects more difficult to understand, especially because it haunts the brains of those who try to analyse it, and because it conceals under the most trivial appearances, those of daily banality for daily newspapers, available to any researcher, the most unexpected revelations about what we least want to know about what we are.

---

[4] Pascal, *Pensées*, 114. (The translations from the *Pensées* are those of W. F. Trotter, see *Pascal's Pensées* (London and Toronto: Dent, 1931). *Trans.*)

I

Critique of
Scholastic Reason

∿

It is because we are implicated in the world that there is implicit content in what we think and say about it. In order to free our thinking of the implicit, it is not sufficient to perform the return of thought onto itself that is commonly associated with the idea of reflexivity; and only the illusion of the omnipotence of thought could lead one to believe that the most radical doubt is capable of suspending the presuppositions, linked to our various affiliations, memberships, implications, that we engage in our thoughts. The unconscious is history – the collective history that has produced our categories of thought, and the individual history through which they have been inculcated in us. It is, for example, from the social history of educational institutions (a supremely banal one, absent from the history of philosophical or other ideas), and from the (forgotten or repressed) history of our singular relationship to these institutions, that we can expect some real revelations about the objective and subjective structures (classifications, hierarchies, problematics, etc.) that always, in spite of ourselves, orient our thought.

Implication and the implicit

Renouncing the illusion of the self-transparency of consciousness and the representation of reflexivity commonly accepted among philosophers (and even accepted by some sociologists, like Alvin Gouldner, who recommends under this name an intimist exploration of the contingencies of personal experience[1]), one has to resign oneself to acknowledging, in the typically positivist tradition of the critique of introspection, that the most effective reflection is the one that consists in objectifying the subject of objectification. I mean by that the one that dispossesses the knowing subject of the privilege it normally grants itself and that deploys all the available instruments of objectification (statistical surveys, ethnographic observation, historical research, etc.) in order to bring to light the presuppositions it owes to its inclusion in the object of knowledge.[2]

These presuppositions are of three different orders. To start with the most superficial, there are those associated with occupation of a position in social space, and the particular trajectory that has led to it, and with gender (which can affect the relationship to the object in many ways, in as much as the sexual division of labour is inscribed in social structures and in cognitive structures, orienting for example the choice of object of study).[3] Then there are those that are constitutive of the *doxa* specific to each of the different fields (religious, artistic, philosophical, sociological, etc.) and, more precisely, those that each particular thinker owes to his position in a field. Finally, there are the presuppositions constituting the *doxa* generically associated with the *skholè*, leisure, which is the condition of existence of all scholarly fields.

Contrary to what is commonly said, especially when people worry about 'ethical neutrality', it is not the first set, in particular religious or political prejudices, which are hardest to apprehend and control. Because they are attached to the particularity of persons or social categories, and are therefore different from one individual to another, from one category to another, they are unlikely to escape the self-interested criticism of those who are driven by other prejudices or convictions.

[1] Cf. A. W. Gouldner, *The Coming Crisis of Western Sociology* (New York: Basic Books, 1970).
[2] The sociology of education, the sociology of cultural production and the sociology of the State, to which I have successively devoted my attention, have thus been for me three stages in a single enterprise of reappropriating the social unconscious which goes beyond declared attempts at 'self-analysis' such as the one presented here – in 'Postscript 1: Impersonal confessions', p. 33 below – or in, for example, an earlier essay in reflexive objectification: cf. P. Bourdieu and J.-C. Passeron, 'Sociology and philosophy in France since 1945: death and resurrection of a philosophy without subject', *Social Research*, 39, no. 1 (Spring 1967), pp. 162–212.
[3] E. Fox Keller, *Reflections on Gender and Science* (New Haven: Yale University Press, 1985). (The opposition between the so-called 'hard' sciences and so-called 'soft' disciplines, in particular art and literature, corresponds fairly closely to the division between the sexes.)

This is not true of the distortions linked to membership of a field and to adherence, which is unanimous within the limits of the field, to the *doxa* which distinctively defines it. The implicit in this case is what is implied in the fact of being caught up in the game, in the *illusio* understood as a fundamental belief in the interest of the game and the value of the stakes which is inherent in that membership. Entry into a scholastic universe presupposes a suspension of the presuppositions of common sense and a *para-doxal* commitment to a more or less radically new set of presuppositions, linked to the discovery of stakes and demands neither known nor understood by ordinary experience. Each field is characterized by the pursuit of a specific goal, tending to favour no less absolute investments by all (and only) those who possess the required dispositions (for example, *libido sciendi*). Taking part in the *illusio* – scientific, literary, philosophical or other – means taking seriously (sometimes to the point of making them questions of life and death) stakes which, arising from the logic of the game itself, establish its 'seriousness', even if they may escape or appear 'disinterested' or 'gratuitous' to those who are sometimes called 'lay people' or those who are engaged in other fields (since the independence of the different fields entails a form of non-communicability between them).

The specific logic of a field is established in the incorporated state in the form of a specific habitus, or, more precisely, a sense of the game, ordinarily described as a 'spirit' or 'sense' ('philosophical', 'literary', 'artistic', etc.), which is practically never set out or imposed in an explicit way. Because it takes place insensibly, in other words gradually, progressively and imperceptibly, the conversion of the original habitus, a more or less radical process (depending on the distance), which is required by entry into the game and acquisition of the specific habitus, passes for the most part unnoticed.

If the implications of inclusion in a field are destined to remain implicit, this is precisely because there is nothing of the conscious, deliberate commitment, or the voluntary contract, about it. The original investment has no origin, because it always precedes itself and, when we deliberate on entry into the game, the die is already more or less cast. 'We are embarked,' as Pascal puts it. To speak of a decision to 'commit oneself' to scientific or artistic life (as in any other of the fundamental investments of life – vocation, passion, devotion) is, as Pascal himself was well aware, almost as absurd as evoking a decision to believe, as he does, with few illusions, in the argument of the wager. To hope that the unbeliever can be persuaded to decide to believe because he has been shown by cogent reasons that he who gambles on the existence of God risks a finite investment to win infinite profit, one would have to believe him disposed to believe sufficiently in reason to be sensitive to the reasons of that demonstration. But, as Pascal himself very well puts it, 'we are as much automatic as intellectual; and hence it comes that the instrument by which conviction is attained is not demonstration alone. How few things are demonstrated! Proofs only convince the mind. Custom is the source of our strongest and most believed proofs. It inclines the automaton, which persuades the mind without its thinking about the matter.'[4] Pascal thus recalls the difference, which the scholastic existence leads one to forget, between what is logically implied and what is practically entailed through the paths of 'habit which, without violence, without art, without argument, makes us believe things'.[5] Belief, even the belief that is the basis of the universe of science, is of the order of the automaton, the body, which, as Pascal never ceases to remind us, 'has its reasons, of which reason knows nothing'.

The ambiguity of the scholastic disposition

But there is no doubt nothing more difficult to apprehend, for those who are immersed in universes in which it goes without saying, than the scholastic disposition demanded by those universes. There is nothing that 'pure' thought finds it harder to think than *skholè*, the first and most determinant of all the social conditions of possibility of 'pure' thought, and also the scholastic disposition which inclines its possessors to suspend the demands of the situation, the constraints of economic and social necessity, and the urgencies it imposes or the ends it proposes. In *Sense and Sensibilia* J. L. Austin refers in passing to the 'scholastic view', giving as an example the fact of enumerating or examining all the possible senses of a word, without any reference to the immediate context, instead of simply observing or using the sense of the word which is directly compatible with the situation.[6]

Developing what is implied in Austin's example, one could say that the 'as if' posture – very close to the 'let's pretend' mode of play which enables children to open imaginary worlds – is, as Hans Vaihinger showed in *The Philosophy of 'As If'*, what makes possible all intellectual speculations, scientific hypotheses, 'thought experiments',

---

[4] Pascal, *Pensées*, 252.
[5] Ibid.
[6] J. L. Austin, *Sense and Sensibilia* (Oxford and New York: Oxford University Press, 1962) , pp. 3–4.

'possible worlds' or 'imaginary variations'.[7] It is what incites people to enter into the play-world of theoretical conjecture and mental experimentation, to raise problems for the pleasure of solving them, and not because they arise in the world, under the pressure of urgency, or to treat language not as an instrument but as an object of contemplation, formal invention or analysis.

Failing to make the connection, suggested by etymology, between the 'scholastic point of view' and *skholè*, philosophically consecrated by Plato (through the now canonical opposition between those who, engaged in philosophy, 'talk at their leisure in peace' and those who, in the courts, 'are always in a hurry – for the water flowing through the water-clock urges them on'[8]), Austin fails to address the question of the social conditions of possibility of this very particular stand-point on the world and, more precisely, on language, the body, time or any other object of thought. He therefore does not realize that what makes possible this view which is indifferent to context and practical ends, this distant and distinctive relation to words and things, is nothing other than *skholè*. This time liberated from practical occupa-tions and preoccupations, of which the school (*skholè* again) organizes a privileged form, studious leisure, is the precondition for scholastic exercises and activities removed from immediate necessity, such as sport, play, the production and contemplation of works of art and all forms of gratuitous speculation with no other end than themselves. (Let it suffice to indicate here – I shall return to this – that, failing to bring out all the implications of his intuition of the 'scholastic view', Austin was unable to see in *skholè* and the scholastic 'language game' the source of a number of fallacies typical of the philosophical thought which, following Wittgenstein and along with other 'ordinary lan-guage philosophers', he endeavoured to analyse and exorcise.)

The scholastic situation (of which the academic world repres-ents the institutionalized form) is a site and a moment of social

---

[7] H. Vaihinger, *The Philosophy of 'As If': A System of the Theoretical, Practical and Religious Fictions of Mankind*, tr. C. K. Ogden (London: Kegan Paul, Trench, Trubner; New York: Harcourt Brace, 1924).

[8] Plato, *Theaetetus*, 172–176c. When he distinguishes those who, 'brought up in freedom and leisure . . . from their youth up, remain ignorant of the way to the agora', from those who have been brought up for 'deceit and requiting wrong with wrong' or who, like shepherds, are 'coarse and uncivilized, for lack of leisure', Plato may seem to be relating the modes of thought he distinguishes to modes of life or upbringing or even to conditions of existence; but this does not prevent him from contrasting virtues – freedom, disinterestedness – and vices – egoism, lying, injustice – grounded in a naturalized social hierarchy, thus opening the way for later analyses, such as Heidegger's, which treat conditions of existence and modes of life ('authentic' or 'inauthentic') as if they were elective lifestyles.

weightlessness where, defying the common opposition between play-ing (*paizein*) and being serious (*spoudazein*), one can 'play seriously' (*spoudaiôs paizein*), in the phrase Plato uses to characterize philo-sophical activity, take the stakes in games seriously, deal seriously with questions that 'serious' people, occupied and preoccupied by the practical business of everyday life, ignore. And if the link between the scholastic mode of thought and the mode of existence which is the condition of its acquisition and implementation escapes atten-tion, this is not only because those who might grasp it are like fish in water in the situation of which their dispositions are the product, but also because the essential part of what is transmitted in and by that situation is a hidden effect of the situation itself.

Learning situations, and especially scholastic exercises in the sense of ludic, gratuitous work, performed in the 'let's pretend' mode, without any real (economic) stake, are the occasion for acquiring, *in addition* to all they explicitly aim to transmit, something essential, namely the scholastic disposition and the set of presuppositions con-tained in the social conditions that make them possible. These condi-tions of possibility, which are conditions of existence, act, as it were, negatively, by default, in particular because they are themselves essen-tially negative, such as the neutralization of practical urgencies and ends and, more precisely, the fact of being detached for a more or less long time from work and the world of work, from serious activ-ity, sanctioned by monetary compensation, or, more generally, of being more or less completely exempted from all the negative experi-ences associated with privation or uncertainty about the morrow. (A quasi-experimental confirmation: for many children of working-class origin, more or less prolonged access to secondary education and to the suspended time between the ludic activities of childhood and adult work, which was previously reserved for bourgeois adolescents, leads to a breaking of the cycle of reproduction of the dispositions which would have prepared them to accept factory work.)[9] The schol-astic disposition which is acquired mainly in experience of education can be perpetuated even when the conditions of its exercise have more or less completely disappeared (with entry into the world of work). But it is truly fulfilled only by inclusion in a scholarly field and especially in one of the fields which, being almost totally limited to the scholastic universe, like the philosophical field and a number of scientific fields, offer the conditions favouring its full development.

[9] For a more detailed analysis of this effect of 'studentification', see P. Bourdieu and P. Champagne, 'Outcasts on the inside', in P. Bourdieu et al., *The Weight of the World* (Cambridge: Polity Press, 1999).

The presuppositions contained in this disposition – the entry requirement demanded by all scholastic universes and the indispensable condition for excelling in one of them – constitute what I shall call, in an oxymoron likely to awaken philosophers from their scholastic slumber, the *epistemic doxa*. Nothing, paradoxically, is more dogmatic than a *doxa*, a set of fundamental beliefs which does not even need to be asserted in the form of an explicit, self-conscious dogma. The 'free' and 'pure' disposition favoured by *skholè* implies (active or passive) ignorance not only of what happens in the world of practice (brought to light by the anecdote of Thales and the Thracian servant girl[10]), and, more precisely, in the order of the *polis* and politics, but also of what it is to exist, quite simply, in the world. It also and especially implies more or less triumphant ignorance of that ignorance and of the economic and social conditions that make it possible.

There is a downside to the autonomy of the scholastic fields, a cost entailed in the social break that is favoured by economic separation. Although it is experienced as free and elective, independence from all determinations is only acquired and exercised in and through an effective distance from economic and social necessity (through which it is closely linked to occupation of privileged positions in the sexual and social hierarchy). The *fundamental ambiguity* of the scholastic universes and of all their productions – universal acquisitions made accessible by an exclusive privilege – lies in the fact that their apartness from the world of production is both a liberatory break and a disconnection, a potentially crippling separation. While the suspension of economic or social necessity is what allows the emergence of autonomous fields, 'orders' (in Pascal's sense) which know and recognize only their specific law, it is also what, in the absence of special vigilance, threatens to confine scholastic thought within the limits of ignored or repressed presuppositions, implied in the withdrawal from the world.

Thus it has to be acknowledged that, though they do not have a monopoly on the scholastic posture, only those who gain entry to the scholastic universes are in a position to realize fully this universal anthropological possibility. Awareness of this privilege forbids one to consign to inhumanity or 'barbarism' those who, because they do not have this advantage, are not able to fulfil all their human potentialities. It also forbids one to forget the limits that scholastic thought

[10] 'While [Thales] was studying the stars and looking upwards, he fell into a pit, and a neat, witty Thracian servant girl jeered at him, they say, because he was so eager to know the things in the sky that he could not see what was there before him at his very feet' (Plato, *Theaetetus*, 174a). *Trans.*

owes to the very special conditions of its emergence, which one must methodically explore in order to try to free it from them.

The genesis of the scholastic disposition

Ethnology and history bear witness that the various dispositions towards the natural world and the social world, and the various anthropologically possible ways of constructing the world – magical or technical, emotional or rational, practical or theoretical, instrumental or aesthetic, serious or ludic, etc. – have very unequal probability, because they are encouraged and rewarded to very unequal degrees in different societies, depending on the degree of freedom with respect to necessity and immediate urgencies that is provided there by the state of the available technologies and economic and cultural resources; and, within a given society, depending on the position occupied within the social space. Although there is no reason to suppose that it is not randomly distributed among different societies and among the different strata of differentiated societies, the anthropological possibility of entering into the detached, gratuitous, ludic relationship with the world that is presupposed by most of the practices considered the most noble encounters very different opportunities for self-realization within those different societies and strata. The same is true of the inclination to adopt a magical attitude towards the world, which was much more improbable for a French philosopher of the 1950s like Jean-Paul Sartre, who evokes such an experience in his *Sketch for a Theory of the Emotions*, than for a Trobriand islander in the 1930s as described by Malinowski. Whereas in the former case this way of seeing the world only arises exceptionally, as an accident provoked by a critical situation, in the latter case it is constantly encouraged and favoured both by the extreme uncertainty and unpredictability of the conditions of existence and by the socially approved responses to those conditions, foremost among which is what is called magic, a practical relation to the world which is instituted in collective rites and thereby constituted as a normal element of normal human behaviour in that society.

Thus the different kinds of 'world-making' have to be related to the economic and social conditions that make them possible. This means that one has to move beyond the 'philosophy of symbolic forms' in Cassirer's sense to a *differential anthropology of symbolic forms*, or, to put it another way, to extend Durkheim's analysis of the social genesis of 'forms of thought' by means of an analysis of the variations in the cognitive dispositions towards the world according to social positions and historical situations. As one moves away from the lower regions of the social space, characterized by the extreme brutality of the economic constraints, the uncertainties diminish and the pressures of economic and social necessity relax. As a consequence, less strictly defined positions, which leave more scope for manoeuvre, offer the possibility of acquiring dispositions that are freer in respect of practical urgencies – problems to solve, opportunities to exploit – and seemingly preadjusted to the tacit demands of the scholastic universes. One of the least visible of the advantages attached to birth lies in the detached, distant disposition – shown, *inter alia*, in what Erving Goffman calls 'role distance' – that is acquired in early experience relatively free from necessity. This disposition, together with the inherited cultural capital with which it is associated, makes an essential contribution towards favouring access to schooling and success in scholastic exercises – especially the most formal ones, which demand the capacity to participate simultaneously or successively in various 'mental spaces', as Gilles Fauconnier puts it – and so towards enabling the final entry into the scholastic universes.

While all learning, even among animals, makes room for play (increasingly so at higher levels of evolution), only the educational system sets up the very special set of conditions that are required in order for the conducts that are to be taught to be able to be performed, outside of the situations in which they are pertinent, in the form of 'serious games' and 'gratuitous' exercises, abstract actions without reference to any useful effect and without dangerous consequences.[11] Learning in school, which, because it is freed from the direct sanction of reality, can offer challenges, tests and problems, similar to real situations but leaving the possibility of seeking and trying out solutions in conditions of minimum risk, is the occasion to acquire, in addition, through habituation, the permanent disposition to set up the distance from directly perceived reality which is the precondition for most symbolic constructions.

The great repression

But the scholastic disposition derives its most significant features from the process of differentiation through which the various fields of symbolic production gained autonomy and constituted themselves as

[11] On this whole point, and especially on the fact that the importance given to didactic interaction and the freedom available to it increase at higher levels of the evolution of animal species, see J. S. Bruner, *Toward a Theory of Instruction* (Cambridge: Harvard University Press, 1966); *Poverty and Childhood* (Detroit: Merrill-Palmer Institute, 1970).

such, thus distinguishing themselves from the economic universe which
was being constituted at the same time. This process is inseparable
from the full-scale symbolic revolution through which European
societies gradually managed to overcome the denial of the economic
on which precapitalist societies were founded and, in a kind of confession made to themselves, to acknowledge explicitly that economic
actions really had the economic ends to which they had always been
oriented.

(The philosophical field is undoubtedly the first scholastic field to
have constituted itself by achieving autonomy with respect to the
developing political field and the religious field, in Greece in the fifth
century BC; and the history of this process of autonomization and
the creation of a universe of argument governed by its own rules is
inseparable from the history of the process which led from analogical
reason (that of myth or rite) to logical reason (that of philosophy).
Reflection on the logic of argumentation, first mythical (with, in
particular, consideration of analogy), then rhetorical and logical,
accompanied the constitution of a field of competition, freed from
the prescriptions of religious wisdom without being dominated by
the constraints of an academic monopoly. In this field, everyone acted
as an audience for everyone else, was constantly attentive to the others
and determined by what they said, in a permanent confrontation which
progressively took itself as its object and was fulfilled in a search for
rules of logic inseparable from a search for rules of communication
and intersubjective agreement.

This prototype of the scholastic world presented in an ideal-typical
form all the features of the scholastic break. For example, myths and
rites ceased to be practical acts of belief obeying a practical logic –
which was ceasing to be understood – and became instead matter for
theoretical astonishment and questioning, or objects of hermeneutic
rivalry, particularly through the introduction of more or less subtle
shifts in the interpretation of the consecrated culture or the distinctive reintroduction of neglected myths such as those of Hecate or
Prometheus. Typically scholastic problems also arose, such as the
question of whether excellence can be taught. The third generation of
sophists and the institutionalization of the school saw the emergence
of the gratuitous intellectual game, eristic (the 'art of disputation'),
and interest in discourse for its own sake, in its logical or aesthetic
form. But the consequences of the institutionalization of *skholè* in an
academic order (the very ones which are recorded in the ordinary,
pejorative, usage of the adjective 'scholastic') appeared with total
clarity in the Middle Ages, when, for example, philosophy, ceasing to
be a way of life, became a purely theoretical and abstract activity,

increasingly reduced to a discourse, articulated in a technical language reserved for specialists.

When, in Renaissance Italy, after a long eclipse, there reappeared a scholastic field in which the process of differentiation of religion and science, analogical reason and logical reason, alchemy and chemistry, astrology and astronomy, politics and sociology, etc. started up again,[12] the first cracks were already opening up. They were steadily enlarged, leading to the complete secession of the scientific, literary and artistic fields, and beginning a process of autonomization with respect to the philosophical field, which, having lost most of its traditional objects, was forced into constant redefinition, especially of its relationship with the other fields and the knowledge they have of their objects.)

Only at the end of a slow evolution tending to strip away the specifically symbolic aspect of the acts and relations of production was the economy able to constitute itself *as such*, in the objectivity of a separate universe, governed by its own rules, those of self-interested calculation, competition and exploitation; and also, much later, in 'pure' economic theory which records the social separation and the practical abstraction of which the economic *cosmos* is the product, while tacitly writing it into the principle of its object construction. But, conversely, it was only by means of a break tending to repress the economic aspect of the specifically symbolic acts and relations of production into the lower world of the economy that the various universes of symbolic production were able to constitute themselves as closed, separate microcosms in which thoroughly symbolic, pure and (from the point of view of the economic economy) disinterested actions were performed, based on the refusal or repression of the element of productive labour that they implied. (The process of autonomization and 'purification' of the various universes is moreover far from complete, both on the side of the economy, which still leaves considerable room for symbolic facts and effects, and on the side of symbolic activities, which always have a denied economic dimension.)

To understand this double break, it is not sufficient to take account of one or another of the various social transformations which have accompanied the development of the economic economy, whether the emergence of 'specialists in practical knowledge' – engineers, technicians, accountants, jurists, doctors – who, as Sartre suggests in his *Plaidoyer pour les intellectuels*, are somehow predisposed, by a

---

[12] A process magnificently described in E. Cassirer, *The Individual and the Cosmos in Renaissance philosophy* (Oxford: Blackwell, 1963).

mysterious expressive correspondence, to fulfil the role of 'organic
intellectuals of the bourgeoisie'; or the rise of a 'corporation' of men
of letters, inclined to extend to politics the principle of critical public
debate which they have set up in the republic of letters, as Habermas
indicates in his analysis of the 'structural transformations of the public space'.[13] In fact, all the new agents, who, it is not untrue to say,
have contributed to the invention of the universal and even, through
the 'Enlightenment philosophers', made themselves its spokesmen,
were able to perform this function only because they were caught up
in relatively autonomous fields whose necessity, which they helped to
bring about, imposed itself on them.

Having freed itself by stages from immediate material preoccupations, in particular with the aid of the profits secured by direct or
indirect sale of practical knowledge to commercial undertakings or
the State, and having accumulated, through and for their work,
competences (initially acquired through education) that could function as cultural capital, they were increasingly inclined and also able
to assert their individual and collective autonomy vis-à-vis the economic and political powers who needed their services (and also vis-à-
vis the aristocracies based on birth, against which they asserted the
justifications of merit and, increasingly, of the 'gift'). But, in return,
the logic of the emerging scholarly fields and of the internal competition made possible by the social break with the universe of the economy and the world of practice, forcing them to mobilize the specific
resources accumulated through previous struggles, at every moment,
in their present struggles, led them to create the specific rules and
regulations of microcosms governed by a social logic favouring systematization and rationalization and so to advance the various forms
(legal, scientific, artistic, etc.) of rationality and universality.

The repression of the material determinations of symbolic practices is particularly visible in the early moments of the autonomization
of the artistic field. Through the permanent confrontation between
artists and patrons, painterly activity progressively asserted itself as a
specific activity, irreducible to a simple labour of material production
that could be evaluated purely in terms of the value of the time spent
and the paint consumed, and consequently claiming the status accorded
to the noblest intellectual activities.[14] The slow, painful process of

---

[13] J. Habermas, *The Structural Transformation of the Public Sphere: An Inquiry into
a Category of Bourgeois Society* (Cambridge: Polity Press, 1989).
[14] Cf. esp. M. Baxandall, *Painting and Experience in Fifteenth Century Italy: A
Primer in the Social History of Pictorial Style* (Oxford: Clarendon, 1972); M. Biagioli,
Galileo Courtier: The Practice of Science in the Culture of Absolutism (Chicago:
University of Chicago Press, 1993).

sublimation through which pictorial practice asserted itself as a purely symbolic activity denying its material conditions of possibility has a clear affinity with the process of differentiation of productive labour and symbolic labour that proceeded at the same time. The emergence of universes which, like the scholastic worlds, offer positions in which one can feel entitled to perceive the world as a representation, a spectacle, to survey it from above and from afar and organize it as a whole designed for knowledge alone, no doubt favoured the development of a new disposition or, one might say, world view, in the literal sense, which found expression as much in the first 'scientific' maps as in the Galilean representation of the world or in pictorial perspective.

(Recently rereading Durkheim's *The Evolution of Educational Thought*, I was again struck by his splendid evocation of how the educated men of the sixteenth century discovered the world-view that I call scholastic: 'It seems then, in a general way, that in the sixteenth century, at least throughout that part of cultivated society whose ideas and sentiments have come down to us through literature . . . a style of life was thought to be realizable and to be in the process of being realized which would be liberated from all preoccupation, unencumbered by any constraint and servitude, a kind of life in which activity would not be forced to submit itself to narrowly utilitarian ends, to canalize itself, to regulate itself so that it could adapt to reality; but it would rather be expended for the sheer pleasure of the expenditure, for the glory and the beauty of the spectacle which it performs to itself when it can be employed in complete freedom, without having to take into account reality and its exigencies.' Durkheim does indeed relate 'the sense of power, of autonomy, of independence, of leisurely, unfettered activity' which was felt by the people of the Renaissance and expressed, in particular, in educational theories in which 'the immediate necessities of life, as well as the urgent need to prepare the child in advance to confront them, seem to have been lost sight of', to the appearance of a new lifestyle, itself linked to new conditions of existence; and he sees very clearly that, beyond their differences, the various educational systems, humanist or erudite, arising from these conditions, were all 'aimed at the sons of a privileged aristocracy for whom the difficulties of serious living did not exist'.)[15]

Perspective, in its historical definition, is no doubt the most accomplished realization of the scholastic vision. It presupposes a single,

---

[15] É. Durkheim, *The Evolution of Educational Thought*, tr. P. Collins (London: Routledge and Kegan Paul, 1977), pp. 218–19.

fixed point of view – and therefore the adoption of the posture of a motionless spectator installed at a point (of view) – and also the use of a frame that cuts out, encloses and abstracts the spectacle with a rigorous, immobile boundary. (It is significant that, to construct a model of vision, Descartes – who, as is well known, gave a privileged place to intuition understood as *vision* – uses, in his *Dioptrics*, the image of an eye placed 'in the expressly made aperture of a window', on the back of which the observer, situated within the *camera obscura*, will see 'perhaps not without admiration and pleasure, a painting that will represent most naturally in perspective all the objects that are outside'.)[16] This singular viewpoint can also be regarded as universal, since all the 'subjects' who find themselves placed there – bodies reduced to a pure gaze, and therefore indifferent and interchangeable – are, like the Kantian subject, assured of having the same objective view, the one of which perspectival representation, as a 'symbolic form of an objectification of the subjective',[17] in Panofsky's phrase, performs the objectification.

Thus perspective presupposes a point of view on which no point of view can be taken; one which, like the frame of the Albertian painter, is that through which one sees (*per-spicere*) but which is not seen. And the only way to get a point of view on this blind spot is to put perspective into historical perspective, as Panofsky does. But fully to understand the process of social construction of this distant, lofty gaze, of the historical invention which is the 'scholastic view', one has to relate it to the whole set of transformations of the relation to the world which accompany the differentiation of the economic order and the symbolic orders. Thus, (freely) transposing Ernest Schachtel's analysis of the process in child development which tends progressively to give pre-eminence to the 'senses of distance', sight and hearing, which can be the basis of an objective, active vision of the world, over the 'senses of proximity', touch and taste, oriented towards immediate pleasure and displeasure,[18] one could hypothesize that the conquest of the scholastic view, objectified in perspective, is accompanied by a distancing from the pleasures of the 'senses of proximity', a distancing which, in the order of individual ontogenesis, privileged by Schachtel, is translated into a progressive repression, no doubt more or less radical depending on the milieu, of early child-hood and its 'shameful' pleasures. And in support of this hypothesis

---

[16] R. Descartes, *Œuvres et Lettres* (Paris: Gallimard, 1953), pp. 205–16, esp. p. 207.

[17] E. Panofksy, *Perspective as Symbolic Form* (New York: Zone Books, 1991).

[18] E. Schachtel, *Metamorphosis: On the Development of Affect, Perception, Attention and Memory* (New York: Basic Books, 1959).

one could even put forward some historical observations: those of
Lucien Febvre, for example, who, in his book on Rabelais, notes the
predominance, in the sixteenth century, of the senses of smell, taste
and touch and the relative rarity of visual references, or those of
Bakhtine, which point to the triumphant presence of the body and its
functions in the premodern popular fair.[19]

The individual and collective conquest of the sovereign gaze, which
sees far in spatial but also in temporal terms, giving the possibility of
foreseeing and acting in consequence, at the cost of a repression of
short-term appetites or a deferment of their satisfaction (through an
asceticism tending to give a strong sense of superiority over ordinary
mortals who have to take each day as it comes) was accompanied by
an intellectualist divorce, without equivalent in any of the great civilizations:[20] a divorce between the intellect, seen as superior, and the
body, seen as inferior; between the most abstract senses, sight and
hearing (with the corresponding arts, painting, 'a mental thing', and
music, whose 'rationalization', analysed by Max Weber, then acceler-
ated, as did its differentiation from dance), and the most 'sensuous'
senses;[21] between the 'pure' taste of the 'pure' arts, those purified by
social processes and procedures of abstraction, such as perspective
or the tone system, and the 'taste of the tongue or gullet' which Kant
refers to – in short, between everything that truly belongs to the
realm of culture, the site of all sublimations and the basis of all
distinctions, and all that belongs to the realm of nature, which is
feminine and popular.[22] These oppositions, translated with total clarity in the cardinal dualism of soul and body (or understanding and
sensibility), are rooted in the social division between the economic
world and the world of symbolic production. The power of symbolic

[19] L. Febvre, *Le Problème de l'incroyance au XVIe siècle, la religion de Rabelais*
(Paris: Albin Michel, 1942); M. Bakhtine, *L'Œuvre de François Rabelais et la culture
populaire au Moyen Age et à la Renaissance* (Paris: Gallimard, 1970).
[20] On the solidarity and interdependence between body and mind in the Chinese
tradition, see J. Gernet, *L'Intelligence de la Chine, le social et le mental* (Paris:
Gallimard, 1994), p. 271. (Around AD 500 Fan Shen asserted the full solidarity
between body and mind: 'My hands and all other parts of my body . . . are all parts of
my mind', ibid., pp. 273–7.)
[21] M. Weber, *Die rationalen und soziologischen Grundlagen der Musik* (Tübingen:
UTB/Mohr-Siebeck, 1972).
[22] On the disgust for the 'facile' and for oral (or sexual) satisfactions as the basis of
the Kantian aesthetic, see P. Bourdieu, *Distinction* (Cambridge: Harvard University
Press, 1984), pp. 486–8. Durkheim himself, like a good Kantian, identifies culture
with asceticism, discipline of the body and its desires and appetites, defined as presocial
and feminine (cf. É. Durkheim, *The Elementary Forms of the Religious Life* (London:
Allen and Unwin, 1915), pp. 312ff.).

appropriation of the world which perspectival vision secures by reducing the diversity of the visible world to the ordered unity whose
conditions of realization are defined by linear perspective is based, as
if on an invisible platform, on the social privilege which is the condition of the emergence of scholastic universes and of the acquisition
and exercise of the corresponding dispositions.

All this is seen particularly well in the invention, in eighteenth-
century England, of the natural park, as analysed by Raymond
Williams. The new organization of land, which turned the English
countryside into a landscape without peasants, that is, into a pure
object of aesthetic contemplation, based on the cult of the 'natural'
and of undulating curves, is part of the world-view of an enlightened
agrarian bourgeoisie which, at the same time as it 'improves' agri-
culture in a grid of straight lines, aims to create a visible universe
totally devoid of any trace of productive labour and any reference to
producers – the 'natural' landscape.[23]

Thus even the beginnings of historical anamnesis recall the original
repression which is constitutive of the symbolic order and which is
perpetuated in a scholastic disposition implying repression of its
economic and social conditions of possibility (conditions which are,
exceptionally, recalled in the confusion that a museum arouses in
visitors who lack the means of satisfying its tacit demands – and
which Zola evokes in a fairly realist manner, albeit still derealized by
literary stylization, in the episode of the visit to the Louvre for
Gervaise's wedding in *L'Assommoir*[24] – or in the disgusted and sometimes indignant rejection that works arising from the artistic disposition arouse in those whose taste has not been formed in 'scholastic'
conditions.[25]

---

[23] R. Williams, 'Pleasing prospects', in *The Country and the City* (London: Chatto
and Windus, 1973), pp. 120–6.

[24] As is shown by the statistics on visits to museums and galleries, the aptitude to
perceive works of art, and more generally the things of the world, as a spectacle, a
representation, a reality with no other end than to be contemplated, is very unequally
distributed. Because it is highly dependent on particular conditions of acquisition,
both in the family and at school, and particular conditions of exercise, such as tour-
ism (an invention of the English aristocracy and bourgeoisie, with the 'Grand Tour'
of art capitals), this disposition, universally demanded of visitors to museums and
galleries, is in no way universal (cf. P. Bourdieu et al., *The Love of Art: European Art
Museums and their Public* (Cambridge: Polity Press, 1991).

[25] The scandalized reactions of manual workers at certain 'art' photographs, which
are violently rejected and condemned for their gratuitous character and their lack
of recognized and immediately recognizable social significance or function, are the
expressions of a taste which can be called 'functionalist' and which is ordinarily
expressed in preferences in everyday life for the 'practical' and the 'substantial'.

The scholastic point of honour

Those who are immersed, in some cases from birth, in scholastic universes resulting from a long process of autonomization are led to forget the exceptional historical and social conditions that make possible a view of the world and of cultural products that is characterized by self-evidence and naturalness. Enchanted adherence to the scholastic point of view is rooted in the sense, which is specific to academic elites, of natural election through gift: one of the least noticed effects of academic procedures of training and selection, functioning as rites of institution, is that they set up a magic boundary between the elect and the excluded while contriving to repress the differences of condition that are the condition of the difference that they produce and consecrate. This socially guaranteed difference, ratified and authenticated by the academic qualification which functions as a (bureaucratic) title of nobility is, without any doubt – like the difference between freeman and slave in past times – at the root of the difference of 'nature' or 'essence' (one could, derisively, speak of 'ontological difference') that academic aristocratism draws between the thinker and the 'common man', absorbed by the trivial concerns of everyday existence. This aristocratism owes its success to the fact that it offers to the inhabitants of scholastic universes a perfect 'theodicy of their privilege', an absolute justification of that form of forgetting of history, the forgetting of the social conditions of possibility of scholastic reason, which, despite what seems to separate them, the universalistic humanism of the Kantian tradition shares with the disenchanted prophets of 'the forgetting of Being'.[26]

Thus it is that, for many philosophers, beyond their philosophical divergences and their philosophical oppositions, Heidegger has been able to become a kind of trustee of the point of honour of the philosophical profession, associating the philosopher's demand for distance from the common world with disdainful distance from the social sciences, pariah sciences studying an unworthy, vulgar object (we know that Heidegger was literally obsessed by the work of the thinkers of the social world, Rickert, who was once his teacher, Dilthey and Max Weber).[27] Evocation of the 'inauthentic' relation that 'ordinary'

---

[26] Cf. P. Bourdieu, *The Political Ontology of Martin Heidegger* (Cambridge: Polity Press, 1991).

[27] On this point, one might read the work by J. A. Barash, *Martin Heidegger and the Problem of Historical Meaning* (Dordrecht and Lancaster: Nijhoff, 1988), which evokes very precisely the whole early period of Heidegger's thought and the confrontation of the author of *Being and Time*, especially in his lectures of the 1920s, with the historical sciences and the problem of history; and the detailed analysis of the

Dasein, or, in more euphemized terms, *Dasein* in the ordinary state of 'people', *das Man*, has to the 'everyday common and ambient world' (*alltägliche Um- und Mitwelt*), the impersonal and anonymous field of action of 'people', is at the heart (and, no doubt, the origin) of a philosophical anthropology that can be read as a kind of rite of expulsion of evil, in other words of the social and of sociology.[28]

To call into question the 'public', the 'public world' (the site par excellence of 'chatter') and 'public time' is to assert not only the philosopher's break with the triviality of 'inauthentic' existence, with the vulgar domain of human affairs, the site of illusion and confusion, with the reign of (public) opinion or the *doxa* – but also his break with the sciences, and in particular the historical sciences. Through their claim to arrive at interpretations endowed with a 'universal validity' (*Allgemeingültigkeit*), in which he sees one of the subtlest forms of 'misappropriation of finitude', these low-born sciences tacitly presuppose the public interpretability of the world and time, which are decreed to be accessible at any time to anyone, that is, to the public man, *das Man*, as an interchangeable being.[29]

Against the 'democratic' or even 'plebeian' character (Cicero long ago denounced the *philosophia plebeia*) of the claim to 'objectivity' and 'universality', and therefore the affirmation, which he sees as inherent in science, of the accessibility of truth to an indifferent, impersonal subject, the 'authentic' philosopher asserts the aristocratic presuppositions that are implied in an unashamed commitment to the privilege of *skholè*, thus offering renewed justifications to the long tradition of philosophical contempt for the *polis*, politics, and the *doxa*, which Husserl himself was already evoking in *The Crisis of*

---

texts (especially lectures) preceding *Being and Time* by T. Kiesiel, *The Genesis of Heidegger's Being and Time* (Berkeley: University of California Press, 1995).

[28] As Louis Pinto has pointed out (in an oral communication), those whom he calls the 'hermeneutists of the everyday', starting with Henri Lefebvre, who, with others, was briefly seduced by the *Lettter on Humanism* (cf. Bourdieu, *The Political Ontology of Martin Heidegger*), have found in the 'analysis' of 'consumer society' a means of reconnecting with an aristocraticism based on condemnation of the people's false needs, which are insatiable (this is Plato's theme of *pleonexia*) and anarchic, and on the claim to demystifying lucidity of those who are able to see *signs* in what, for others, is a mere deception.

[29] The identification of the universal with the 'inauthentic' is expressed with particular clarity in Heidegger's correspondence with Elisabeth Blochmann: 'The new life that we want, or rather that wants to germinate in us, has renounced the aim of being universal, that is to say inauthentic, and extensive' (cf. M. Heidegger, *Correspondance avec Karl Jaspers, suivi de Correspondance avec Elisabeth Blochmann* (Paris: Gallimard, 1996), pp. 216–17 and also 267–8).

European Sciences.[30] Making the experience of the singular *Dasein*
as 'being-for-death' the only authentic route to the past, he asserts that
the philosopher, with his unique lucidity as to the role of the historian's
preconceptions (*Vorgriffe*) in unveiling the meaning of the past, is
alone able to succeed where the conventional methods of the historical sciences inevitably fail, and to ensure an authentic reappropriation
of the original meaning of the past.

   In a *tour de force* that is close to being a conjuring trick, Heidegger
conducts his antirationalist battle against the sciences, and especially
the social sciences, with the aid of a mode of thought that is specific
to the social sciences, since he bases his critique of the limits of
scientific thought on a restatement of the dependence of criteria of
rationality on a historicity of truth of which the sciences do not
have mastery. But, simultaneously, he distances himself from the historical sciences, which, because they are linked to a particular image
of the world (*Weltbild*) and accept only the truth provided by human
methods of explanation, forget the limits of human reflection and the
opacity of Being. Only the fundamental ontology of finite existence is
able to give a new unity to historical sciences floundering in anarchy
and to recall that the preconceptions of these sciences derive not
from cultural values (as Dilthey or Weber may suppose) but from the
essential historicity of the historian, the condition of possibility of
the uncovering of the meaning of a past that would otherwise remain
irremediably hidden.

   Thus, perhaps because he was confronted with historical sciences
that were particularly active and particularly well armed with philosophical tools (neither Rickert nor Dilthey, still less Weber, waited
for him before reflecting on the historical sciences), perhaps also because his position and his trajectory inclined him that way, Heidegger
presents, especially in the works of his youth, a particularly acute
manifestation of the *hubris* of thought without limits. At the cost of
much ignorance and some inconsistencies, he gives a particularly
trenchant formulation of the conviction that philosophers sometimes
have of being able to think the historical sciences better than they
think themselves, to adopt a more lucid, more profound and more
radical standpoint on their object and their relation to that object,
and even, without any other weapons than those of pure and solitary
reflection, to produce a knowledge superior to that available from
the collective research and plebeian instruments of science, the symbol
of which is perhaps statistics (explicitly mentioned in the famous

[30] E. Husserl, *The Crisis of European Sciences and Transcendental Phenomenology*,
tr. D. Carr (Evanston, Ill.: Northwestern University Press, 1970), p. 125.

passage on *das Man*), which cancels out in the mediocrity of the average the radical singularity of the *Dasein* – only the 'authentic' *Dasein*, of course: who cares about that of *das Man*?

The strategies which Heidegger used in his struggle against the social sciences of his day, especially the one which consists in turning their own achievements against those sciences, were revived or reinvented by the 'avant-garde' of French philosophy in the 1960s. The social sciences, strongly rooted, since Durkheim, in the philosophical tradition, in particular because of the need to confront philosophy, sometimes on its own territory, in order to assert their autonomy and specificity against its hegemonic pretensions, had by then managed to occupy a dominant position, with works like those of Lévi-Strauss, Dumézil, Braudel or even Lacan, confusedly conflated under the journalistic label 'structuralism', within the university field and the intellectual field. All the philosophers of the moment had to define themselves relative to them in a relationship of antagonism tending towards annexation and in a kind of conscious or unconscious double game, sometimes taken to the point of dual membership (marked, in particular, by recourse to the '-ology' effect – 'archaeology', 'grammatology', etc. and other would-be scientific flourishes), thereby rediscovering – without needing to be the least bit Heideggerian – strategies of supersession rather similar to those that Heidegger used against these sciences.

Radical doubt radicalized

So, only if they were to take the risk of really calling into question the philosophical game to which their existence as philosophers is linked, or their recognized participation in this game – and not simply through the displays of radical subversion in which 'academic anti-academicism' has always revelled – would philosophers be able to secure the conditions for a genuine freedom with respect to everything which authorizes and entitles them to call themselves and think themselves philosophers and which, in exchange for this social recognition, confines them in the presuppositions inscribed in the posture and professional position of philosopher. Only a critique aiming to make explicit the social conditions of possibility of what is defined, at each moment, as 'philosophical' would be able to make visible the sources of the philosophical effects that are implied in those conditions. This alone would fulfil the intention of liberating philosophical thought from the presuppositions inscribed in the position and dispositions of those who are able to indulge in the intellectual activity designated by the term 'philosophy'. For, while it has to be pointed out that the philosopher, who likes to think of himself as *atopos*, placeless, unclassifiable, is, like everyone, comprehended in the space he seeks to comprehend, this is not done in order to debase him. On the contrary, it is to try to offer him the possibility of some freedom with respect to the constraints and limitations that are inscribed in the fact that he is situated, first, in a place in social space, and also in a place in one of its subspaces, the scholastic fields.

To those who ask why, and above all by what right, one can call for such a 'liberation' of philosophy, I will reply first that one has to liberate philosophy in order to liberate the social sciences from the reactive – not to say reactionary – critique that philosophy never ceases to make of them, being content, most of the time, to orchestrate unwittingly the commonest vision of these sciences. Thus, turning against social science the 'philosophy of suspicion' that they so readily attribute to it, the so-called 'postmodern' philosophers almost all concur in denouncing the scientific ambition that the social sciences affirm by definition. Inclined to see an assertion as just a disguised injunction or order, to see logic as a 'thought police', to see the claim to scientificity as a mere 'truth effect' designed to secure obedience or as a disguised aspiration to hegemony inspired by the will to power – when, that is, they do not go so far as to transform sociology, a somewhat undisciplined discipline, into a disciplinarian discipline, authoritarian, even totalitarian and thought-policing, they can, sometimes in contradiction with their conscious and declared political options, restore a philosophically and politically acceptable form to the most obscurantist accusations and anathemas that spiritualistic (and conservative) criticism has always made of the sciences, and especially the social sciences, in the name of the sacred values of the person and the imprescriptible rights of the 'subject'.

But I also have the conviction that there is no more philosophical activity, even if it is bound to scandalize any normally constituted 'philosophical mind', than analysis of the specific logic of the philosophical field and of the dispositions and beliefs socially recognized at a given moment as 'philosophical' which are generated and flourish there, thanks to philosophers' blindness to their own scholastic blindness. The immediate harmony between the logic of a field and the dispositions it induces and presupposes means that all its arbitrary content tends to be disguised as timeless, universal self-evidence. The philosophical field is no exception to this rule. Sociological critique is therefore not a mere preliminary, preparing the ground for a more radical and more specific philosophical critique: it leads to the principle of the 'philosophy' of philosophy, which is tacitly engaged in the social practice that, in a given place and time, is defined as philosophical.

Because the 'philosopher' is nowadays almost invariably a *homo academicus*, his 'philosophical mind' is shaped by and for a university field, and steeped in the particular philosophical tradition that this field hands down and inculcates: subtly ranked canonical authors and texts which provide the 'purest' thought with its guidelines and references (here as elsewhere, national syllabuses [*programmes*], written or unwritten, produce nationally 'programmed' minds);[31] problems arising from historically constituted debates, perpetuated through educational reproduction; recurrent major oppositions, often condensed into couples of antithetical terms, in which some people have chosen to see, in appropriately portentous style, 'the binary oppositions of western metaphysics', but which stem in fact, more trivially, from the dualistic structure into which the philosophical field tends, like other fields, to be organized (with, in particular, in the case of France, the constant opposition between a pole close to science, concerned with epistemology, the philosophy of science, and logic, and a pole close to art and literature in its objects and mode of expression, and oriented towards the aesthetic and aestheticism, like the current 'postmodernism'); concepts which, despite their apparent generality, are always inseparable from a situated, dated semantic field and, through it, from a field of struggles itself limited to the frontiers of a language and a nation; theories more or less truncated and rigidified by the routine of educational transmission, which eternizes them only by dehistoricizing and derealizing them, etc.

I believe that the radical doubt implied in recalling the social conditions of philosophical activity, particularly through the freedom it can give with respect to the conventions and conformisms of a philosophical universe which has its own common sense, could enable one to shake the system of barriers that the philosophical system has set up to block awareness of the scholastic illusion (in which the celebrated texts of Plato on *skholè* and the cave, or Heidegger on *Das Man* are central components). The implicit philosophy of philosophy that is rooted in this illusion, no doubt supported and encouraged by the confidence or hegemonic ambition linked to occupation of a high position (at least in France) in the university field, is manifested in particular in a number of major common presuppositions: deliberate

---

[31] C. Soulié, 'Anatomie du goût philosophique', *Actes de la Recherche en Sciences Sociales*, no. 109 (Oct. 1995), pp. 3–28; and R. Rorty, J. B. Schneewind and Q. Skinner (eds), *Philosophy in History: Essays on the Historiography of Philosophy* (Cambridge: Cambridge University Press, 1984).

forgetting or denial of history or, which amounts to the same thing, refusal of any genetic approach or any real historicization;[32] the illusion of 'foundation', which springs from the claim to adopt a point of view on the other sciences which they cannot take on themselves, to found them (theoretically) and not to be founded by them (historically); the refusal to objectify the objectifying subject, which is ruled out as 'reductionism', together with its extension, aesthetic fundamentalism.

But a radical doubt based on a critique of scholastic reason could, above all, have the effect of showing that the errors of philosophy, from which the 'ordinary language philosophers', essential allies, seek to free us, often have as their common root *skholè* and the scholastic disposition. This is the case, it seems to me – to cite only a few of the kinds of errors which immediately spring to mind – when Wittgenstein denounces the fallacy that understanding a word and learning its meaning are a mental process implying the contemplation of an 'idea' or the targeting of a 'content', or when Moore points out that when we see something blue, we are not aware of the concept of 'blueness'. Similarly, when Ryle distinguishes between 'knowing that' and 'knowing how', between theoretical knowledge and practical knowledge (of a game, a language, etc.) or when Wittgenstein reminds us that stating judgements is only one of the possible ways of using language and that 'I am in pain' is not necessarily an assertion, but can also be a manifestation of pain, or when Strawson criticizes the logicians for having concentrated on sentences 'relatively independent of their context', or Toulmin invites us to distinguish the ordinary use of the expression of probability from the use of probabilistic statements in scientific inquiry, they are all pointing to tendencies of thought which belong to the scholastic 'language game' and which, as such, are liable to eclipse the logic of practice to which the exploration of ordinary language can lead us.

In other words, one can, as I have always tried to, draw on the analyses that the ordinary language philosophers, and also the pragmatists, especially Peirce and Dewey, have made of the generic tendencies of philosophy – which, as Austin says, have nothing to do with the personal weaknesses of any particular philosopher – to give its full generality and its full force to the critique of scholastic reason. Conversely, an analysis of the scholastic position and disposition would no doubt supply the principle for a radicalization and systematization of the critique of the ordinary philosophical use of language

---

[32] On the dehistoricization of the history of philosophy, see 'Postscript 2: Forgetting history', p. 43 below.

and of the fallacies it encourages, and also for a critique of the gulf between scholastic logics and the logic of practice, which, there is every reason to think, is better expressed in ordinary, non-scholastic language than in the socially neutralized and controlled language that prevails in scholastic universes.

POSTSCRIPT I

Impersonal Confessions

To take away the objectifying brutality of the analysis I have sketched here of the philosophical habitus of a generation of French philosophers that has the particularity of having imposed its particularities on the whole world, and so, perhaps, to overcome a few resistances, I think it may be useful to perform an exercise in reflexivity by trying to outline the broad features of my years of philosophical apprenticeship. I do not intend to deliver the kind of so-called 'personal' memories that provide the dismal backdrop for academic autobiographies – awestruck encounters with eminent masters, intellectual choices interlaced with career choices. What has recently been presented under the label of 'ego history'[33] still seems to me very far from a genuine reflexive sociology: happy academics (the only ones asked to perform this academic exercise . . .) have no history, and one is not necessarily doing them a service, or a service to history, in asking them for unmethodical histories of uneventful lives.

So I shall speak very little about myself, the singular self, in any case, that Pascal calls 'hateful'. And if I nonetheless never cease to speak about myself, it will be the impersonal self that the most personal confessions pass over in silence, or refuse, on account of its very impersonality.[34] Paradoxically, perhaps nothing nowadays appears

[33] Alludes to a series launched under this title by Pierre Nora and soon aborted. *Trans.*
[34] Louis Marin, to whom I dedicate this postscript, has brilliantly explored, in relation to Pascal, the question 'who is "I"?' (cf. L. Marin, *Pascal et Port-Royal* (Paris: PUF), 1977, esp. pp. 92ff.).

more hateful than this interchangeable self that is revealed by the sociologist and socio-analysis (and also, though it is less apparent, and so better tolerated, psychoanalysis). Whereas everything prepares us to enter the regulated exchange of narcissisms, of which a certain literary tradition has established the code, the effort to objectify this 'subject' which we are led to think universal because we have it in common with all those who are the product of the same social conditions encounters violent resistance. Anyone who takes the trouble to break with the self-indulgence of nostalgic evocations in order to make explicit the collective privacy of common experiences, beliefs and schemes of thought, in other words some of the unthought which is almost inevitably absent from the sincerest autobiographies because, being self-evident, it passes unnoticed and, when it surfaces in consciousness, is repressed as unworthy of publication, is liable to offend the narcissism of the reader who feels objectified, despite himself, by proxy and, paradoxically, all the more cruelly the closer he is to the author of the work of objectification – unless the catharsis induced by the awakening of consciousness is expressed, as sometimes happens, in liberated and liberating laughter.

I must first say, and this will be my only 'confidence', that it is likely that if I can now, with some chance of success, conceive the project of recreating the vision of the academic and intellectual world that I had in the 1950s, not in terms of its most deceptively unique features but of what was most banally common about it, including the illusion of singularity, this is because I was unable to be satisfied very long with the bedazzlement of the *oblat miraculé*.[35] This was a relatively rare experience, without being unique (I also found it in Paul Nizan, in particular through Sartre's very fine preface to *Aden Arabie*), which no doubt inclined me towards an objectifying distance – the posture which normally makes a good informant – from the deceptive seductions of the Alma Mater.

It is on the basis of this experience that I shall try to reconstruct the space of possibles as it presented itself to me as a member of a particular category of adolescents, the philosophy students of the École Normale (the 'normaliens philosophes') having in common a whole set of properties linked to the fact of being at the heart and the peak of an educational institution though separated, among themselves, by secondary differences related, in particular, to their social trajectory. Like an initiate such as the author of the *Hopi Sun* who recounts his experience to an ethnologist, I would like to evoke, at least in

---

[35] Oblate: the pupil of humble origins who 'gives everything' and owes everything to the educational system. *Trans.*

broad terms, the rites of institution which tended to produce the inner conviction and commitment which, in the 1950s, were the condition for entry into the tribe of philosophers – and to try to determine why and how one became a 'philosopher', a word whose ambiguity enables the most modest philosophy teacher to give himself the status of philosopher in the full sense of the word and which helped to generate in apprentice 'philosophers' the ambiguity of ambitions and the enormous overinvestment which are excluded by better determined choices, more directly adjusted to the real chances, such as that of candidates for a post of art teacher, who are little inclined to see themselves as 'artists'.

I cannot relate here the whole mechanics of the election which, from the *concours général* and the *classes préparatoires* to the *concours*, leads the elect (and especially the *miraculés*) to elect the School which has elected them, to recognize the criteria of election which have constituted them as an elite.[36] The logic which determined the 'vocation' of 'philosopher' was probably not very different: one simply submitted to the hierarchy of the disciplines by moving (the more so, no doubt, the more success one had had) towards what Jean-Louis Fabiani calls 'the crowning discipline'.[37] (Until the 1950s, philosophy surpassed all other disciplines in prestige and the choice of philosophy over mathematics in secondary school and beyond was not necessarily a negative choice based on lesser success in the sciences.) To make things clearer, at the risk of shocking a profession which disowns such hierarchical dispositions, I will say that, without having the same mechanical rigour, the choice of philosophy was not very different in its principle from the choice which leads those best placed in some major competitions to choose the corps of mining engineers or the finance inspectorate. One became a 'philosopher' because one had been consecrated and one consecrated oneself by securing the prestigious identity of 'philosopher'.

The choice of philosophy was a manifestation of status-based assurance which reinforced that assurance (or arrogance). This was especially true at a time when the whole intellectual field was dominated by Jean-Paul Sartre and when the *khâgnes*,[38] notably with Jean Beaufret, the addressee of Heidegger's *Letter on Humanism*, and the entrance examination for the École Normale itself, with its jury

---

[36] I have done so in *The State Nobility: Elite Schools in the Field of Power*, tr. L. C. Clough (Cambridge: Polity Press, 1996).

[37] J.-L. Fabiani, *Les Philosophes de la République* (Paris: Éditions de Minuit, 1988), p. 49.

[38] *khâgne*: lycée class preparing for the entrance examinations for the Grandes Écoles. *Trans.*

consisting of Maurice Merleau-Ponty and Vladimir Jankélevitch, were or seemed to be summits of intellectual life.

Khâgne was the heart of the apparatus of production of French-style intellectual ambition in its most elevated form, that is, philosophical ambition. The total intellectual, the model of which had just been invented and imposed by Sartre, was called for by the education dispensed in the *khâgne*, which offered a vast range of disciplines – philosophy, literature, history, ancient and modern languages – and which, through training in the dissertation *de omni re scibili*, the centre of the whole system, encouraged a self-confidence verging on triumphant unawareness of ignorance. Belief in the omnipotence of rhetorical invention was bound to be encouraged by the skilfully staged exhibitions of philosophical improvisation: I am thinking of masters like Michel Alexandre, a belated disciple of Alain, who used his prophetic poses to cover the weaknesses of a philosophical discourse reduced to the resources of reflection without historical basis, or Jean Beaufret, who initiated his dazzled pupils into the arcana of the thinking of Heidegger, and who, as an exemplary incarnation of professorial aristocraticism, was closer than it seems to the old Alainian tradition (a number of 'philosophers' trained in the *khâgnes* of the 1950s combined enthusiasm for Heidegger with admiration for Alexandre).

In short, *khâgne* was the place where the status-based legitimacy of a socially recognized academic 'nobility' was constructed. Simultaneously, it inculcated the sense of elevation which imposes the highest intellectual ambitions on any 'philosopher' and forbids him to stoop to certain disciplines or certain objects, notably those that concern the specialists of the social sciences; and it took the shock of 1968, for example, to bring the philosophers trained in the *khâgnes* of the late 1940s (Deleuze and Foucault, in particular) to consider the problem of power and politics, albeit in a highly sublimated mode.

Just as – as Norbert Elias points out – the nobleman remains a nobleman even if he is a mediocre fencer (whereas the best of fencers does not become a nobleman), the socially recognized 'philosopher' is separated from non-philosophers by a difference of *essence* which can in no way be associated with a difference of *competence* (the definition of which varies moreover from one era, or national tradition, to another). This sense of caste dignity implies a sense of 'placement' (as on the sports field or the Stock Exchange) which manifested itself especially in intellectual preferences, with the most ambitious students attaching themselves by predilection to esoteric and obscure texts, including those which, as in the case of Husserl and Heidegger, were practically inaccessible for lack of translations (their major works were not translated until the 1960s, in other words when the excitement that surrounded them had died down). The same went for the choice of subjects for dissertations and theses or the professors who would supervise them, which was guided by a practical knowledge of the space of possibles and, more precisely, a sense of the hierarchies among the masters and the prospects, both 'spiritual' and 'temporal', which were promised through them.[39]

The sense of the game removes the need for cynicism: by making explicit what ordinarily remains implicit, even in biographies, analysis encourages a finalist, calculating view of the strategies of academic investment. This reductive vision, which is often located in the standpoint of Thersites, which is the source of so much writing about intellectuals, is particularly false just when it seems to apply most irresistibly, as in the case of great intellectual and academic successes. In fact, the great initiates do not need to choose in order to make the right choice, and this is one of the reasons why they are chosen: it is by this strange commitment, at once total and distant, of the 'learned ignorance' (*docta ignorantia*) that is inherent in the sense of the game that 'true vocations' which know nothing of the base calculations of careerist ambition are customarily recognized (it will be understood that I do not speak in my own name but am only seeking to capture the tone and tenor of the dominant discourse). Successful initiation, the one which gives access to that caste within a caste, the 'philosophes normaliens', secures the essential privilege of all 'well-born' persons, an adaptation to the game so immediate and so total that it seems to be innate and gives its possessors the supreme advantage of not needing to calculate in order to win the rarest of the profits offered by the game.

But this caste is also a corps whose members are united by solidarities of interest and affinities of habitus that create what has to be called an *esprit de corps* – however strange that expression may seem when applied to a set of individuals each persuaded of his or her total uniqueness. One of the functions of rites of institution is indeed that it creates a commonality and communication of unconsciouses which make possible the discreet conflict between close adversaries, the hidden borrowing of themes or ideas which each one may sincerely believe are his own because they are the product of schemes of invention similar to his own, tacit references and allusions intelligible only within the small circle of intimates. One only has to look in this light

---

[39] This point is developed further in P. Bourdieu, *Homo Academicus*, tr. P. Collier (Cambridge: Polity Press, 1988), pp. 120ff. and in Soulié, 'Anatomie du goût philosophique'.

at what has been written since the 1960s to discover, behind the deceptive display of proclaimed differences, a profound homogeneity of problems, themes and schemes of thought. To take an extreme example, only the transfiguration resulting from a complete change of theoretical context prevents people from seeing in the Derridean slogan 'deconstruction' a very free variation on Bachelard's theme, which has become an academic *topos*, of the break with precon- structions, inherent in the construction of the scientific object, which has been simultaneously orchestrated at the 'scientific' or 'scientistic' pole of the field of philosophy (especially by Althusser) and of the social sciences.

It was on the basis of this profound agreement as to the place and rank of philosophy that the divergences which gave rise to the trajectories leading to the opposing positions in the philosophical field in the 1960s were defined. They concerned above all the way to situate oneself in relation to the previous state of the field and to claim the *succession* – either in continuity, for those who sought to occupy positions of temporal power within the university field, or through rupture, for those who aimed at prestigious positions within the intellectual field where the status of successor can only be achieved through revolutionary subversion. The complexity of the relationship between the two generations, and the subterranean com- plicities between members of the same generation, are seen clearly in the almost universal recognition accorded to Georges Canguilhem. A fellow-student at the École Normale of Sartre and Aron, from whom he was separated by his lower-class provincial origin, Canguilhem could be invoked by the occupants of opposite positions in the uni- versity field. As an exemplary *homo academicus* – for a long time, and with great rigour, he served as inspector general for secondary education – he could serve as an emblem for academics who occu- pied positions homologous to his own in the agencies responsible for reproduction and consecration of the corps; but as the advocate of a tradition of history of science and epistemology who, at the height of the triumph of existentialism, represented the last bastion of serious- ness and rigour, he was consecrated, with Gaston Bachelard, as the *maître à penser* of philosophers more remote from the heart of the academic tradition, such as Althusser, Foucault and some others; it was as if his central yet minor position in the university field and the quite rare, even exotic dispositions that had predisposed him to occupy it had designated him to play the role of a totemic emblem for all those who sought to break with the dominant model and who constituted themselves as an 'invisible college' by rallying around him.

Sartre's domination was indeed never uncontested and those (of whom I was one) who sought to resist 'existentialism' in its fashionable or academic forms could draw support from a set of dominated currents: a history of philosophy very closely linked to the history of the sciences, the 'prototypes' of which were represented by two major works, *Dynamique et Métaphysique leibniziennes*, by Martial Guéroult, a graduate of the École Normale and professor at the Collège de France, and *Physique et Métaphysique kantiennes*, by Jules Vuillemin, then a young lecturer at the Sorbonne and a contributor to *Les Temps Modernes*, another *normalien*, who succeeded Guéroult at the Collège de France; and an epistemology and history of the sciences represented by authors such as Gaston Bachelard, Georges Canguilhem and Alexandre Koyré. Often of working-class and provincial origin, or brought up outside France and its academic traditions, and attached to non-standard university institutions, like the École des Hautes Études or the Collège de France, these marginal and temporally dominated authors (to whom one should add Eric Weil), hidden from public notoriety by the celebrity of the dominant figures, offered a recourse to those who, for various reasons, sought to react against the fascinating but rejected image of the total intellectual, present on all the fronts of thought.

The concern for seriousness and rigour which led to a shunning of fashionable enthusiasms (and which inclined a number of teachers of philosophy to oppose to Sartre a Heidegger they had barely read) also led some to search for another antidote to the 'facile' aspect of existentialism, often identified with a literary and somewhat fatuous exaltation of *le vécu* ('lived experience'), in a reading of Husserl (translated by Paul Ricœur or Suzanne Bachelard, the daughter of the philosopher, herself a historian of science) or among those phenomenologists who were most inclined to see phenomenology as a rigorous science, such as Maurice Merleau-Ponty, who also offered an opening towards the human sciences. In that context, the journal *Critique*, edited by Georges Bataille and Eric Weil, representing the two poles of a secondary opposition between those who looked towards the dominated pole of the philosophical field, also offered ways out, by opening access to an international and transdisciplinary culture, an escape route from the closure effect exerted by every elite school. (The reader will have understood that in this evocation of the space of 'philosophical possibles' which seemed to present itself to me at that time are expressed the often very strong and always lively admirations I felt in my early twenties, and the particular point of view from which my representation of the university field and of philosophy arose.)

So it would be possible to produce as one wished the appearances either of continuity or break between the 1950s and the 1970s, depending on whether or not one takes account of the dominated figures of the 1950s who provided the launch-pad for some of the leaders of the anti-existentialist revolution in philosophy. But just as – except perhaps for Bachelard, who sprinkled his writings with ironic comments on the peremptory assertions, particularly as regards science, of the existentialist masters – the dominated thinkers of the 1950s provided both in their lives and in their works many indications of their submission to the dominant philosophical model, so too the new dominant figures of the 1970s did not perhaps carry through to the end the revolution they had undertaken against the foundation of the domination of the total philosopher; and those of their works that are most liberated from the grip of academia still bear the marks of the hierarchy, inscribed both in the objective structure of institutions – with, for example, the opposition between the major thesis, the vehicle of the most ambitious, original and 'brilliant' developments, and the minor thesis, formerly written in Latin, devoted to humble products of erudition or the human sciences – and in cognitive structures, in the form of the opposition between the theoretical and the empirical, the general and the specialized.

Their concern to maintain and mark their distance from the social sciences, which was asserted all the more strongly perhaps because those sciences threatened their hegemony and because they were discreetly appropriating a number of their achievements, no doubt helped to conceal from the philosophers of the 1970s and their readers that the break they were making with the politically correct naiveties of personalist humanism was simply leading them back to the 'philosophy without a subject' that the (Durkheimian) social sciences had advocated from the beginning of the century. And this enabled the minor polemic of the 1980s to try to swing back the pendulum by proclaiming the 'return of the subject' against those who, in the 1960s, had themselves announced a 'philosophy without a subject', against the 'existentialists' who, like Sartre and the young Raymond Aron (of *Introduction to the Philosophy of History*), had themselves rebelled in the 1930s and the immediate postwar years against the 'totalitarian' empire of the objectivist philosophy of the human sciences . . .

I cannot conclude this impersonal confession without mentioning what seems to me to be the most important but most invisible property of the philosophical universe of that place and that moment – and perhaps of all times and all countries – namely *scholastic enclosure*, which, while it also characterizes other summits of academic life, Oxford or Cambridge, Yale or Harvard, Heidelberg or Göttingen, no doubt takes one of its most exemplary forms with the École Normale (or *khâgne*). Much has been said, in celebration of it, about the privilege of that enclosed world, set apart from the vicissitudes of the real world, in which most of the French philosophers whose message now inspires American campus radicalism were students in or around the 1950s.

(And this is surely no accident. American universities, especially the most prestigious and the most exclusive, are *skholè* made into an institution. Very often situated far away from the major cities – like Princeton, totally isolated from New York and Philadelphia – or in lifeless suburbs – like Harvard in Cambridge – or, when they are in the city – like Yale in New Haven, Columbia on the fringes of Harlem, or the University of Chicago on the edge of an immense ghetto – totally cut off from the adjacent communities, in particular by the heavy police protection they provide, they have a cultural, artistic, even political life of their own, with, for example, their student newspaper which relates the parish-pump news of the campus. This separate existence, together with the studious atmosphere, withdrawn from the hubbub of the world, helps to isolate professors and students from current events and from politics, which is in any case very distant, geographically and socially, and seen as beyond their grasp. The ideal-typical case, the University of California Santa Cruz, a focal point of the 'postmodernist' movement, an archipelago of colleges scattered through a forest and communicating only through the Internet, was built in the 1960s, at the top of a hill, close to a seaside resort inhabited by well-heeled pensioners and with no industries. How could one not believe that capitalism has dissolved in a 'flux of signifiers detached from their signifieds', that the world is populated by 'cyborgs', 'cybernetic organisms', and that we have entered the age of the 'informatics of domination', when one lives in a little social and electronic paradise from which all trace of work and exploitation has been effaced?)

The effects of scholastic enclosure, reinforced by those of academic elitism and the prolonged coexistence of a socially very homogeneous group, inevitably favour an intellectualocentric distance from the world. The social and mental separation is, paradoxically, never clearer than in the attempts – often pathetic and ephemeral – to rejoin the real world, particularly through political commitments (Stalinism, Maoism, etc.) whose irresponsible utopianism and unrealistic radicality bear witness that they are still a way of denying the realities of the social world.

The distance I have progressively taken from philosophy no doubt owes a lot to what are called the chance events of existence, in

particular a forced stay in Algeria, which one could say, without looking further, was at the origin of my 'vocation' as an ethnologist and
then as a sociologist. But I would not have been responsive to the call
to understand and testify which I then felt if I had not been aware for
a long time of a dissatisfaction with the philosophical game, even in
its severest and most rigorous form, which still held my interest. And,
rather than to have, myself, to indulge in confidences, I shall simply
quote a passage from the correspondence of Ludwig Wittgenstein,
which Jacques Bouveresse, a wonderful interpreter, brought to my
attention, and which expresses rather well a good part of my feelings
about philosophy: 'What is the use of studying philosophy if all that
it does for you is to enable you to talk with some plausibility about
some abstruse questions of logic, etc., & if it does not improve your
thinking about the important questions of everyday life, if it does not
make you more conscientious than any . . . journalist in the use of the
dangerous phrases such people use for their own ends?'[40]

---

[40] Quoted in N. Malcolm, *Ludwig Wittgenstein: A Memoir* (London: Oxford University Press, 1958), p. 39.

POSTSCRIPT 2

Forgetting History

In *The Conflict of the Faculties*, Kant starts out from the observation that, in contrast to the 'higher faculties' of theology, law or medicine, whose authority is directly guaranteed and validated by the temporal powers, the 'lower faculty' of mathematics, philosophy, history, etc. has no other basis than 'reason of the scientific population'. Deprived of any temporal delegation, philosophy is thus forced to make a theoretical virtue out of a historical necessity: refusing the foundation in social reason which it is in any case refused, it claims to found itself in (pure) reason, at the cost of theoretical acrobatics worthy of Baron Münchhausen, and so to offer the other faculties the only foundation valid in its eyes, a foundation in reason, which, although they do not know it, they sadly lack.

The refusal of thinking about genesis, and above all of thinking about the genesis of thought, is no doubt one of the major principles of the resistance that philosophers put up, more or less universally, against the social sciences, especially when these dare to take as their object the philosophical institution and, by the same token, the philosopher himself, the 'subject' par excellence, and when they refuse him the social extraterritoriality he grants himself and which he means to defend. The social history of philosophy, which aims to refer the history of philosophical concepts or systems to the social history of the philosophical field, seems to deny the very essence of an act of thought that is regarded as irreducible to the contingent, anecdotal circumstances of its apparition.

The priests of the philosophical cult are jealous defenders of their monopoly of the history of philosophy, which is thus kept from the profane hands of historical science. They subject canonical texts, eternized by the forgetting of the historical process of canonization from which they spring, to a dehistoricizing reading which, without even needing to assert belief in the irreducibility of philosophical discourse to any social determination, brackets off everything that links the text to a field of production and, through it, to a historical society.

The principle of absolutizing works by dehistoricizing them is also set out very clearly in the various 'philosophical' solutions to the contradiction, as old as the teaching of philosophy, which arises from the existence of a plurality of philosophical visions, each claiming exclusive access to a truth which they claim to be single. If we leave aside the belief in a *philosophia perennis*, capable of perpetuating itself, always self-identical, in endlessly new forms of expression, or the eclectic and, thereby, typically academic conviction which consists in seeing the philosophies of the past as self-sufficient wholes that are both intrinsically necessary (as formally coherent 'systems', amenable to a strictly internal analysis) and non-exclusive, like artistic representations (as Martial Guéroult does), or even complementary, as expressions of different axiomatics (as Jules Vuillemin does), these solutions can be reduced to three philosophies of the history of philosophy, associated with the names of Kant, Hegel and Heidegger. Beyond their differences, they have in common the fact that they abolish history as such, by bringing together at the same point alpha and omega, *arkhè* and *telos*, past thought and the present thought which thinks it better than it thought itself – to use Kant's formula, which every historian of philosophy spontaneously reinvents as soon as he seeks to give a sense to his undertaking.

The archaeological vision of the history of philosophy that Kant proposes looks to the 'philosophizing history of philosophy' to replace the empirical genesis – which demeans the dignity of the thinking subject – with the transcendental genesis; to replace 'the chronological order of books' with 'the natural order of the ideas which must successively develop on the basis of human reason'. It is on this condition that the history of philosophy can manifest itself in its truth as the history of reason, a logical development leading to the emergence of true philosophy, that is, critical philosophy, the supersession of dogmatism and scepticism.[41] Realized, completed philosophy thus

---

[41] On this whole question, see the excellent book by Lucien Braun, *Histoire de l'histoire de la philosophie* (Paris: Éditions Ophrys, 1973), pp. 205–24; and also his *Iconographie et philosophie. Essai et définition d'un champ de recherche* (2 vols, Strasbourg: Presses Universitaires de Strasbourg, 1996).

appears as what makes it possible to understand all the philosophies of the past philosophically, that is to say totally unhistorically, to perceive them as essential options, grounded in the very nature of the human mind, of which critical philosophy deduces the possibility.

Thus is justified an *a priori* history which can only be written *a posteriori*, once the ultimate history has sprung into existence, as if *ex nihilo*, to close, conclude and crown (while owing it nothing) the whole empirical history of the previous philosophies which it supersedes while making it possible to understand them as they truly are: 'The other sciences can grow little by little through combined efforts and additions. The philosophy of pure reason must be drawn up (*entworfen*) all at once because it is a question here of determining the very nature of knowledge, its general laws and its conditions, and not of haphazardly trying out one's judgement.'[42] Philosophy does not and cannot have a genesis; even when it comes only at the end, it is the beginning, and a radical beginning, since it springs forth all at once as a totality: 'A philosophical history of philosophy is not possible either empirically or historically, but rationally, that is to say, *a priori*. For, although it establishes facts of reason, it does not borrow them from the historical narrative but draws them from human reason, as philosophical archaeology.'[43]

The social significance of the 'break' between the empirical and the transcendental, between experience as 'fact' and the forms manifested in it, which transcendental reflection constitutes as conditions of objectivity inscribed in the subject of knowledge, is seen most clearly in the distinction between the vulgar history of philosophies and 'philosophical archaeology' as an '*a priori* history' which establishes 'facts of reason' by drawing them, not, contrary to all appearances, from the raw 'facts' of historical experience, but from human reason alone. Indeed, one is forced to wonder whether, more generally, like 'philosophical archaeology', history dehistoricized by philosophical sublimation, the transcendental is not always a kind of empirical, philosophically transfigured and thereby denied.

Only with Hegel does the specifically philosophical philosophy of the history of philosophy achieve its fulfilment: the last of philosophies is indeed the ultimate philosophy, the conclusion and goal of

[42] B. Erdmann, *Reflexionen Kants zur Kritik der reinen Vernunft* (Leipzig 1882–4), quoted by Braun, *Histoire de l'histoire de la philosophie*, p. 212.
[43] Cf. Reike, *Lose Blätter aus Kants Nachlass*, vol. 2, p. 278, quoted by Braun, *Histoire de l'histoire de la philosophie*, p. 215. On the distinction between the logical order and the chronological order of the events produced by empirical causality as the foundation of an *a priori* history of philosophy in Johann Christian Grohmann, see Braun, pp. 235ff.

all previous philosophies, the end of history and of the philosophy of history. 'Philosophy as such, the last, contains all that has been produced by the work of millennia: it is the result of all that has preceded it. This development of philosophy, considered historically, is the history of philosophy.'[44] The end of the history of philosophy is philosophy itself, which works itself out by working out the philosophical history of that history, in order to extract Reason from it: 'Philosophy derives its origin from the history of philosophy, and conversely. Philosophy and the history of philosophy are the image of one another. To study this history is to study philosophy itself, and in particular logic.' But philosophy is identified with its history not in order to reduce it to the historical history of philosophy, still less to history as such, but so as to annex history to philosophy, making the course of history an immense course in philosophy: 'The study of the history of philosophy is the study of philosophy itself, and it cannot be otherwise.' Just when one seems closest to a banally historical history of philosophy, one remains separated from it *toto coelo*, as Hegel liked to say, because this very particular history is in fact ahistorical.

The chronological order of the unfolding of philosophies is also a logical order; and the necessary sequence of philosophies, which is that of Mind developing according to its own law, has primacy over the secondary relationship between the various philosophies and the societies from which they arose. 'The relationship of political history to philosophy does not consist in being the cause of philosophy.' The philosophical history of philosophy is a reappropriation that is performed in and through a selective, unificatory awakening of consciousness which supersedes and conserves the principles of all the philosophies of the past. As an *Erinnerung* it is a theoretical redemption, a theodicy, which saves the past by integrating it into the ultimate and therefore eternal present of absolute knowledge: 'It is not as a sequence, founded in reason, of phenomena that contain and reveal what reason is that this history reveals itself as a reasonable thing ... And it is precisely the task of philosophy to recognize that, in so far as its own phenomenon is history, the latter is only determined by the Idea.' The philosophies of the past, with all the determinations they owe to their roots in a determinate epoch of history, are treated as mere stages in the development of Mind, that is, of philosophy: 'The course of history does not show us the Becoming of things foreign to us, but the Becoming of ourselves and of our own knowledge.'

[44] G. W. F. Hegel, *Hegel's Lectures on the History of Philosophy* (London: Routledge and Kegan Paul; New York, Humanities Press, 1963).

And one ends up wondering whether, at least in the case of the man who was one of the supreme incarnations of the (German) professor of philosophy, the philosophical history of philosophy was not the principle of the philosophy of history.

There remains the theory of the return to the origin, which makes the philosopher (or the professor of philosophy) the guardian and interpreter of the sacred texts of philosophy – a role often also claimed by the philologists – assigning him the role of revealing what was delivered in its truth at the beginning. This model of the history of philosophy as the elucidation of a truth revealed at the origin (*arkhè*) finds its accomplishment in Heidegger's theory of truth as 'un-veiling' and anamnesis, which gives its highest justification to one of the most prestigious forms of the typically professorial practice of comment-ary. This theory authorizes and encourages the *lector* to see himself as an authentic *auctor*, either prophet or heresiarch, who, by a return to the (Greek) origins, beyond the era of metaphysics and Plato who inaugurates it, reveals to his contemporaries the long obscured and forgotten truth of a revelation of truth, inscribed in a history which is in no way accidental but which belongs to the 'history of Being'.

Thus, the ambition of being one's own foundation is inseparable from the refusal to take note of the empirical genesis of that ambition and, more generally, of thought and its categories. It is clear that resistance to historicization is rooted not only in the habits of thought of a whole corporation, acquired and reinforced by the routine teach-ing and exercises of ritualized practice, but also in the interests attached to a social position. Consequently, to combat this forgetting of his-tory (worthy of Heidegger's 'forgetting of Being') which, because it stems from belief, is barely amenable to the arguments of reason, I am tempted to set authority against superstition and to refer the devotees of hermeneutic philosophy, a strictly 'philosophical' reading of the texts consecrated by tradition as philosophical, to the various passages of the *Tractatus* in which Spinoza defines the programme for a genu-ine science of cultural products. Spinoza there invites the interpreters of the Books of the Prophets to subject these works to a 'historical examination' seeking to determine not only 'the life, the conduct, and the studies of the author of each book, who he was, what was the occasion, and the epoch of his writing, whom did he write for, and in what language', but also 'into whose hands it fell . . . by whose advice it was received into the Bible, and . . . how all the books now univer-sally recognized as sacred, were united into a single whole.'[45] This

---

[45] B. Spinoza, *Tractatus Theologico-Politicus*, in *The Chief Works of Benedict de Spinoza*, tr. R. H. M. Elwes (London: George Bell and Sons, 1905), vol. 1, p. 103.

magnificently sacrilegious programme, which is only now beginning to be carried out in the area of analysis of philosophical texts, contradicts point by point all the presuppositions of the liturgical reading, which, in a sense, is perhaps not as absurd as it might seem from the standpoint of a rather narrow reason, since it grants the canonical texts the false eternization of ritual embalming.

2

The Three Forms of Scholastic Fallacy

∿

If one has to recall the social conditions of the formation of the scholastic disposition, this is not done with a sterile and facile (because always somewhat self-indulgent) intention of denunciation. It is not a question of judging that situation of withdrawal from an ethical or political standpoint – as has often been done, in the past, by condemning one tradition or another, German idealism for example, as a 'philosophy of professors'; still less of denigrating the mode of thought that it makes possible, which, arising from a long historical process of collective liberation, is the basis for humanity's rarest conquests. It is simply a question of trying to determine whether, and how, it affects the thought that it makes possible and, consequently, the very form and content of what we think. The logic in which this reminder is situated is that of epistemological questioning, and not of political denunciation (which has almost always made it possible to dispense with the former) – a fundamental questioning, since it bears on the epistemic posture itself and on the presuppositions entailed by the fact of being able to withdraw from the world so as to think it.

Having said this, analysis of the consequences flowing from ignorance of the effects of unconsciously universalizing the vision of the world associated with the scholastic condition is not a gratuitous exercise of pure speculation. The scholastic 'automaton' which is the product of the incorporation (and therefore the forgetting) of the constraints of the scholastic condition is a systematic principle of error – in the realm of knowledge (or science), the realm of ethics (or law, and of politics) and in the realm of aesthetics, three areas of practice which have constituted themselves as fields by breaking away from the urgencies of practice and also by dissociating themselves from philosophy. The three forms of fallacy, being founded on the same principle – the universalizing of a particular case, the vision of the world that is favoured and authorized by a particular social condition, and on the forgetting or repression of these social conditions of possibility – and thus linked by kinship, support and justify each other, and this makes them stronger and more resistant to critique.

Scholastic epistemocentrism

Having observed the ignored or repressed difference between the common world and the scientific worlds, one can endeavour, without 'primitivist' nostalgia or 'populist' exaltation, to conceptualize what remains practically inaccessible to any self-respecting scholastic thought: the logic of practice. And this must be done by trying to carry through to the end the analysis that even the boldest of philosophies often abandon in mid-course, at the point where it would encounter the social. To do this, one has to reverse the movement that is exalted by the myth of the cave, the professional ideology of the professional thinker, and return to the world of everyday existence, but armed with a scientific thought that is sufficiently aware of itself and its limits to be capable of thinking practice without destroying its object. Put less negatively, it is a question of understanding, first, the primary understanding of the world that is linked to experience of inclusion in this world, then the – almost invariably mistaken and distorted – understanding that scholastic thought has of this practical understanding, and finally the – essential – difference between practical knowledge – reasonable reason – and the scientific knowledge – scholastic, theoretical, reasoning reason – that is generated in autonomous fields.

The effects of scholastic distortion are all the more significant and scientifically disastrous when the people that science takes as its object are more remote from academic universes in their conditions. This is true whether they are members of the societies traditionally studied by ethnology (which, failing to objectify its scholastic unconscious, is often less freed than it seems to be and thinks it is from the essentialist presuppositions of Lévy-Bruhl's evocation of the 'primitive mentality') or occupants of the lower positions in social space. When he fails to analyse the 'theoretical posture' that he adopts towards his object, the social conditions which make it possible and the gap between these conditions and those which underlie the practices he is analysing, or, more simply, when he forgets that, as Bachelard puts it, 'the world in which one thinks is not the world in which one lives', the ethnologist trapped in his scholastic ethnocentrism can indeed see a difference between two 'mentalities', two natures, two essences, like Lévy-Bruhl – and others, more discreetly, after him – when he is in fact confronted with a difference between two socially constructed modes of construction and comprehension of the world: the scholastic one which he tacitly sets up as the norm, and the practical one which he has in common with men and women seemingly very distant from him in time and social space, and in which he cannot recognize the practical mode of knowledge (often magical, syncretic, in a word, prelogical) which is also his own in the most ordinary acts and experiences (those of jealousy, for example) of ordinary existence. Scholastic ethnocentrism leads him to cancel out the specificity of practical logic, either by assimilating it to scholastic knowledge, but in a way that is fictitious and purely theoretical ('on paper' and without practical consequences), or by consigning it to radical otherness, to the non-existence and worthlessness of the 'barbarous' or the 'vulgar', which, as Kant's notion of 'barbarous taste' pertinently reminds us, is nothing other than the barbarian within.

It is in the unmade 'choices' of ordinary scientific practice more than in epistemological or deontological declarations of principle (which, especially if he is an ethnologist, forbid him any manifestation of social superiority) that the scholastic unconscious, and the 'spectator's theory of knowledge', as Dewey puts it, are manifested. Projecting his theoretical thinking into the heads of acting agents, the researcher presents the world as he thinks it (that is, as an object of contemplation, a representation, a spectacle) as if it were the world as it presents itself to those who do not have the leisure (or the desire) to withdraw from it in order to think it. He sets at the origin of their practices, that is to say, in their 'consciousnesses', his own spontaneous or elaborated representations, or, worse, the models he has had to construct (sometimes against his own naive experience) to account for their practices.

We are no less separate, in this respect, from own practical experience than we are from the practical experience of others. Indeed, simply because we pause in thought over our practice, because we turn back to it to consider it, describe it, analyse it, we become in a sense absent from it; we tend to substitute for the active agent the reflecting 'subject', for practical knowledge the theoretical knowledge which selects significant features, pertinent indices (as in autobiographical narratives) and which, more profoundly, performs an essential alteration of experience (the one which, according to Husserl, separates retention from memory, protention from project). The forgetting of this inevitable transmutation, and of the inevitable boundary it sets up between 'the world in which one thinks' and 'the world in which one lives' is so natural, so profoundly consubstantial with theoretical thought, that it is very unlikely that anyone who is immersed in the scholastic 'language game' will be able to come and point out that the very fact of thought and discourse about practice separates us from practice. It takes, for example, all the subversive energy of a Wittgenstein to suggest that the utterance 'I am in pain', even if it presents itself in the form of an assertion, is no doubt just a variety of pain behaviour, liking moaning or crying out.

This clearly means that science should make it its aim not to adopt practical logic for itself, but to reconstruct that knowledge theoretically by including in the theory the distance between practical logic and theoretical logic, or even between a 'practical theory' – folk knowledge or folk theory, as Schutz and the ethnomethodologists put it – and a scientific theory. To do this requires a constant effort of reflexivity, the only means, *and itself scholastic*, of fighting against scholastic inclinations. It is customarily ignored that the description of descriptions or of spontaneous theories itself presupposes a scholastic break with the recorded activity that has to be put into the theory; and that apparently humble and submissive forms of scientific work, such as 'thick description', imply and impose on reality a preconstructed mode of construction which is none other than the scholastic view of the world. It is clear, for example, that in his 'thick description' of a cock-fight, Geertz 'generously' credits the Balinese with a hermeneutic and aesthetic gaze which is none other than his own; and it is then natural that, having failed to put explicitly into his description of the social world the 'literarization' that his description has imposed on it, he should follow through the logic of his error of omission and declare, against all reason, in his preface to *The Interpretation of Culture*, that the social world and the whole set of social relations and realities are simply 'texts'.[1]

Like reason, which, according to Kant, tends to situate the principle of its judgements not in itself but in the nature of its objects, *scholastic epistemocentrism* engenders a totally unrealistic (and idealist)

---

[1] C. Geertz, *The Interpretation of Culture: Selected Essays* (New York: Basic Books, 1973) and H. Geertz and C. Geertz, *Kinship in Bali* (Chicago: University of Chicago Press, 1975).

anthropology. Imputing to its object what belongs in fact to the way of looking at it, it projects into practice (with, for example, rational action theory) an unexamined social relation which is none other than the scholastic relation to the world. Taking various forms depending on the traditions and the domains of analysis, it places a metadiscourse (a grammar, a typical product of the scholastic standpoint, as with Chomsky) at the origin of discourse, or a metapractice (law, in the case of a number of ethnologists, who have always been inclined to juridism, or, as with Lévi-Strauss, the rules of kinship, with the aid of play on the different senses of the world 'rule', which Wittgenstein has taught us to distinguish) at the origin of practices.

Because he forgets what defines its specificity, the social scientist credits agents with his own vision, and in particular an interest in pure knowledge and pure understanding which is normally alien to them. This is the 'philologism' which, according to Bakhtine, tends to treat all languages like dead languages, fit only for deciphering; it is the intellectualism of the structuralist semiologists who treat language as an object of interpretation or contemplation rather than an instrument of action and power. It is also the epistemocentrism of the hermeneutic theory of reading (or, *a fortiori*, of the theory of the interpretation of works of art conceived as 'reading'): through an unjustified universalization of the presuppositions inscribed in the status of *lector* and in academic *skholè* – the condition of possibility of that very particular form of reading which, performed at leisure and almost always repeated, is methodically oriented towards extraction of an intentional and coherent meaning – they tend to conceive every understanding, even practical understanding, as an *interpretation*, a self-aware act of deciphering (the paradigm of which is translation).

Indulging in an unjustifiable form of 'projection of self into the other' (as the phenomenologists liked to say) which draws authority from the professional myth of reading as 're-creation', they read the *auctores* of the present or the past as *lectores*. The work as it presents itself, that is, as an *opus operatum*, totalized and canonized in the form of a corpus of 'complete works' torn from the time of its composition and capable of being run through in all directions, obscures the work in the process of construction and above all the *modus operandi* of which it is the product. And this leads them to proceed as if the logic that emerges from the retrospective, totalizing, detemporalizing reading of the *lector* had, from the beginning, been at the heart of the creative action of the *auctor*. They thereby ignore the specific logic of the process of invention, which, even in the most formal explorations, is always the implementation of a disposition of practical sense which discovers and understands itself as it unfolds in the work in which it is realized.[2]

Practical logics

The scholastic vision dispenses with a methodical consideration of the difference between the theoretical viewpoint and the practical viewpoint, which, setting aside any intention of pure speculation, is obligatory in the conduct of the most concrete operations of research in the social sciences – conducting an interview, describing a practice, drawing up a genealogy, etc. To perform the conversion of the gaze that is required for correct understanding of practice perceived in terms of its own logic, one has to take a theoretical viewpoint on the theoretical viewpoint and draw out all the theoretical and methodological consequences of the (in one sense too obvious) fact that vis-à-vis the situation and the behaviours that he observes, the scientist (ethnologist, sociologist, or historian) is not in the position of an active agent, involved in the action, invested in the game and its stakes; that, faced with one of the marriages recorded in the genealogies he collects, he is not in the position of a father or mother who wants a marriage, and a good marriage, for their son or daughter. Yet it is rare for this difference in viewpoints, and in the associated interests, to be really taken into account in the analysis. This is true even in the case of the ethnologist, who has every reason to see himself as excluded from the game by his status as an outsider and therefore condemned, whether he likes it or not, to a quasi-theoretical viewpoint (even if he finds encouragement to forget the limits inherent in his viewpoint, not so much in his more or less successful attempts to 'participate' as in the complicity he often receives from his informants – especially the 'elders' – when he unwittingly imposes the scholastic viewpoint on them, especially by his questions which incline and encourage them to adopt a theoretical viewpoint on their own practice). And it is no doubt the powerful, fascinating experience of being a stranger that makes him forget, in the literary self-indulgence of exoticism, that he is no less a stranger to his own practice than to the strange practices he observes, or rather, that his own practice is no less strange to him, in its truth as practice, than the strangest practices of other people, with which it shares, in its trivial self-

[2] See 'Postscript: How to read an author', p. 85 below.

evidence, one essential thing, but so hard to think, namely the logic of practice.

It is sufficient to succeed in placing oneself – *in thought*, by means of a theoretical and empirical effort (and not through the magic of some form of intuition or emotional participation) – at the point of view of the agent practically engaged in universes in which the essential part of the circulation of economic and, above all, symbolic capital takes place through matrimonial exchanges, to be led to see behaviours such as the practices associated with marriage, from the initial negotiations to the final ritual, as oriented *strategies* (and not rules) aimed at maximizing the material and symbolic profits secured through the marriage. The same theoretical conversion of the theoretical gaze leads to the discovery that the ritual action (and, by the same token, the recitation of myth) that objectivist anthropology sees in terms of logic and algebra is much closer, in reality, to a gymnastics or dance taking advantage of all the possibilities offered by the 'geometry' of the body – right/left, up/down, in front/behind, etc. – and oriented towards perfectly serious and often very urgent ends. Plato pointed out that the 'the philosopher is a mythologist'; but it is also true that the mythologist (in the sense of the analyst of myths) is often a philosopher, which leads him to forget that symbolic systems, such as ritual practice, are coherent and signifying, but only up to a point. This is because they have to comply with a twofold condition: on the one hand to manifest a certain constancy in the use of mythic symbols and operators, and, on the other hand, to remain practical, that is, economical, easy to use and turned towards practical ends, towards the realization of wishes, desires, often vital ones, for the individual and above all for the group.

Thus, it is only when – at the cost of an effort of learning about others and their practice, which, it has to be said, does not come without learning about oneself and one's own practice – one has managed to make oneself more attentive and more receptive to practice as it is practised that one has some chance of observing and recording some of the features of ritual behaviours which structuralist logicism, supported by the whole social logic of a scholastic universe that prides itself on its logical logic, its models, preferably mathematical ones, would lead one to ignore or set aside as simple misfirings of the mythic algebra, devoid of meaning or interest – ambiguous acts, polysemous objects (underdetermined or indeterminate), made possible by the relative indeterminacy of acts and symbols, not to mention the partial contradictions and the fuzziness arising from the uncertain abstraction which governs the whole process, giving it its practical coherence, which also means its flexibility, its openness, everything that makes it 'practical' and therefore predisposed to respond at the least cost (especially in logical development) to the urgencies of existence and practice.[3]

Among many examples, I shall only mention here the ambiguities of the Kabyle ritual of the last sheaf, which, as if hesitating between a cycle of resurrection of the grain and a cycle of death and resurrection of the field, treats the last sheaf, in some areas, as a female personification of the field (referred to as the 'betrothed') onto which the male rain, sometimes personified as *Anzar*, is called down, and elsewhere as a male (phallic) symbol of the 'spirit of the grain', destined to return for a time to dryness and sterility before inaugurating a new cycle of life by pouring down as rain onto the parched earth. Or again, the ambiguities of rain, which, by virtue of its celestial origin, partakes of solar masculinity while evoking, in another respect, moist, terrestrial femininity, so that, depending on the occasion, it can be treated either as fecundating or fecundated. The same is true of an operation like the scheme of swelling, depending on whether it is associated with phallic virility and semen, which causes swelling, or with the earth, the womb, which swells, like beans or wheat in the pot.

Among the practical determinants of the functioning of practical logic, one of the most determining is no doubt the fact that actions, even the most ritualized and repetitive ones, are necessarily linked to time by their movement and their duration. Objectivist hermeneutics, which fails to observe that the *economical coherence* appropriate to behaviours that are necessarily subject to the urgency of practical purposes is made possible by the fact that they unfold in time, destroys that logic by constructing schemas and models which telescope the successive moments of practice (for example, gift and countergift). It considers 'monothetically', to put it in Husserlian terms, that is, in simultaneity, sequences of symbolic practices which 'polythetically', that is, in succession and discontinuity, unfold polysemous mythico-ritual symbols, thus protected against the confrontation and contradiction that one encounters as soon as one makes a systematic collection, for example, by trying to reconstitute the calendar of agrarian, culinary, etc., rites and practices; which play on the connotations and harmonics of the symbols on the basis of the urgencies and demands of the situation, taking advantage of the logical liberties which come from being staggered in time (and which theoretical synchronization destroys, as Socrates was already aware when he used it to throw his interlocutors into confusion).

---

[3] I only sketch here analyses which I have developed in detail in *The Logic of Practice* (Cambridge: Polity Press, 1990), esp. pp. 200–70.

As for the principle of this minimum coherence, it cannot be anything other than analogical practice founded on the *transfer of schemes*, which takes place on the basis of acquired equivalences facilitating the substitutability and the substitution of one behaviour for another and making it possible, through a kind of practical generalization, to master all problems of similar form capable of arising in new situations. This economical use of polysemy, fuzzy logic, vagueness, approximation, and this art of sequencing practices linked by a more or less observable 'family likeness' is, moreover, not restricted to archaic worlds. At the risk of surprising, I could evoke here some forms of practical logic which, though our theories do not allow for them, we often indulge in, especially in the political order, when, for example, we put into play vague sets of imprecise metaphors and approximate metaphors – liberalism, liberation, liberalization, flexibility, free enterprise, deregulation, etc. – or even in the intellectual order, where there have flourished, and still flourish, syncretic ideologies, obtained by mixing themes and schemes borrowed from various thinkers – among the German 'conservative revolutionaries' of the 1930s, degeneration, decomposition, totality, etc. – in varying proportions, according to the audience, the circumstances and the occasion, which leave each of their users the possibility of projecting their commonest drives and interests with the illusion of the most extreme originality.

The scholastic barrier

Like the ethnological inquiry, the sociological survey is the occasion for distortions which are simply a particular form of the structural misunderstandings which are set in place whenever a professional – lawyer or doctor, professor or engineer – enters into relation with a lay person, a stranger to the scholastic vision, without realizing that he is confronted not only with a different language, but with another way of constructing the given (of a dispute or an illness, for example), presupposing the implementation of a profoundly different system of dispositions. A number of failures which then arise in communication are attributable to the difficulty of moving from the notion applicable in everyday practice to the specialist notion – legal, medical, mathematical, etc. – that is to say, of adopting the disposition which is presupposed by its adequate use in the field in question, which leads one to accentuate, even absolutize, certain connotations of the words demanded by the field (for example, the mathematical, sociological or artistic connotation of the word 'group'). So long as these

languages (which, as in the case of law or philosophy, are only partially independent of ordinary language) are addressed to listeners
and users who are prepared, without even realizing it, to adopt the
principle of selection among the various connotations which prevails
in that field (and which is announced in the founding tautologies:
philosophical texts must be read philosophically, works of art must
be contemplated aesthetically – and not religiously, or erotically –
etc.), there is no need to specify the sense in which they are meant.

But the gap becomes clear whenever this agreement of dispositions
ceases to be assured: when, for example, a *plaint*, in the sense of a
simple expression of pain, dissatisfaction or discontent, has to be
turned into a plaint in the legal sense, the declaration of a wrong or
an injustice before a legal authority, or into a universal demand,
before a delegate, a representative or spokesperson. The frequently
observed disappointment that the most deprived agents experience
on contact with the courts is only the limiting case of the structural
frustration to which they are condemned in all their relations with
bureaucratic authorities. The difficulty is no less, even if it is less
evident, whenever an unformulated need, expectation or aspiration
has to be stated *formally*, as an *official* request, to a social security
office or any other welfare agency. And what can one say of the
seemingly so banal transformation presupposed by the legal formalization of a promise, the one which occurs, almost automatically,
as if independently of the parties to it, through the intervention of a
law officer such as a *notaire*, the guarantor of the regularity of the
required formalities, the drafting of the contract, the recording and
witnessing of the signatures, application of the seal, quasi-sacramental
enunciation of the commitments, etc.? Like the priest in his own
domain, the 'ministerial officer' is the sherpa of a mysterious, risky
passage which brings a singular, ad hoc act into the order of law,
thereby converting it into a legal act destined to be considered hence-
forward (notably by all the legal officials who may have cognizance
of it) as entitled to produce all the juridical effect attached to the
category of acts in which it has been formally inscribed (sale, purchase, lease, etc.).

What is involved, in all these cases (and the same would be true
for the patient–doctor relation), is not just the mastery of a specialist
language and particularly its terminology; it is the profound transformation that is imperatively required for crossing the scholastic frontier.
This transformation, although unrecognized in epistemological or methodological reflection, is also in question in the relationship between
the sociological surveyor and the surveyed. It happens very often
that, having failed to question the questionnaire or, more profoundly,

the position of the agent who produces or administers it, and who has the leisure to detach himself from the self-evidences of ordinary existence in order to ask himself some extra-ordinary questions or to ask some ordinary questions in an extra-ordinary way, the sociologist asks the respondents to be their own sociologists, by asking them directly the question he is asking himself about them (I am thinking of questions, countless times used and countless times approved, at least tacitly, by the guardians of methodological orthodoxy, of the type: 'Do you think social classes exist?' or 'In your view, how many social classes are there?'). Worse, one finds questioners (especially among specialists in 'public opinion') who will pose questions to which the respondents can always provide a minimum yes-or-no answer, but which they have never posed themselves before having them imposed on them, and which they could not really pose themselves (that is, produce by their own means) unless they were disposed and prepared by their conditions of existence to adopt on the social world and on their own practice the point of view from which those questions were produced, that is, unless they were quite other than what they are, which is exactly what the survey is trying to understand. And the trap that scholastic questions open for the person who asks them, in his positivist naivety, is all the greater because they may sometimes apparently elicit responses (a yes or a no) which, when they are not simple concessions of indifference or politeness, often spring from practical dispositions of habitus, triggered by tacit reference to a personal situation in its singularity (for example, a general question about the future of technical education may receive a response generated on the basis of the problems directly encountered in that system by the respondent's son or daughter).[4]

Reflecting on the practice of polling organizations, together with analysis of the conditions of access to the scholastic posture, helped me greatly to become aware of the effects of the gap between the intention of the questioner and the extrascholastic preoccupations of the respondents, which is the source of the distortions performed by the self-blind questioning of the doxosophers[5] (apparent experts in appearances who can deceive other 'semi-experts' – journalists or politicians – only because they deceive themselves). The method adopted in the survey whose findings are presented in *The Weight of*

[4] I was able to confirm this by carrying out a second interview on the meaning of their answers with people previously subjected to a standard example of scholastic questioning (a questionnaire by the polling agency SOFRES).

[5] The Platonic notion of 'doxosophers' (*doxosophoi*), which can be translated as seeming scholars or scholars of appearances, of opinion (*doxa*), is used here to refer to opinion pollsters. *Trans.*

the World[6] was primarily intended to try – at the cost of a permanent effort of reflexivity – to neutralize the distortions which the structural gap inherent in some forms of the survey relationship can introduce into communication. Being anxious to avoid proceeding as if the disposition to consider one's own experience and one's own practice as an object of knowledge to be thought and spoken about were a universal disposition, we set out to bring to the order of discourse, that is, a quasi-theoretical status, certain experiences of people who do not have access to the conditions in which one acquires the scholastic disposition. This was done not only by taking care to avoid introducing a scholastic bias through epistemocentric questions which would call for the scholastic disposition, but also by assisting those respondents who were furthest from the scholastic condition in an effort of self-understanding and self-knowledge which, like the 'self-concern'[7] which it presupposes, is ordinarily reserved for the world of *skholè*.

I have taken these few examples from ethnology and sociology rather than, as I might, from linguistics or, above all, economics, where the scholastic illusion reigns unchallenged, because of the failure to consider the economic conditions of compliance with the laws of the economic world, which the theory thus constitutes as the universal norm of practices. They will suffice, I think, to show that unawareness of everything that is implied in the scholastic viewpoint leads to the fallacy of putting 'a scientist in the machine' (to adapt Ryle's famous title) by crediting agents with the reasoning reason of the scientist reasoning about their practices (and not the practical reason of the scientist acting in everyday life); or, more precisely, by proceeding as if the constructs (theories, models or rules) that one has to produce in order to make practices or works intelligible to an observer who can only grasp them from outside after the event (with the aid of instruments of thought whose use takes time, such as genealogies or statistics) were the effective and efficient principle of those practices.

Digression: A critique of my critics

I hesitated for a long time before deciding to discuss here the misreadings that are very often made of my work. And if I have overcome the temptation to ignore them – a strong one because the

[6] P. Bourdieu et al., *The Weight of the World: Social Suffering in Contempory Society* (Cambridge: Polity Press, 1999), esp. Pierre Bourdieu, 'Understanding'.
[7] *le 'souci de soi'* – which is the title of volume 1 of Michel Foucault's *Histoire de la Sexualité. Trans.*

preconceptions which inspire them often seem to me obvious and likely to denounce themselves for any reader in good faith – it is above all in order to pursue as far as possible the concern to explain, and to explain myself.

I have tried to show on what conditions and at the cost of what effort one can really implement the famous 'principle of charity' (which I would here rather call the principle of generosity) in the confrontation with an author of the present or the past.[8] And, being convinced that every cultural producer, without distinction, has a right to such treatment, I feel entitled to claim it for my own work (generosity in no way implies indulgence, and the harshest critiques, when based on real knowledge and understanding, are probably the most fruitful, and if I were not afraid of appearing to give way to indulgence myself, I would like to list all those who, by their private or public criticisms, have helped me to discover and, I think, move beyond the limits of my research). The most reductive critiques, often coming from eager young rivals who, as in all fields, see the interpellation of more consecrated competitors, sometimes reduced to a form of defamation (with, for example, classificatory insults – 'Marxist', 'holistic', 'determinist', etc.), as a shortcut towards visibility more convenient than producing work of their own, almost always spring from two principles: the theoreticist derealization associated with the scholastic view of the *lector*, and the dehistoricization resulting from an inability or refusal to situate a type of thought in the space of possibles in relation to which it was constructed.

The *lector*'s reading strives to find sources, always partial, often imaginary (reminding one of those art historians who transpose the iconological approach into periods for which it is no longer justified and flaunt their wealth of culture and imagination in enumerating the references – to classical painting, contemporary popular images, contemporary photographs, etc. – suggested to them by a painting of Manet's). It does so with the intention, so typical of *academica mediocritas*, of explaining the unknown in terms of the already known, the academic variant of the slogan 'nothing new under the sun', a favourite theme of conservative thought, and of demonstrating that 'known' authors are, like everyone else, simply readers of other known authors. (I am thinking of those who have applied themselves to cataloguing the earlier uses of the notion of *habitus*, not with a view to showing the originality of the latest usage – though that usage is the principle of their intervention – but with the aim of destroying it.

[8] Cf. P. Bourdieu, *The Rules of Art: Genesis and Structure of the Literary Field* (Cambridge: Polity Press, 1996), and 'Postscript: How to read an author', p. 85 below.

To them, I would recall the often-quoted response that Pascal, though very critical of Descartes, made to those who wanted to attribute the *cogito* to St Augustine: 'In truth, I am very far from saying that Descartes is not its true author, even if he only learned of it by reading that great saint; for I know how much difference there is between casually writing a word, without thinking any longer or more extensively about it, and seeing in that word an admirable sequence of consequences, which proves the distinction of material and spiritual natures, and making it a firm and sustained principle of a whole physics, as Descartes claimed to do. For, without examining whether he effectively succeeded in what he claimed, I will suppose that he did, and it is on that supposition that I say that this word is as different in his writings from the same word in those of others who have uttered it in passing, as a man full of life and strength from a dead man.'[9] A very elegant way of underlining that one kind of critique is only an irreproachable form of murder.)

But the clearest misunderstanding stems from the fact that the *lector*'s reading is an end in itself, and that it is interested in texts, and in the theories, methods or concepts that they convey, not in order to do something with them, to bring them, as useful, perfectible instruments, into a practical use, but so as to gloss them, by relating them to other texts (under cover, on occasion, of epistemology or methodology[10]). This reading thus sweeps away what is essential, that is to say, not only the problems that the concepts aimed to name and resolve – understanding a ritual, explaining the variations in behaviour in relation to credit, saving or fertility, accounting for differential rates of educational success or museum-going, etc. – but also the space of theoretical and methodological possibles which led those problems to be posed, at that moment, and in those terms (for example, the forced choice between objectivism and subjectivism incarnated, at a particular moment, by this or that exemplary representative of structuralism or phenomenology), and which it is indispensable to reconstruct through historical work, in particular because it may have been transformed by the new solutions that the texts subjected to critique have provided to these problems.

[9] Pascal, 'Art de persuader', in *Pensées et Opuscules*, ed. L. Brunschvicg (Paris: Hachette, 1912), p. 193.
[10] I shall never cease to regret that epistemological reflection on the social sciences has largely been abandoned to the specialists of these disciplines, who do not always have the necessary competence and serenity, and that, with some remarkable exceptions (I am thinking of Jean-Claude Pariente, for example), the philosophers have kept away from them, at least in France, no doubt because the caste barrier between the disciplines is higher there.

The very logic of the commentary, which subjects the *opus oper-atum*, a definitively totalized and, as it were, posthumous totality, to an artificial synchronization and decontextualization, leads one to ignore or even cancel out the very movement and effort of research, with its tentative beginnings, its sketches, its rectifications, and the specific logic of a practical sense of theoretical orientation (or, to put it another way, of a scientific habitus), which, at every moment, in a mixture of audacity and prudence, advances provisional concepts that construct themselves as they become more specific and are corrected through the facts that they make it possible to produce; all of which happens, insensibly, through successive refinements and revisions, without any need to resort to self-critiques as spectacular as the errors they are supposed to correct.

The best example would no doubt be the notion of strategy, which forced itself on me in the search for solutions to quite specific problems of ethnology (matrimonial strategies) and sociology (reproduction strategies) and which has had a decisive role in the progress of historical studies devoted to kinship in western societies, by marking a clear break with the structuralist vocabulary of the rule and the theory of action as execution that it implied. How could I have been unaware that in introducing one of the key words of game theory and of the 'intentionalist' view of action into a diametrically opposite paradigm, I would lay myself open to all the critical questioning provoked by a displaced concept, one that was therefore unstable, uncertain and always, as it were, out on a limb? And I think that a more 'practical' reading, guided by the need for the research tools that my texts offered, which would also have been both more demanding and more indulgent than the 'magisterial' critique, would, paradoxically, have been able to exploit that conscious and controlled ambiguity in order to move beyond the alternatives of consciousness and the unconscious and to try to analyse the specific forms of knowledge and even reflection that practice engages.

But what does the scholastic reading ultimately *do*? Opting for sterile genealogies rather than considering the space of possibles in relation to which a concept was developed, and which would give a more accurate idea of its theoretical function, it accentuates, to the point of absurdity, the aspect that the concept had already had to exaggerate, sometimes to excess, in order to break with the dominant representation(s) by 'twisting the stick in the other direction'. Thus, against the scholastic illusion which tends to see every action as springing from an intentional aim, and against the socially most powerful theories of the day which, like neomarginalist economics, accept that philosophy of action without the slightest questioning, the theory of habitus has the primordial function of stressing that the principle of our actions is more often practical sense than rational calculation, or, against the discontinuist, actualist view which is common to philosophies of consciousness (of which the paradigmatic expression is found in Descartes) and to mechanist philosophies (with their stimulus–response model), the past remains present and active in the dispositions it has produced; or again, against the atomistic view put forward by some experimental psychology, which seeks to analyse separate (aesthetic, affective, cognitive, etc.) aptitudes or attitudes, and against the representation (accredited by Kant) which counterposes noble, so-called 'pure' tastes to elementary, or alimentary, tastes, social agents have, *more often than one might expect*, dispositions (tastes, for example) that are more systematic than one might think.

One only has to push these features to the extreme – presenting habitus as a kind of *monolithic* principle (whereas, especially in the case of Algerian subproletarians, I have many times pointed to the existence of cleft, tormented habitus bearing in the form of tensions and contradictions the mark of the contradictory conditions of formation of which they are the product); as an *immutable principle* (whatever degree of reinforcement or inhibition it has received); as *inexorable* (conferring on the past the power to determine *all* future actions); and *exclusive* (leaving no room in any circumstances for conscious intention) – to be able to claim an easy triumph over a caricatured adversary of one's own making. How can one fail to see that the degree to which a habitus is systematic (or, on the contrary, divided and contradictory) and constant (or fluctuating and variable) depends on the social conditions of its formation and exercise, and that this can and must therefore be measured and explained empirically? Or that one of the interests of the theory of habitus is that it reminds us that the probability of achieving 'rational' action, far from being fixed *a priori*, by the diktat of one or another of the stylized theories of action which *homo academicus* loves to 'compare and contrast', depends on social conditions amenable to empirical inquiry, that is to say, on the social conditions of production of dispositions and on the – organic or critical – social conditions of their exercise?

This critique of critiques reveals in any case how difficult it is to discern, in the misunderstandings one observes, the part that is attributable to intentional malevolence, which a superficial look would no doubt lead one to overestimate, and the part that is due to the tendencies inherent in the logic of competition within the field, or, still more strongly, to the tendencies inscribed in the scholastic situation and in the deeply buried dispositions of the scholastic worldview. One might conclude from this that critical reflexivity can, here too, bring not only additional knowledge, but also something like a beginning of wisdom.

Moralism as egoistic universalism

A number of universalistic manifestos or universal prescriptions are no more than the product of (unconscious) universalizing of the particular case, that is, of the privilege constituting the scholastic condition. This purely theoretical universalization leads to a fictitious universalism so long as it is not accompanied by any reminder of the repressed economic and social conditions of access to the universal or by any (political) action aimed at universalizing these conditions in practice. To grant 'humanity' to all, but in a purely formal way, is to exclude from it, under an appearance of humanism, all those who are deprived of the means of realizing it.

Thus, the representation of political life that Habermas proposes, on the basis of a description of the emergence of the 'public sphere' as it developed in the major European countries in the eighteenth century, with all the institutions (newspapers, clubs, coffee-houses, etc.) which accompany and support the development of a civic culture, obscures and represses the question of the economic and social conditions that would have to be fulfilled in order to allow the public deliberation capable of leading to a rational consensus, that is, a debate in which the competing particular interests would receive the same consideration and in which the participants, conforming to an ideal model of 'communicative action', would seek to understand the points of view of the others and to give them the same weight as their own.[11] How indeed can it be ignored that, even within the scholastic worlds, cognitive interests are rooted in strategic or instrumental social interests, that the force of arguments counts for little against the arguments of force (or even against desires, needs, passions and, above all, dispositions), and that domination is never absent from social relations of communication?

But I would fear I might fail to respect the principle of generosity if I were to offer a necessarily rapid and superficial critique of a complex body of thought, constantly evolving and rooted in a long historical tradition, which, to do it justice, would have to be discussed at length (thus the theory of public deliberation, theorized later as 'communicative reason', preserves a variant of the distinction, dear

[11] J. Habermas, *The Theory of Communicative Action* (Cambridge: Polity Press, 1987) and *Knowledge and Human Interests* (Cambridge: Polity Press, 1987).

to Kant – and Rousseau – between *Willkür*, or the 'general will', and *Wille*, or the 'will of all' understood as the aggregation of particular wills, and pursues the argument of Rousseau who insisted on the argumentative character of the working out of the 'general will'). For that reason I prefer to try to bring out what seems to me to be the *generative formula* of Habermas's thought as regards politics, so as to make it amenable not to a theoretical commentary or critique, but to a confrontation with experience, to which, it has to be said, it does not spontaneously lend itself. It seems to me in fact that – and here he is close to the characteristic effect of German philosophy as described by Marx[12] – Habermas subjects social relations to a twofold reduction, or, which amounts to the same thing, a twofold depoliticization, which surreptitiously throws the political back onto the terrain of ethics. He reduces political power relations to relations of communication (and to 'the force without violence of argumentative discourse which makes it possible to reach agreement and bring about consensus'), that is, to relations of 'dialogue' from which he has in practice removed the power relations that take place there in a transfigured form.[13] The essentialist analysis of language, and of 'intercomprehension' understood as its supposed logically immanent *telos*, thus takes place within a purportedly 'sociological' theory of 'non-violent' (*zwanglos*) communication and in a 'communicative ethic' which is a simple reformulation of the Kantian principle of the universalization of moral judgement and no longer has anything in common with what is uncovered by a sociology of relations of symbolic power; and which, above all, purely and simply abolishes the question of the conditions that have to be fulfilled, both in inter-individual relations and in the political order, to usher in the 'kingdom of ends' ('Reich der Zwecke',

---

[12] When reading Habermas's descriptions of the 'ideal discursive situation' and of the 'communicative ethics' that is generated there as if by miracle, one cannot help thinking of the pages that Marx devotes, in the Manifesto of the Communist Party, to the German philosophers and the consummate art with which they transformed 'the utterance of the will of the revolutionary French bourgeoisie' into an expression of 'the laws of pure Will, of Will as it was bound to be, of true human will generally' (K. Marx and F. Engels, *Manifesto of the Communist Party* (Peking: Foreign Languages Press, 1972), p. 65). The analogy is rough and ready, and an oversimplification. But it is certain that, while it is never possible to reduce a body of thought to its social uses and effects, Habermas's work has owed part of its universal appeal to the fact that it gave the stamp of great German philosophy to pious considerations on democratic dialogue, too obviously marked by the naiveties of Christian humanism (A. Wellmer, *Ethik und Dialog. Elemente des moralischen Urteils bei Kant in der Diskursethik* (Frankfurt: Suhrkamp, 1986).

[13] I have developed this critique further in *Language and Symbolic Power* (Cambridge: Polity Press, 1991).

as Kant says in *Grundlegung zur Metaphysik der Sitten*) that goes by the name of 'communicative action'.

One then only has to go back to the 'public sphere' as it exists in reality, to understand that the epistemocentric illusion which leads Habermas to make the universality of reason and the existence of universalizable interests the basis of rational consensus is based on unawareness (or repression) of the conditions of access to the political sphere and of the factors of *discrimination* (such as sex, education or income) which limit the chances of access not only, as is often said, especially with reference to women, to positions in the political field, but, more profoundly, to articulated political opinion ('to opine [*doxazein*] is to speak,' said Plato) and consequently to the political field.

For, if we regard opinion polls as an opportunity to grasp empirically the conditions of access to political opinion, and consider not only, as people usually do, the answers given, but also the chances of giving or not giving any answer at all, and their variations in relation to various criteria, then we find that the capacity to adopt the necessary posture to respond in a truly pertinent way to the scholastic problematic that the 'pollsters' unwittingly impose is not, as one might expect, distributed randomly – or equally – but depends on various factors such as sex, occupation or level of education. The propensity and aptitude to give an answer (especially to complex questions similar to those that political commentators and 'political scientists' discuss) tends to decline, in favour of abstention and confessions of ignorance, as one moves down the hierarchy of occupations, incomes and qualifications.[14] This finding clearly raises a question as decisive for science as for politics, but one that is disdainfully ignored by 'political science' (no doubt because discovery of this kind of invisible property qualification is a scandal for the 'democratic' mind or, more profoundly, offends belief in the sacred values of the 'person'): the question of the economic and social conditions of access to political opinion, legitimately (and scholastically) defined as articulated and general discourse about the world.

The observation that the inclination and aptitude to express interests, experiences and opinions in words, to seek coherence in judgements and to ground it in explicit and explicitly political principles depend directly on educational capital (and secondarily on the weight of cultural capital relative to economic capital) has something deeply shocking about it. And I only fear that those who are so attached to

---

[14] I analysed these statistical variations more precisely in 'Public opinion does not exist', in *Sociology in Question* (London: Sage, 1993), pp. 149–57.

their 'democratic' or even 'egalitarian' habits of thought that they cannot tell the difference between an observation and a wish, a constative proposition and a performative judgement, will read these analyses – which at least credit the most deprived with the fact of their dispossession – as subtly conservative assaults on 'the people', its 'struggles' and its 'culture'.[15] The flagrant inequality of access to what is called personal opinion is a challenge for the democratic conscience, for the ethical good will of the do-gooders, and also, more profoundly, for the intellectualist universalism that is at the heart of the scholastic illusion. Is there a single philosopher concerned for humanity and humanism who does not accept the central dogma of the rationalist faith, that the faculty of 'judging well', as Descartes put it, of discerning good from evil, truth from falsehood, by a spontaneous, immediate inner feeling, is a universal aptitude of universal application?

Constructed in the eighteenth century against the Church, which claimed a monopoly on the legitimate production of judgements on the world, the idea of 'opinion' and the idea of 'tolerance' that is bound up with it as the affirmation that all opinions, whoever produces them, are equivalent, expressed above all the claim to the right to unrestricted production for the new *small independent cultural producers*, the writers and journalists, whose role was growing in parallel with the emergence of specialized fields and the development of a market for the new cultural products and then of the press and parties as agencies producing specifically political opinions. It was only among some of the founders of the Third Republic, in France, that the idea of personal opinion, inherited from the Enlightenment, was explicitly associated with that of compulsory secular schooling, which was thought necessary in order to give a real basis for universal access to the judgement supposedly expressed in universal suffrage. This connection between education and opinion, which seemed obvious at the beginning both to the supporters and the opponents of universal suffrage, has been little by little forgotten, or repressed.

The presuppositions contained in that genesis survive in the 'democratic' *doxa* which supports all political thought and practice. This *doxa* makes political choice a judgement and a *purely political* judgement,

---

[15] To acknowledge that the most deprived are, contrary to all populist illusions, also deprived of the political 'means of production' is to deny to the 'iron laws of oligarchies' the universal validity that conservative thought ascribes to them. The concentration of power in the hands of mandated representatives is a consequence of dispossession and of the unconditional entrusting of self which it favours, one which is destined to diminish as the extension of education increases access to the instruments of production of political opinion.

implementing explicitly political principles – rather than the practical schemes of the *ethos*, for example – to give an articulated response to a problem perceived as political. This amounts to presupposing that the citizens all possess to the same degree the mastery of the instruments of political production, which are necessary in order to identify a political question as such, to understand it and to respond to it in accordance with their interests, giving an answer that is congruent with the whole set of choices generated from political principles adjusted to those interests. The opinion poll, which calls upon all the persons questioned, without distinction, to produce a 'personal opinion' (as shown by the recurrent and insistent 'What do *you* think?' and 'In *your* view . . .') or to choose, by their own means, without any assistance, between several ready-made opinions, brings out into broad daylight the presuppositions which constitute the *doxa* of 'political science' (a *doxa* so strongly protected by its self-evidence that any theoretical questioning of the presuppositions of the democratic unconscious is likely to be immediately denounced as an assault on democracy). And, through the variations of the rates of non-response and 'Don't know' according to various economic and, especially, cultural variables, it makes it possible to observe the symbolic effects of misrecognition that one produces, without needing to want to do so, or to know one is doing it, by acknowledging everyone's equal right to personal opinion without giving everyone the real means of realizing this formally universal right.

The intellectualist illusion, a typically scholastic one, which supports all political thought and action, is reinforced in this case by the effects of the scholastic cult and culture of the personal and of the 'person'. And it would not be hard to show that the opposition between what is taken to be 'personal' – 'personal ideas', 'personal style', 'personal opinions' – and everything that is impersonal – the Heideggerian *Das Man*, the common, the trivial, the collective, the borrowed – is at the heart of the ethical and aesthetic *doxa* which underlies academic judgements, and that it takes its place very naturally in the system of parallel oppositions which, with another set organized around the opposition between the 'comfortable' (*aisé*) and the 'poor', are the basis of the whole symbolic order, with the division between the rare, distinguished, select, unique, exclusive, different, original, incomparable, on the one hand, and, on the other, the common, vulgar, banal, nondescript, ordinary, average, trite, and all the related distinctions between brilliant and dull, fine and gross, delicate and crude, high and low. It is not only in literature that, as Gide put it, 'only what is personal is of value.' And, ignoring the subtleties (analysed elsewhere) of the different forms (especially bourgeois and petit-bourgeois) of the pretension to 'personal opinion', I would simply like to indicate that the intellectualist universalism through which the universal thinker credits all humans with access to the universal is very deeply rooted, in this case, in the supremely elitist faith in personal opinion, which can coexist with belief in the universality of access to 'enlightened judgement' only by means of an immense repression of the conditions of access to this distinctive and distinguished opinion.[16]

(One only has to relate this 'discovery', which concerns both social reality and 'science' and its unconscious, to the one I made in my early work on Algeria, in the early 1960s, to see that, like access to opinion, access to enlightened economic choice, in the act of purchasing, borrowing or saving, has economic conditions of possibility, and that equality in freedom and in 'rationality' is equally fictitious in either case. I was able to establish empirically that, below a certain level of economic security, provided by stable employment and a basic level of regular income, allowing some grip on the present, economic agents can neither conceive nor perform most of the behaviours which presuppose an effort to take a grip on the future, such as the management of resources over time, saving, measured recourse to credit or the control of fertility. In short, there are economic and cultural conditions for access to what is regarded as rational economic behaviour. Failing simply to ask the question, albeit a typically economic one, of these conditions, economic science treats the prospective and calculating disposition towards the world and time as a natural datum, a universal gift of nature, whereas we know that it is the product of a quite particular individual and collective history.[17])

There are historical conditions for the emergence of reason. And every representation, whether or not it aspires to be scientific, which is based on the forgetting or the deliberate concealment of these conditions tends to legitimate the most unjustifiable of monopolies, the monopoly of the universal. And so, at the risk of being attacked from both sides, one has to make the same refusal both to the advocates of an abstract universalism which ignores the conditions of access to the universal – those who are privileged in terms of gender, ethnicity or social position, who not only have a *de facto* monopoly over the conditions of appropriation of the universal but also grant themselves a legitimation of their monopoly – and to the advocates

[16] On the various spontaneous 'philosophies' of opinion, see P. Bourdieu, 'Questions de politique', *Actes de la Recherche en Sciences Sociales*, 16 (Sept. 1977), pp. 55–89.
[17] P. Bourdieu, *Travail et travailleurs en Algérie* (Paris and The Hague: Mouton, 1964).

of a cynical, disenchanted relativism. Whether in the relations between nations or within nations, abstract universalism generally serves to justify the established order, the prevailing distribution of powers and privileges – the domination of the bourgeois, white, Euro-American heterosexual male – in the name of the formal requirements of an abstract universal (democracy, human rights, etc.) dissociated from the economic and social conditions of its historical realization, or, worse, in the name of an ostentatiously universalist condemnation of any claim for rights for a particular group and, consequently, of all 'communities' based on a stigmatized particularity (women, gays, blacks, etc.). On the other hand, sceptical or cynical rejection of any form of belief in the universal, in the values of truth, emancipation, in a word, Enlightenment, and of any affirmation of universal truths and values, in the name of an elementary form of relativism which regards all universalistic manifestos as pharisaical tricks intended to perpetuate a hegemony, is another way, in a sense a more dangerous one, because it can give itself an air of radicalism, of accepting things as they are.

There is, appearances notwithstanding, no contradiction in fighting *at the same time against* the mystificatory hypocrisy of abstract universalism *and for* universal access to the conditions of access to the universal, the primordial objective of all genuine humanism which both universalistic preaching and nihilistic (pseudo-) subversion forget. The critique of formally universalist critique, which is the condition for a permanent *Aufklärung* of *Aufklärung*, is all the more necessary because the propensity to universalize the particular case, the root of all forms of ethnocentrism, is in this case supported by all the appearances of generosity and virtue. The *imperialism of the universal* that is implied in assimilationist annexation of verbal universalism can take place in the relations of domination within a single nation through a universalization of educational demands not accompanied by a similar universalization of the means of satisfying them. The educational institution, in so far as it is capable of imposing more or less universal recognition of the cultural law while being very far from being able to distribute so widely the knowledge of the universal culture needed in order to obey it, gives a fallacious, but socially very powerful, basis to the epistemocratic sociodicy.[18]

Annexationist violence can also be exerted in the relations of symbolic domination between States and societies having unequal access to the conditions of production and reception of what the dominant nations are able to impose on themselves (and therefore on their own

---

[18] In the sense of justification of society, of the established order.

dominated categories) and to impose on others as universal in politics, law, science, art or literature. In both cases the dominant way of
being, tacitly turned into a norm, the accomplished realization of the
essence of humanity (all forms of racism are essentialist), tends to be
asserted with the appearances of naturalness by virtue of the universalization which constitutes the particularities resulting from historical discrimination, either as unmarked, neutral, universal attributes
(male, white, etc.), or negative, stigmatized 'natures'. Defined as short-
comings linked to a 'mentality' ('primitive', 'female', 'working-class'),
in other words to a nature (which is sometimes proclaimed as such,
contrary to all reason, by the victims of this naturalization) or a
quasi-nature whose historical character is obliterated, the distinctive
properties of the dominated category ('black', 'Arab', in particular,
nowadays) cease to be seen as deriving from the particularities of a
collective and individual history marked by a relation of domination.

And, by a simple reversal of cause and effect, it is thus possible to
'blame the victims' by making their nature responsible for the dispos-
sessions, mutilations and deprivations they are made to suffer. Among
countless examples, some of the most remarkable of which were
generated by the colonial situation, a particularly choice example can
be found in the writings of Otto Weininger, who, in a work claiming
to represent Kantian philosophy, described Jews and women as the
most pernicious incarnations of the threat of heteronomy and disorder to which the project of *Aufklärung* is exposed. Regarding the
name and attachment to the name as 'a necessary dimension of human
personhood', he reproached women for the ease with which they
gave up their own names and took their husbands', concluding,
magisterially, that 'woman is essentially nameless and is so because
she, by definition [*seiner Idee nach*], lacks personhood'.[19] We see
here the paradigm of all the fallacies of racist hatred, examples of
which can be found every day in statements and behaviours directed
at all dominated and stigmatized groups – women, homosexuals,
blacks, immigrants, the dispossessed – who are thus declared responsible for the destiny that is made for them, or summoned to conform
to 'the universal' as soon as they mobilize to claim the rights to
universality which they are in fact denied.

Pascal warns us against 'two extremes: to exclude reason, to admit
reason only'.[20] The modicum of reason which, through long historical

[19] Cf. O. Weininger, *Geschlecht und Charakter. Eine prinzipielle Untersuchung*
(Munich: Matthes and Seitz, 1980), quoted by E. L. Santner, *My Own Private Germany: Daniel Paul Schreber's Secret History of Modernity* (Princeton: Princeton University Press, 1996), pp. 141–2.
[20] Pascal, *Pensées*, 253.

struggles, has been established in history must be endlessly defended, first through an endless critique of the fanaticism of reasoning reason and the abuses of power that it justifies and which, as Hegel noted, engender irrationalism; and then, above all, through the struggles of a *Realpolitik* of reason, which to be effective cannot, as we have seen, be limited to the regulated confrontations of a rational dialogue that knows and recognizes no other force than that of arguments.

The impure conditions of a pure pleasure

The third dimension of the scholastic illusion is aesthetic universalism, of which Kant gave the purest expression in an inquiry into the conditions of possibility of the judgement of taste which makes no mention of the social conditions of possibility of that judgement – those that are manifestly presupposed by 'the disinterested play of sensibility' or 'the pure exercise of the faculty of feeling', in short, what is called the transcendental use of sensibility. Aesthetic pleasure, the 'pure pleasure that *must* be able to be felt by every man', as Kant puts it, is the privilege of those who have access to the conditions in which the so-called 'pure' disposition can be constituted. More precisely, it is based on two sets of conditions: on the one hand, the emergence, through a long evolutionary process, of an autonomous universe, the artistic field, freed from economic and political constraints, and knowing no other law than the law it sets for itself, which means, ultimately, that of art with no other end than itself; and, on the other hand, the occupation, within the social world, of positions in which the 'pure' disposition which gives access to 'pure', purely aesthetic, pleasure can be formed, in particular through upbringing or schooling, and in which, once formed, it can be exercised and, through use, be maintained and perpetuated. (One could, incidentally, say exactly the same of rational or enlightened economic choice, which presupposes on the one hand the existence of an economic cosmos enabling calculation and forecasting to be possible and favouring the development and exercise of the dispositions towards calculation and forecasting that it needs in order to function; and on the other hand access to the conditions in which prospective and calculating dispositions can be formed and exercised, and therefore reinforced.)

All aesthetic reflection must in fact take as its starting point the no doubt somewhat trivial statistic that the mathematical probability of visiting a museum or gallery is closely tied to the level of education, or, more precisely, to the number of years spent in school, which, in France at least, gives very little space to artistic education, so that it must be concluded that the scholastic situation as such exerts a specific effect. This indisputable datum is there to remind us that the propensity to seek and experience aesthetic delight at objects consecrated as works of art by being exhibited in the separate, sacred and sacralizing spaces called museums, which are as it were the institutionalization of the constituting point of view (*nomos*) of the artistic field, is in no way natural or universal. Being the product of particular conditions, this inclination is in fact the monopoly of a privileged minority (although nothing justifies reserving for a few, with the myth of the 'eye', a potential capacity to recognize beauty and to experience aesthetic pleasure which may or may not encounter its social conditions of realization).

In contrast to the frankly aristocratic tradition which, from Plato to Heidegger, ratifies theoretically the difference between the elect and the excluded in matters of thought, art or morality by legitimating it with a more or less explicit sociodicy, universalistic humanism apparently recognizes the right of all to the universal achievements of humanity – but it simply presents, as a characterization of the 'subject' in its universality, an analytic of the experience of the cultivated 'subject' in its particularity (scientific, ethical or aesthetic). It too thus ratifies the difference, but in a more concealed way, through simple omission of the social conditions which make it possible, thereby setting up as the norm of all possible practice the one which has benefited from these forgotten or ignored conditions. And this ratification has very little chance of being contested: it can only satisfy those who, having the universal as their particularity (in this area or elsewhere), feel entitled to feel themselves universal and to demand universal recognition of the universal which they incarnate so perfectly and which they often justify, especially in their own eyes, by a cultural proselytism which can, moreover, coexist with a concern to mark or maintain difference; but it will also be accepted, paradoxically (there is, whether one likes it or not, very little 'resistance' in these matters), by all those who, being excluded from the conditions of access to the universal, have often internalized the prevailing law, which (thanks, in particular, to the work of the educational system) is constituted as a universal norm, generating demands and lacks – sufficiently deeply to feel themselves, if not deprived, then dispossessed, at least on some occasions, or even crippled and in some way diminished.

When one remembers the very particular social conditions of possibility of the judgement 'aspiring to universal validity' which, according to Kant, the judgement of taste is, one is inevitably obliged to set limits to its pretensions to universality and, by the same token, those of the Kantian aesthetic. While that aesthetic may be granted a limited validity, as a quasi-phenomenological analysis of the aesthetic experience that is accessible to certain cultivated 'subjects' in certain historical societies, it immediately has to be added that the unconscious universalizing of the particular case that it performs by forgetting its own historical conditions of possibility, that is, its own limits, has the effect of constituting a particular experience of the work of art (or of the world) as the universal norm of all possible aesthetic experience, and of tacitly legitimating those who have the privilege of access to it.

The populist aestheticism which leads some to credit working-class people with a 'popular aesthetic' or a 'popular culture' is another effect, perhaps the most unexpected one, of the scholastic illusion: it performs a tacit universalization of the scholastic viewpoint which is not accompanied by the slightest real intention of universalizing its conditions of possibility. Instead of note being taken of the social conditions of the suspension of practical interests that a 'pure' aesthetic judgement presupposes, the economic and social privilege which makes the aesthetic viewpoint possible is granted by tacit implication to all men and women, but fictitiously, and only *on paper*. One cannot, in fact, without contradiction, describe (or denounce) the inhuman conditions of existence that are imposed on some, and at the same time credit those who suffer them with the real fulfilment of human potentialities such as the capacity to adopt the gratuitous, disinterested posture that we tacitly inscribe – because it is socially inscribed there – in notions such as 'culture' or 'aesthetic'.

One understands the laudable concern to *rehabilitate*: that is probably what motivated me when, for example, I tried to show that the apparently most conventional and stereotyped photographic compositions which people in the most deprived categories produce, especially to solemnize the solemn moments of family life, or the astonished or indignant comments they make about photographs that aspire to art, obey principles which are coherent but diametrically opposed to those of the Kantian aesthetic (which does not entitle one to refer to them as an aesthetic, except, perhaps, in quotation marks).[21] It was the same concern which encouraged Labov to try to show that the language of adolescents from the black ghettos can vehicle theological analyses as refined as the artfully verbose and euphemized, sometimes impenetrably obscure, discourse of students at Harvard.[22]

---

[21] Cf. P. Bourdieu et al., *Photography: A Middle-brow Art* (Cambridge: Polity Press, 1990).
[22] W. Labov, *Language in the Inner City: Studies in the Black English Vernacular* (Philadelphia: University of Pennsylvania Press, 1972).

But this should not mask the fact that, for example, in contrast to the language of the pupils of the elite schools, the inventive and colourful language (tending therefore to offer intense aesthetic satisfactions) of Harlem adolescents remains totally devoid of value on the educational markets and all similar social situations, starting with recruitment interviews. The social world, with its hierarchies which are not so easily relativized, is not relativist . . .

The cult of 'popular culture' is often simply a purely verbal and inconsequential (and therefore pseudo-revolutionary) inversion of the class racism which reduces working-class practices to barbarism or vulgarity. Just as some celebrations of femininity simply reinforce male domination, so this ultimately very comfortable way of respecting the 'people', which, under the guise of exalting the working class, helps to enclose it in what it is by converting privation into a choice or an elective accomplishment, provides all the profits of a show of subversive, paradoxical generosity, while leaving things as they are, with one side in possession of its truly cultivated culture (or language), which is capable of absorbing its own distinguished subversion, and the other with its culture or language devoid of any social value and subject to abrupt devaluations (like the 'broken English' Labov refers to) which are fictitiously rehabilitated by a simple operation of theoretical false accounting.

It follows that 'cultural policies' directed towards the most deprived are condemned to oscillate between two forms of hypocrisy (as is clearly visible nowadays in the treatments accorded to ethnic minorities, especially immigrants). On the one hand, in the name of a respect that is at once condescending and without consequences for cultural particularities and particularisms that are largely imposed and suffered, and which are thereby redefined as choices – I am thinking of the use some conservative thinking makes of 'respect for difference' or that inimitable invention of some American specialists on the ghettos, the 'culture of poverty' – one encloses the dispossessed in their condition by failing to offer them the real means of realizing their restricted possibilities. On the other hand, as the educational system now does, one universally imposes the same demands without any concern for equally universally distributing the means of satisfying them, thus helping to legitimate the inequality that one merely records and ratifies, while additionally exercising (first of all in the educational system) the symbolic violence associated with the effects of real inequality within formal equality. (This is a fairly depressing conclusion when one knows that, in modern States at least, the possibility for the dominated to reappropriate something like a culture of their own with the aim of ennobling it is more or less totally ruled out by the effect of the forces of cultural imposition, and deculturation, foremost among which is the educational system, which is effective enough to destroy marginal traditional cultures – with the collaboration of the mass media – without being capable of giving broad access to the central culture.)

Thus, disregard of the – ignored or repressed – social conditions of the experience of beauty and the conditions of its real universalization is sufficient in itself to bear witness to the tacit adherence of the universalistic thinker to the very particular, privileged, social conditions of his would-be universalistic aesthetic experience. But the *Critique of the Faculty of Judgement*[23] provides another, more direct, confession: the rigorous architecture of the theory of aesthetic judgement, the only one perceived by the spontaneously complicit commentary of the *lectores*, conceals a hidden discourse, that of the scholastic unconscious, which expresses the horror of 'barbarous taste', 'the taste of the tongue, the palate and the gullet', the purely sensual antithesis of the 'pure' taste which has all the attributes of universality. And perhaps a similar confession, no less paradoxical in appearance, has to be detected in those who take up arms to defend universalism only when they see the emergence of effective movements of protest against the most flagrant denials of universalism, which are immediately denounced as particularist dissidence.

The ambiguity of reason

One only has to recall the social conditions of the emergence of universes in which the universal is generated to find it impossible to share in the naively universalistic optimism of the first *Aufklärung*: the advent of reason is inseparable from the progressive autonomization of social microcosms based on privilege, sites for the progressive invention of modes of thought and action that are theoretically universal but monopolized in practice by a few. The resulting ambiguity explains how people can indulge simultaneously or alternately in aristocratic contempt for the domestic barbarism of the 'vulgar' and in universalistic moralism, an unconditional generosity towards an unconditioned 'humanity', whether exotic or domestic.

---

[23] See the Postscript to *Distinction* (Cambridge: Harvard University Press, 1984) for Bourdieu's critique of Kant's *Critique of the Faculty of Judgement* and of Derrida's commentary on it. *Trans.*

The same ambiguity is seen in the relationship between dominant and dominated nations – or provinces and regions annexed to the central State, its language and culture, etc. Thus the revolutionaries of 1789, who took the French State to a higher degree of universality than most contemporary nations (with the *Code Civil*, the metric system, decimal currency and so many other 'rational' inventions), immediately invested their universalistic faith in an imperialism of the universal which served the interest of a national (or nationalist) State and its dignitaries. As a result, they aroused reactions as opposed, albeit equally comprehensible, as the universalistic enthusiasm of those who, like Kant, were attentive to the luminous aspect of the message, and the reactive nationalism of which Herder became the theoretician. In any case, those aspects of the reactionary mystique of the nation which are most repugnant to the universalistic conviction, and the irrationalist pathos which so often accompanies it, become more comprehensible when seen as a distorted riposte to the ambiguous aggression of the imperialism of the universal (a riposte of which the contemporary homologue might be some forms of Islamic fundamentalism).

The *obscurantism of the Enlightenment* can take the form of a fetishism of reason and a fanaticism of the universal which remain closed to all the traditional manifestations of belief and which, as is shown for example by the reflex violence of some denunciations of religious fundamentalism, are no less obscure and self-opaque than what they denounce. But, above all, in so far as it is made possible by privilege – a privilege that is not aware of itself – reason contains the potentiality of an abuse of power: produced in fields (legal, scientific, etc.) based on *skholè* and objectively engaged (especially through their links with the educational system) in the division of the labour of domination, it has a rarity which causes it always to function as (cultural or informational) capital and also, in so far as the economic and social conditions of its production remain misrecognized, as symbolic capital and therefore both as a source of material and symbolic profits and as an instrument of domination and legitimation. It even offers the supreme form of legitimation, with *rationalization* (in both Freud's and Weber's senses) or, more precisely, universalization, which is the sociodicy par excellence. The legal or mathematical formalization which materializes the scholastic separation in a barrier of opaque and necessary symbolism, allowing one to write propositions valid for an indifferent universal x, can give the air of the most irresistible universality to the most arbitrary content.

(Whatever the respect that the *homo scholasticus* slumbering in me may feel for the theoretical construction built up by John Rawls, I cannot subscribe to a formal model in which the 'things of logic' too visibly eclipse or crush the 'logic of things'.[24] It is surely clear that, as has often been suggested, the dogmatic character of Rawls's argument for the priority of basic liberties is explained by the fact that he tacitly credits the partners in the original position with a latent ideal which is none other than his own, that of a *homo scholasticus* attached to an ideal vision of American democracy.[25] And, above all, how can one forget the conditions that have to be fulfilled in order for the author and his readers to be able to accept the scholastic presuppositions of this analysis of the presuppositions of the social contract – particularly the one which consists in depriving the contracting parties of any information concerning the respective social properties, in short, reducing them to the state of interchangeable individuals, as in neoclassical theories? It is impossible to grant anything other than an arbitrary and quasi-ludic adherence to the typically scholastic mental experience which, as in Habermas – who, despite the apparent differences, largely attributable to the difference between theoretical traditions, is very close to Rawls – tends to reduce a question of politics (already a somewhat unreal one) to a problem of rational ethics: to imagine that we are trying to organize social and economic institutions with people whose agreement we must obtain, but on the basis that we know nothing about the tastes, talents or interests of the two sides, nothing about the social position that each will occupy or of the society in which they will live. And it is impossible not to think that what Rawls calls the 'veil of ignorance', that is, the idea that a theory of justice must say what our rights and rules of cooperation would be if we were to know nothing of what is ordinarily opposed to perfect impartiality, is a fine evocation, a useful one in the end, of the abstraction on which the economic orthodoxy from which Rawls has adopted his mode of thought is, often unwittingly, based.)

The State nobility finds the principle of its sociodicy in the educational system and in the qualifications which are presumed to guarantee its competence. The nineteenth-century bourgeoisie based its legitimacy on the distinction between the 'deserving poor' and the rest, who were morally condemned for their fecklessness and immorality. The

---

[24] J. Rawls, *A Theory of Justice* (Cambridge: Harvard University Press, 1971). For an insight into the deep affinity which, beyond the proclaimed differences, exists between Rawls and Habermas, see J. Habermas, 'Reconciliation through the public use of reason: remarks on political liberalism', *Journal of Philosophy*, no. 3 (1995), pp. 109–31.

[25] Cf. H. L. A. Hart, 'Rawls on liberty and its priority', in N. Daniels (ed.), *Reading Rawls* (New York: Basic Books, 1975), pp. 238–59.

State nobility also has its 'poor' (or, in the current terminology, the 'excluded'), who, rejected from work – the source of the means of existence but also of justifications for existing – are condemned, sometimes in their own eyes too, in the name of what is now supposed to determine and justify election and exclusion, namely competence, the *raison d'être* and legitimation that the State alone is supposed to guarantee, through rational, universal procedures. The myth of the 'natural gift' and the racism of intelligence are at the centre of a sociodicy, experienced by all dominant groups, beyond the differences in their declared ethical and political commitments, which makes (educationally measured) 'intelligence' the supreme principle of legitimation and which, in a civilization of 'performance' where success is everything – imputes poverty and failure not to idleness, improvidence or vice, but to stupidity.

Any project for a reform of understanding which counts solely on the force of rational preaching to advance the cause of reason remains a prisoner of the scholastic illusion. One therefore has to appeal to a *Realpolitik* of the universal, a specific form of political struggle aimed at defending the social conditions of the exercise of reason and the institutional bases of intellectual activity, and at endowing reason with the instruments which are the conditions of its fulfilment in history. Acknowledging the unequal distribution of the social conditions of access to the universal – a challenge to or denial of humanistic preaching – this kind of politics can make it its aim to work towards favouring access everywhere and by all means to all the instruments of production and consumption of the historical achievements that the logic of the internal struggles of the scholastic fields institutes as universal at a given moment in time (while taking care not to turn them into fetishes and to strip them, by remorseless critique, of all that they owe merely to their social function of legitimation).

It can also aim to rehabilitate practical reason and to subvert the social division between theory and practice in representations and in practices. This opposition, deeply rooted in the scholastic unconscious, dominates the whole of thought. Functioning as an absolute principle of division, it makes it impossible to discover that, as Dewey reminds us, appropriate practice (speaking a language or riding a bicycle, for example) is knowledge and that it even contains a quite particular form of reflection. It imposes itself on thought and practice through the hierarchies that it underlies, even in intellectual and artistic life (between the 'pure' and the 'applied', the 'scientific' and the 'technical', the 'artistic' and the 'decorative', etc.) and also through a number of dichotomies of academic discourse, such as the Kantian distinction between understanding and sensibility, which masks the fact that there is no use of sensibility which does not already imply the use of intellectual capacities.

This opposition, constantly reinforced by the scholastic point of honour, which, with all the forms of logicism implied in 'rational action', inscribes for example reasoning reason in the universality of a nature, is what stands in the way of the construction of an expanded and realistic rationalism of the reasonable and of prudence (in the Aristotelian sense of *phronesis*), capable of defending the specific reasons of practical reason, without falling into the exaltation of practice and of the tradition which one kind of irrationalist, reactionary populism has opposed to rationalism; and capable of imposing effective (that is, educationally sanctioned) recognition of the plurality of the forms of 'intelligence' and combating by every means the *destiny effect* daily exerted by educational verdicts based solely on the most formal forms of this polymorphous capacity.

Digression: A 'habitual' limit to 'pure' thought

To give a sense of how difficult it is to cross this frontier between theory and practice which makes it impossible to produce an adequate knowledge of practical knowledge and to ground a theory of reason capable of making a place for it, I would like to cite here a text by Husserl in which one sees the challenge that this knowledge 'without consciousness' represents even for the philosophers most disposed and prepared to recognize the specific logic of primary experience: 'Our life-world in its originality, which can be brought to light only by the destruction of those layers of sense, is not only (. . .) a world of logical operations, not only the realm of the pregivenness of objects as possible judicative substrates, as possible themes of cognitive activity, but it is also the world of experience in the wholly concrete sense which is commonly tied in with the word "experience". And this commonplace sense is in no way related purely and simply to cognitive behaviour; taken in its greatest generality, it is related, rather, to a habituality [*Habitualität*] which lends to him who is provided with it, to him who is "experienced", assurance in decision and action in the ordinary situations of life (. . .) just as, on the other hand, by this expression we are also concerned with the individual steps of the "experience" by which this habituality is acquired. Thus this commonplace, familiar and concrete sense of the word "experience" points much more to a practically active and evaluative mode of behaviour than specifically to one that is cognitive and judicative.'[26] While recognizing the specificity of what, in another tradition, is called 'knowledge by acquaintance',[27] and the 'experience' it secures, and while explicitly relating it to *Habitualität* (or perhaps for that very reason), Husserl denies it the status of knowledge. For him it has to be seen as a 'practically active and evaluative' rather 'cognitive and judicative' mode of behaviour – as if unconscious acceptance of the opposition between theory and practice and especially, perhaps, the refusal of the trivially genetic mode of explanation were stronger than his desire to return to things themselves and forbade him to cross the sacred boundary.

One is thus led to wonder whether it was not because they were compelled by social drives strong enough to give them reasons to overcome the aversion to everything associated with practice that it has mainly been conservative thinkers, hostile to the rationalist tradition, like Heidegger, Gadamer and, in another tradition, Michael Oakeshott,[28] who have been able to set out some of the properties of practical knowledge, with the aim of rehabilitating tradition against exclusive faith in reason. The interest of Oakeshott's thought lies in the fact that it explicitly establishes the link, elsewhere obscured or tacit, between interest in practical reason and political hostility towards the rationalist tendency to devalue practical traditions in favour of explicit theories – which he calls ideologies – or to consider everything that is consciously planned and deliberately executed as

---

[26] E. Husserl, *Experience and Judgment: Investigations in a Genealogy of Logic*, tr. J. S. Churchill and K. Ameriks (London: Routledge and Kegan Paul, 1973), p. 52. One would have to show how, in his late works, Husserl endlessly oscillated between a transcendental theory of the pure Ego, habitus then being no more than a kind of *constantia sibi* of the pure subject, capable of positing constant 'persistent aims', and an anthropological theory of the empirical Ego as *Habitualität*, the words habitus and *Habitualität* as he uses them being the very site of the tension arising from his somewhat desperate efforts to save the subject: 'Within the absolute stream of consciousness of a monad, certain formations of unity occur, but ones which are thoroughly different from the intentional unity of the real Ego and its properties. To those formations belong unities such as the persistent "opinions" of one and the same subject. They can, in a certain sense, be called "habitual", though there is no question here of a habitus as what has become customary, the way the empirical subject might acquire "real" dispositions which would then be called customary. The habitus that we are concerned with pertains not to the empirical, but to the pure, Ego' (E. Husserl, *Ideas Pertaining to a Pure Phenomenology and to a Phenomenological Philosophy. Second Book: Studies in the Phenomenology of Constitution* (Dordrecht, Boston and London: Kluwer, 1989), p. 118).

[27] In English in the original. *Trans.*

[28] M. Oakeshott, *Rationalism in Politics and Other Essays* (London: Methuen, 1967).

superior to what has been unconsciously established over the course of time.

The supreme form of symbolic violence

Through oppositions like that between theory and practice, the whole social order is present in the very way that we think about that order. It follows that the anthropological sciences are condemned to make their goal not only knowledge of an object, like the natural sciences, but knowledge of the knowledge – practical or scientific – of a given object of knowledge, and indeed of any possible object of knowledge. This does not mean that, like philosophy, which assigns itself a similar mission, they claim to occupy an absolute position, without a 'beyond', such that they cannot themselves become objects of knowledge, especially for a particular form of historical knowledge. They have no choice but to strive to know the modes of knowledge, and to know them historically, to historicize them, while subjecting to historical critique the very knowledge that they apply to them.

Rationality – the rationality which the historical sciences claim for themselves in asserting the status of science and distinguishing themselves from the status of simple 'discourse' (to which Foucault himself wanted to reduce them) – is, logically, a central stake in historical struggles, no doubt because reason, or at least rationalization, tends to become an increasingly decisive historical force. The form par excellence of symbolic violence is the *power* which, beyond the ritual opposition between Habermas and Foucault, is exercised *through rational communication*, that is, with the (extorted) adherence of those who, being the dominated products of an order dominated by forces armed with reason (such as those which act through the verdicts of the educational institution or through the diktats of economic experts), cannot but give their acquiescence to the arbitrariness of rationalized force.

It will no doubt be necessary to mobilize ever more resources and technical and rational justifications in order to dominate, and the dominated will have to make ever more use of reason to defend themselves against ever more rationalized forms of domination (I am thinking for example of the political use of opinion polls as instruments of rational demagogy). The social sciences, which alone can unmask and counter the completely new strategies of domination which they sometimes help to inspire and to arm, will more than ever have to choose which side they are on: either they place their rational instruments of knowledge at the service of ever more rationalized domination, or they rationally analyse domination and more especially the contribution which rational knowledge can make to *de facto* monopolization of the profits of universal reason. Awareness and knowledge of the social conditions of that logical and political scandal, the monopolization of the universal, indicate without ambiguity the ends and the means of a permanent *political struggle* for the universalization of the means of access to the universal.

How to Read an Author

I fear that my critique of the *lector*'s reading will fall victim to the derealizing neutralization that this reading precisely performs. And, knowing that here I am touching on the very foundation of scholastic belief, I would like not only to explain, or prove my point, but make it felt, and in that way overcome routine, or lift resistance, by using, as a kind of parable, the case of Baudelaire, who, through successive readings and rereadings, has, more than any other writer, suffered the effects of canonization, an eternization that dehistoricizes and derealizes, while making it impossible to recreate 'the inimitable grandeur of beginnings' to which, in a quite different context, Claude Lévi-Strauss refers.

With Baudelaire we are faced with a problem of *historical anthropology* just as difficult as those that arise for the historian or ethnologist from the deciphering of an unknown society. But, because of the false familiarity we derive from long academic frequentation, we are not aware of it. One of the most hackneyed topics of the discourse of celebration of the 'classics', which has the effect of sending them into limbo, as if outside time and space, far away, in any case, from the debates and battles of the present, consists paradoxically in describing them as our contemporaries, those closest to us – so contemporary and so close that we do not doubt for an instant the apparently immediate understanding (in reality mediated by our whole education) that we think we have of their work.

Yet we are, without realizing it, perfect strangers to the social universe in which Baudelaire found himself, and in particular to the intellectual world with which and against which he evolved and which, in return, he profoundly transformed and indeed *revolutionized*, by helping to create the literary field, a radically new world, but one that, for us, is self-evident. Being ignorant of our ignorance, we efface the most extraordinary aspects of Baudelaire's life, namely the efforts he had to make to bring about that extra-ordinary reality, the literary microcosm as the 'economic world reversed'. Like Manet, another great heresiarch, Baudelaire is the victim of the success of the revolution he brought about: the categories of perception that we apply to his actions and his works, and which are the product of the world resulting from that revolution, make them appear normal, natural, self-evident; and the most heroic breaks have become the inherited privileges of a caste, now within the scope of every hack writer intent on transgression and the most mediocre celebrant of the academic cult of anti-academicism.

If this is indeed the case, then the sociology (or social history) that is always accused of being 'reductive' and of destroying the creative originality of the writer or artist is in fact capable of doing justice to the singularity of the great upheavals that ordinary historiography obliterates. By reducing history to a rhapsody of small details collected without any principle of relevance, ordinary historiography can dispense with the immense effort that is needed in order to construct the social universe of *objective relationships* in relation to which the writer had to define himself in order to construct himself and which cannot necessarily be reduced to those the historiographer records, that is, to the *real interactions* with writers or artists actually encountered and frequented: Hugo, Gautier or Delacroix are as important in this space as Charles Asselineau, Banville, Babou, Champfleury or Pierre Dupont.

This exhortation to a genuine historical anthropology of Baudelaire can draw support from a text by Baudelaire, who wrote, in his first article on the Universal Exhibition of 1855: 'I ask any man of good faith, provided always he has done a little thinking and travelling: what would a modern Winckelman (we are full of them, the nation is bursting with them and lazy people adore them) – what, I say, would a modern Winckelman do, what would he say, at the sight of a Chinese product, a strange product, weird, contorted in shape, intense in colour, and sometimes delicate to the point of fading away? And yet this object is a sample of universal beauty; but if it is to be understood, the critic, the viewer, must bring about within himself a transformation, which is something of a mystery, and, by a phenomenon of will-power acting on his imagination, he must learn by his own effort to share in the life of the society that has given birth to this unexpected bloom. Few men have received – in full – the divine grace of cosmopolitanism; but all men may acquire it to a greater or lesser degree. The most richly endowed in this respect are the lone travellers . . . No scholastic veil, no academic paradox, no pedagogic utopia has interfered with their vision of the complex truth. They know the admirable, the immortal, the inevitable relation between form and function. They are not ones to criticize; they contemplate, they study. If instead of a pedagogue I were now to take a man of the world, an intelligent one, and were to transport him to a distant land, I feel sure that though his surprises on disembarking would be great, though his process of acclimatization might be more or less long, more or less difficult, his sympathy would sooner or later become so keen, so penetrating, that it would create in him a whole new world of ideas, a world that will become part and parcel of him and accompany him as memories until his death. Those odd-shaped buildings that began by offending his academic eye (every people is academic in judging others, every people is barbaric when being judged) . . . this whole world of new harmonies will slowly enter into him, penetrate him patiently.'[29]

Baudelaire, the *auctor* par excellence, sets out clearly the principles of a reading which ought to incite the *lectores* that we always are to some degree to perform a reflexive analysis of the social position of the *lector* and make a critique of the 'academic eye' a preliminary to every reading, and especially to the reading of *auctores*.[30] The *lector* is indeed never more exposed to structural misreading than when he is dealing with the *auctor auctorum*, the writer who invented the writer. In this case, the effects of ignorance of the historical and cultural distance between the literary world that Baudelaire found and the one he left us are redoubled by the effects of ignorance of the social distance between *lector* and *auctor*: the derealization, the

[29] C. Baudelaire, 'The Universal Exhibition of 1855: the Fine Arts', *in Selected Writings on Art and Artists*, tr. P. E. Charvet (Harmondsworth: Penguin, 1972), pp. 115–17.

[30] One would no doubt find many occurrences of this critique of the professorial critique. In the same text on the Universal Exhibition, for example, there is a condemnation of the 'pedantry' and 'erudition' (ibid., p. 119) of the 'sworn professors' that had already been seen in the 'Études sur Poe': 'But the point these pundits [les professeurs-jurés] have not thought of is that in the life process, some complication, some combination of circumstances, may arise which their schoolboy wisdom has not reckoned with' ('Further notes on Edgar Poe', in *Selected Writings on Art and Artists*, p. 189). And we know that Baudelaire often condemned didacticism both in painting and in art criticism (cf. for example 'The Salon of 1859', in ibid., p. 318).

dehistoricization and the 'banalization', as Max Weber says of the priestly treatment of prophetic charisma, that are performed by the routine, scheduled repetition of scholastic commentary have the effect of making bearable what would be unbearable, of gaining universal acceptance for what would be unacceptable, at least for some people.

By way of a practical illustration of what the effect of 'resurrection' (the Kabyles say that 'to cite is to resuscitate') produced by a real historicization might be, I would like to offer a somewhat particular way of reading a text of Baudelaire's taken from a commentary on *Prométhée délivré* by Senneville (the pseudonym of Louis Ménard): 'This is philosophical poetry. – What is philosophical poetry? – What is M. Edgar Quinet? – A philosopher? – Er, er! – A poet? – Oh! Oh!'[31] To reactivate the quite extraordinary violence of this text, one only has to transpose it to the present (as in exercises in old grammar books where one had to put a sentence 'into the present'), with the aid of an intuition of the homologies: 'This is philosophical poetry. – What is philosophical poetry? – What is Mr X (enter here the name of a present-day poet-philosopher) or Mr Y (a contemporary philosopher-poet or philosopher-journalist)? – A philosopher? – Er, er! – A poet? – Oh! Oh!' The effect of 'debanalization' is striking; so much so that I could not cite the names of contemporary writers that spring to mind without appearing somewhat scandalous, or indecent. Thus, the actualization – in the sense of making present, actual – performed by structural historicization is a genuine reactivation. It helps to give the text and its author a form of transhistoricity which, in contrast to the derealization associated with eternization by academic commentary, has the effect of making them active and effective, and available, when the case arises, for new applications, especially those performed by the *auctor*, who is capable of reviving in practice a practical *modus operandi*, in order to produce an *opus operatum* without precedent.

But how does such a reading differ from the wild projection, based on vague supposed analogies, to which the *lector* so often surrenders (especially when he wants to play the *auctor* by conceiving and experiencing his reading as a second 'creation')? The effort to *put oneself in the place* of the author is only valid if one has acquired the means of constructing that place as such, as a *position*, a point (the basis of a point of view) in a social space that is nothing other than the literary field within which the author is situated. Then, 'the critic, the viewer' (as Baudelaire himself puts it) is able to 'bring about within himself a transformation, which is something of a mystery', and, 'by

---

[31] C. Baudelaire, *Œuvres complètes*, ed. C. Pichois (Paris: Gallimard, 1985), vol. 2, p. 9.

a phenomenon of will-power acting on his imagination', can learn to *'share in the life of the society that has given birth* to this unexpected bloom'. And he may even, as I have in my exercise of socio-logical grammar, expose a strategy that can be observed in different states of the fields of cultural production, the strategy of seeking to combine the properties and profits associated with membership of two different fields (the philosophical field and the literary field, or the philosophical field and the journalistic field, etc.) without combining the competences and accepting the corresponding costs (which is what Baudelaire's 'Er, er!' and 'Oh! Oh!' say in their terribly economic way).

Thus, to be able really to understand Baudelaire's work, and to participate *actively*, without the true or false modesty of the *lector*, in the 'creative' activity, one has to acquire the means of 'sharing in the life of the society that has given birth' to this unprecedented oeuvre, in other words the literary universe in which and against which the 'creative project' took shape, and, more precisely, the space of artistic (poetic) possibilities objectively offered by the field at the moment when the author was working to define his artistic intention. This is an inaugural moment, when one has more chance of grasping the historical principles of the *genesis* of the oeuvre, which, once its difference is invented and affirmed, will develop in accordance with its internal logic, which is more independent of the circumstances.

The field in which and against which Baudelaire defines himself is, it seems to me, dominated by a principal opposition according to the degree of autonomy with respect to external demands, especially ethical ones. On the one hand, there is a strongly autonomous 'pure' poetry which asserts its indifference towards political or moral commitment or the personal lyricism of intimate experience, as with Théophile Gautier (especially the preface to *Mademoiselle de Maupin* and *Émaux et Camées*), and its refusal to give way to lyrical effusions or the expression of age-old anxieties, as with Leconte de Lisle. At the other pole is a poetry more open to the world, with the spiritualists – moralistic eulogists of Nature, like Victor de Laprade, a Lamartinian and Christian poet converted into a pantheistic worshipper of the world;[32] and, opposed to the former in a second dimension, the 'École Moderne', associated with the name of Maxime Du Camp (and the *Revue de Paris*), who, in his *Chants modernes*, celebrates industry, progress, etc., and explicitly rejects the cult of form and the pictorial effects of Théophile Gautier.

---

[32] Here one ought to cite the 1855 letter on nature to Desnoyers, in which Baudelaire refuses 'the singular new religion' in the name of true spirituality (C. Pichois and J. Ziegler, *Baudelaire* (Paris: Julliard, 1987), pp. 301–3).

Baudelaire sets himself against both polar positions while granting to each and taking from each that by which it is most directly opposed to the other: in the name of the cult of pure form, which places him on the radical wing of autonomous literature, he refuses submission to external functions and the respect for official norms, whether it be the moralizing precepts of the bourgeois order for the spiritualistic poets or the cult of work for the 'École Moderne'. But he rejects just as strongly the social withdrawal of the devotees of pure form (to which must be added the 'pagan school' or 'the Greek poet, M. de Banville') in the name of the exaltation of the incantatory function of poetry, the critical imagination, the complicity between poetry and life, and 'modern feeling', as Asselineau puts it.

With this *unprecedented combination* of socially exclusive position-takings, he brings into existence, *in a site of high tension*, a hitherto impossible position, springing from the linking of aesthetic avant-gardism with ethical avant-gardism, two distinct and even quasi-irreconcilable positions. And, as if to add pain to his difficulty in living, he refuses either to make it an aesthetic axiom, like the Romantics, or, worse, the Bohemians, or to flee from it into the 'serene contemplation of divine forms', like the Parnasse school; he rejects the escape from the present and the real of the 'very erudite antiquarians' (including the painter Gérome, 'a mind full of curiosity for the past and eagerness to learn', 'who substitutes the entertainment provided by a page of erudition for the pleasure of pure painting'[33]) as much as the concern for 'instruction' and, like Hugo, 'the expression of moral truths', the 'crowning modern heresy', according to Edgar Allan Poe.[34]

Thus one would need to unfold the whole space of the relationships designated by refusals, rejections, revolts, rages, often directed against two writers at once, two conceptions of poetry, art or literature that are themselves irreconcilable: twofold refusals that the 'coincidence of contraries' they imply makes all the more *violent* and incommunicable, unacceptable, incomprehensible, even for the man who utters and experiences them and who is forced to see himself and live his life as a kind of abnormal anomaly, or – since a language still has to be found – a 'demon' ('I mean that modern art has an essentially demonic tendency').[35]

All that, the answer will certainly come, is well known. And how could it be otherwise, after so many commentaries, so many holy 'readings', so many pious *lectores*? But is it just a matter of 'reading',

[33] Baudelaire, 'The Salon of 1859', p. 318.
[34] Baudelaire, 'Further notes on Edgar Poe', pp. 207–8.
[35] Baudelaire, *Œuvres complètes*, p. 168.

as predicated by the *lector* who presupposes that authors and readers raise questions of 'reading' and not questions of life and death? Partly because his statutory modesty as a humble interchangeable celebrant of the prophetic word (this is Weber's definition of priesthood) forbids it, partly because his dispositions and the logic of his competition with his peers incline him to the prudent minutiae of erudition which, because it does not see the *field of battle* as such, dissolves the violence of the desperate, painful clashes of creation in the endless enumeration of minor disputes and petty quarrels, the *lector* is bound to forget that for Baudelaire, the question of poetry, the poet's life and art of living, is the object of an *absolute investment*, total and unreserved, an enterprise into which one flings oneself bodily, at the risk of self-destruction. And this raises the question of *controlled ruin*, vigilance in perdition – especially in the use of drugs, the symbol and means of a new relationship between art and existence. This new relationship manifests itself in ethical transgression presented as the fulfilment of an art refusing moral exemplarity and acknowledging only its own laws, or in the 'dark and desolate talent'[36] of those artists who, like Edgar Allan Poe, are 'in search of a bizarre ideal'.[37]

And here one would need to reconsider Baudelaire's literary and art criticism, in which and through which the *auctor auctorum* labours to 'produce' himself (here, for once, we can say 'create' himself) as an *auctor*, and in which the *lectores*, even when they speak (not without condescension) of 'author's criticism', have only seen the criticism of a *lector*. This would presuppose that one was able to reconstitute – in order to place Baudelaire within it – the field of criticism that was then taking shape, with on one side academic criticism, for which paintings were a pretext for writings that were oriented towards the exhibition of knowledge, and on the other the all-purpose hacks and scribblers (*Le Petit Journal*) who chiefly aimed to please a bourgeois readership, if need be with mockery and sarcasm. From 1846, Baudelaire marked a sharp break with the tacit presuppositions of this universe whose apparent dissensions mask a profound consensus. The break is at once practical (he does not just talk about art, he *lives* the part of the artist) and theoretical: he asks criticism to submit itself to the internal logic of the work, to 'enter without preconceptions into the deep intention of each painter', and also to render in and by a specific evocation the specific language – that of forms and colours – instead of 'seeking to astonish by means that are alien to the art in question'. It would be futile to seek to establish whether, in doing so,

[36] 'Edgar Allan Poe, his life and works', in Baudelaire, *Selected Writings on Art and Artists*, pp. 162ff.
[37] 'Further notes on Edgar Poe', p. 207.

he is transposing and generalizing the idea of autonomous poetry that he is in the process of inventing (as might be suggested by his claim to the poet's right to judge the great painters and great musicians: 'It seemed to me that this music [Wagner's] was *my own*') or whether he seeks, and finds, in the works and lives of the artists, and in his analysis of them, the justification and inspiration for his heroic effort to construct the figure of the artist as a *creator*.

Caught between his aversion to the historical or philosophical thematics of academic painting and his equally strong aversion to the flat representation of reality in the manner of Courbet and the landscape or genre painters, he struggles in vain, with much contradiction and confusion, to imagine a route beyond these alternatives. The supersession that he could not find in painting, where, despite his willingness to adopt the viewpoint of the *auctor*, he was reduced to the status of *lector*, he found in a poetry divested of the ornaments and preciosities of Parnassian neo-academicism and capable, in its intense simplicity, of escaping both 'rococo romanticism' and the trivialities of realistic or sentimental evocation.

Thus, against the dehistoricization which historical erudition paradoxically produces, the historical reconstruction – barely *sketched* here – of the structure of the literary space and of the possibilities or impossibilities that it offers brings to light the *impossible position* in which Baudelaire placed himself – for reasons no doubt deriving in part from the psychological and social sufferings linked to his experience of the family microcosm, condensed in his relation to his mother, the matrix of his relation to the institution and, more generally, to the whole social order. This position, generating an extraordinary *tension* and *violence*, was produced, one could even say invented, by Baudelaire himself, by setting himself in opposition to positions which were opposed to each other, and by trying to bring together properties and projects that were profoundly opposed and socially incompatible, *without conciliatory concessions*.

If, as I believe, this model is valid for all the authors of great *symbolic revolutions*, this is no doubt because what they have in common is that they find themselves placed before a space of already made possibles, which, for them and them alone, designates in advance a *possible to be made*. This impossible possible, both rejected and called for by the space which defines it, but as a void, a lack, is what they then strive to bring into existence, against and despite all the resistances which the emergence of this structurally excluded possible induces in the structure which excludes it and in the comfortably installed occupants of all the positions constitutive of that structure.

3

The Historicity of Reason

~∞~

The sociologist might seem to be threatened with a kind of schizo-phrenia, in as much as he is condemned to speak of historicity and relativity in a discourse that aspires to universality and objectivity, to characterize belief in an analysis implying the suspension of all naive adherence, to subject scholastic reason to a critique that is inevitably scholastic in its conditions of possibility and its forms of expression – in short, seemingly to destroy reason in a rational argument, like patients who comment on what they say or do in a metadiscourse that contradicts it. Or is that simply an illusion, arising from a reluct-ance to accept the historicity of scientific or legal reason?

Traditionally, to historicize is to relativize, and indeed, historic-ally, historicization has been one of the most effective weapons in all the battles of the *Aufklärung* against obscurantism and absolutism and, more generally, against all the forms of absolutization or natur-alization of the historical and therefore contingent and arbitrary principles of a particular social universe. Paradoxically, however, it is perhaps on condition that reason is subjected to the test of the most radical historicization, in particular by destroying the illusion of foundation by recalling the arbitrariness of beginnings and by historical and sociological critique of the instruments of historical and sociological science itself, that one can hope to save it from arbitrariness and historical relativization. This would be done, in particular, by trying to understand how, and on what conditions, the rules and regularities of social games capable of forcing egoistic drives and interests to surpass themselves in and through regulated conflict can be set up in things and in bodies.

Violence and law

'Custom creates the whole of equity, for the simple reason that it is accepted. It is the mystical foundation of its authority; whoever carries it back to first principles destroys it. Nothing is so faulty as those laws which correct faults. He who obeys them because they are just obeys a justice which is imaginary and not the essence of law; it is quite self-contained, it is law and nothing more. He who will examine its motive will find it so feeble and so trifling that, if he be not accustomed to contemplate the wonders of human imagination, he will marvel that one century has gained for it so much pomp and reverence. The art of opposition and of revolution is to unsettle established customs, sounding them even to their source, to point out their want of authority and justice. (. . .) [The people] must not see the fact of usurpation; law was once introduced without reason, and has become reasonable. We must make it regarded as authoritative, eternal, and conceal its origin, if we do not wish that it should soon come to an end.'[1]

Thus the only possible foundation of law is to be sought in history, which, precisely, abolishes any kind of foundation. At the origin of law, there is nothing other than arbitrariness (in both senses), 'the fact of usurpation', violence without justification. Genesis amnesia, which arises from exposure to custom, masks what is spelled out in the brutal tautology: 'law is law, and nothing more.' Anyone who wants to 'examine its motive', its *raison d'être*, and 'sound it even to its source', that is, ground it by going back to the first beginning, like philosophers, will never find anything other than this kind of principle of sufficient unreason.

In the beginning, there is only custom, the historical arbitrariness of the historical institution which becomes forgotten as such by trying to ground itself in mythic reason, with theories of contract, the origin myths of the democratic religions (which have recently received their gloss of rationality with John Rawls's *A Theory of Justice*[2]), or, more routinely, by becoming naturalized and so acquiring a recognition rooted in misrecognition: 'What are our natural principles but principles of custom . . . ?'[3] Nothing is more futile, then, in these matters

---

[1] Pascal, *Pensées*, 294.
[2] J. Rawls, *A Theory of Justice* (Cambridge: Harvard University Press, 1971).
[3] Pascal, *Pensées*, 92.

than the ambition of reason which aspires to ground itself, proceeding by rigorous deduction from 'principles': 'Philosophers have much oftener claimed to have reached it, and it is here they have all stumbled. This has given rise to such common titles as *First Principles*, *Principles of Philosophy*, and the like, as ostentatious in fact, though not in appearance, as that one which blinds us, *De omni scibili*.'[4]

Manifestly, Pascal is thinking of Descartes. However, making a strict division between the order of knowledge and the order of politics, between the scholastic 'contemplation of truth' (*contemplatio veritatis*) and the 'usage of life' (*usus vitae*), the otherwise so intrepid author of *The Principles of Philosophy* recognizes that outside of the former domain, doubt is not appropriate: like all the modern prophets of scepticism, from Montaigne to Hume, to the great astonishment of his commentators, he always refrained from extending the radical mode of thought he had inaugurated in the order of knowledge into the realm of politics (one remembers how prudently he spoke of Machiavelli) – perhaps because he realized that he would have condemned himself, as Pascal predicted, to the ultimate discovery, which is bound to destroy the ambition of grounding everything in reason, that the 'fact of usurpation', 'once introduced without reason, has become reasonable'.

But the force of custom never completely cancels out the arbitrariness of force, the basis of the whole system, which always threatens to appear in broad daylight. Thus the police recalls by its existence the extralegal violence on which the legal order is based (and which the philosophy of law, particularly Kelsen, with his theory of 'fundamental law', seeks to obscure). The same is true, albeit more insidiously, of the critical breaks in the history-less course of the 'order of successions' introduced by *coups d'État*, extreme actions of extraordinary violence which break into the cycle of reproduction of power, or, less dramatically, the inaugural moments when an agent socially designated for legitimate exercise of physical or symbolic violence (a king, minister, judge, professor, etc.) is invested with a new mandate. With the *coup d'État*, whether understood in its classical sense (recalled by Louis Marin, commenting on Naudé) of an exceptional action which a government resorts to in order to ensure what it sees as the salvation of the State, or in the modern, more restricted, sense of a violent undertaking in which an individual or a group seizes power or changes the Constitution, it is the violence and arbitrariness of the origin and, by the same token, the question of the justification of

---

[4] Pascal, *Pensées*, 72.

power that are brought back to the surface in 'the explosion, the violence, the shock of the absolute of force', as Marin again puts it. It is the break with the 'legitimate' exercise of power as a representation of force capable of making itself *recognized* simply by making itself *known*, of being shown without being exercised.[5] The exhibition of force, in military parades, but also in judicial ceremonial, as analysed by E. P. Thompson, implies an exhibition of the mastery of force, thereby kept in the status of a potential force, which could be used but is not used. To show it is to show that it is strong enough, and sufficiently sure of its effects not to need actual use. It is a denial (in the real sense of *Verneinung*) of force, an affirmation of force which is inseparably a negation of force, the very one which defines a 'civilized' police force, capable of forgetting and making it forgotten that it is a force and so converted into legitimate violence, misrecognized and recognized, into symbolic violence. (If, like *coups d'État*, 'police violence' arouses outrage, this is perhaps because it threatens the practical belief which creates 'the force of law and order', a force that is recognized as legitimate because it is capable of being used – especially by not really being used – in favour of the very people who undergo it.)

Nomos and *illusio*

Arbitrariness is also the basis of all fields, even the 'purest' ones, like the worlds of art or science. Each of them has its 'fundamental law', its *nomos* (a word that is normally translated as 'law' and would be better rendered as 'constitution', a term which better recalls the arbitrary act of institution, or as 'principle of vision and division', which is closer to the etymology).[6] There is nothing to be said of this law, except, with Pascal, that 'it is law, and nothing more.' It is only stated (on the rare occasions when it is stated at all) in the form of tautologies. Irreducible to and incommensurable with any other law, it cannot be related to the law of any other field and the regime of truth that the field imposes. This is particularly clear in the case of the artistic field, whose *nomos* as asserted in the second half of the nineteenth century ('art for art's sake') is the inversion of that of

---

[5] L. Marin, 'Pour une théorie baroque de l'action politique', preface to G. Naudé, *Considérations politiques sur les coups d'État* (Paris: Éditions de Paris, 1989), pp. 7–65, esp. pp. 19–20.

[6] I intend to set out the theory of fields more systematically in a future work. For the moment, the reader is referred to my book *The Rules of Art* (Cambridge: Polity Press, 1996).

the economic field ('business is business'). There is, as Bachelard observes, the same incompatibility between the 'legal mind' and the 'scientific mind':[7] for example the refusal of all approximation, the will to dispel vagueness, a source of disputes, can lead a lawyer to assess the value of a plot of land at a precise number of francs, which is absurd in the eyes of the scientist.

This means that once one has accepted the viewpoint that is constitutive of a field, one can no longer take an external viewpoint on it. The *nomos*, a 'thesis' which, because it is never put forward as such, cannot be contradicted, has no antithesis. As a legitimate principle of division which can be applied to all the fundamental aspects of existence, defining the thinkable and the unthinkable, the prescribed and the proscribed, it must remain unthought. Being the matrix of all the pertinent questions, it cannot produce the questions that could call it into question.

Each field, like the Pascalian 'order', thus involves its agents in its own stakes, which, from another point of view, the point of view of another game, become invisible or at least insignificant or even illusory: 'All the glory of greatness has no lustre for people who are in search of understanding. The greatness of clever men is invisible to kings, to the rich, to chiefs, and to all the worldly great. The greatness of wisdom (...) is invisible to the carnal-minded and to the clever. These are three orders differing in kind.'[8] To confirm Pascal's propositions, one only has to observe where the stakes and prizes offered by each of the different fields cease to be perceptible and attractive (it is one of the ways of testing their limits). For example, the career ambitions of a senior civil servant can leave a researcher indifferent, and the reckless investments of an artist, or journalists' struggles for access to the front page, are almost unintelligible to the banker (the quarrels of the artist or writer with a bourgeois father are more than a simple *topos* of hagiography) and also, no doubt, for everyone external to the field, which very often means for superficial observers.

Digression: Common sense

It follows from this that the world of common sense well deserves its name: it is the only truly common place where those who are confined to it, for lack of access to the scholastic disposition and to the

[7] G. Bachelard, *Le Nouvel Esprit scientifique* (Paris: Librairie Félix Alcan, 1934).
[8] Pascal, *Pensées*, 793.

historical conquests of the world of science, can, exceptionally, find one another and find grounds for understanding one another, as can all those who have a place in one or another of the scholastic universes (for whom it also offers the only common referent and the only common language for them to talk among themselves about what goes on within each of these universes enclosed in its idiosyncrasy and its idiolect). Common sense is a stock of self-evidences shared by all, which, within the limits of a social universe, ensures a primordial consensus on the meaning of the world, a set of tacitly accepted commonplaces which make confrontation, dialogue, competition and even conflict possible, and among which a special place must be reserved for the principles of classification, such as the major oppositions structuring the perception of the world.

These classificatory schemes (structuring structures) are, essentially, the product of the incorporation of the structures of the fundamental distributions which organize the social order (structured structures). Being, as a consequence, common to all the agents participating in that order, they are what makes possible the agreement in disagreement of agents who are situated in opposite positions (high/low, visible/obscure, rare/common, rich/poor, etc.) and who are characterized by distinctive properties, themselves different or opposite in social space. In other words, they are what makes it possible for all agents to refer to the same oppositions (such as high/low, up/down, rare/common, light/heavy, rich/poor, etc.), to think the world and their position in the world, while sometimes giving opposite signs and values to the terms they counterpose: thus the same freedom of manners may be seen by some as 'shameless', impolite, rude, and by others as 'unaffected', simple, unpretentious, natural.

Common sense is to a large extent national because most of the major principles of division have so far been inculcated by or reinforced by educational institutions, one of whose main missions is to construct the nation as a population endowed with the same 'categories' and therefore the same common sense. The disorientation one experiences in a foreign country, which is not entirely overcome by mastery of the language, stems largely from the countless little discrepancies between the world as it presents itself at each moment and the system of dispositions and expectations constituting common sense. The existence of transnational fields (scientific ones, in particular) creates specific common senses which call the national common sense into question and it favours the emergence of a scholastic view of the world that is (more or less) common to all the *scholars* of all countries.

Instituted points of view

The process of differentiation of the social world which leads to the existence of autonomous fields concerns both being and knowledge. In differentiating itself, the social world produces differentiation of the modes of knowledge of the world. To each of the fields there corresponds a fundamental point of view on the world which *creates* its own object and finds in itself the principle of understanding and explanation appropriate to that object. To say, with Saussure, that 'the point of view creates the object' means that the same 'reality' is the object of a plurality of representations that are socially recognized but partially irreducible to each other – like the points of view socially instituted in the fields of which they are the product – although they have in common a claim to universality. (Because each field as a 'form of life' is the site of a 'language game' which gives access to different aspects of reality, one may question the existence of a general rationality, transcending regional differences, and, however intense the desire for reunification, one must no doubt, like Wittgenstein, abandon the search for something like a language of all languages.)

The principle of vision and division and the mode of knowledge (religious, philosophical, juridical, scientific, artistic, etc.) which prevails in a field, in association with a specific form of expression, can only be known and understood in relation to the specific legality of that field as a social microcosm. For example, the 'language game' that is called philosophical can only be described and understood in its relationship with the philosophical field as a 'form of life' within which it is current. The structures of thought of the philosopher, the writer, the artist or the scientist, and therefore the limits of what presents itself to them as thinkable or unthinkable, are always partly dependent on the structures of their field, and therefore on the history of the positions constituting the field and of the dispositions they favour. The epistemic unconscious is the history of the field. And it is clear that, to secure some chance of really knowing what one is doing, one has to unfold what is inscribed in the various relations of implication in which the thinker and his thought are caught up, that is, the presuppositions he engages and the inclusions or exclusions he unwittingly performs.

Every field is the institutionalization of a point of view in things and in habitus. The specific habitus, which is demanded of the new entrants as a condition of entry, is nothing other than a specific mode of thought (an *eidos*), the principle of a specific construction of reality, grounded in a prereflexive belief in the undisputed value of the instruments of construction and of the objects thus constructed (an *ethos*). (In reality, what the new entrant must bring into the game is not the habitus that is tacitly or explicitly demanded there, but a habitus that is practically compatible, or sufficiently close, and above all malleable and capable of being converted into the required habitus, in short, congruent and docile, amenable to restructuring. That is why operations of co-option, whether in the recruitment of a rugby player, a professor, a civil servant or a policeman, are so attentive not only to the signs of competence but also to the barely perceptible indices, generally corporeal ones – dress, bearing, manners – of dispositions to be, and above all to become, 'one of us'.)

To take just one example, the aesthetic disposition, tacitly demanded by the artistic field (and its products) and inculcated by its structures and its functioning, which inclines agents to perceive works of art as they ask to be perceived, that is to say, aesthetically, as works of art (and not as ordinary objects in the world), is inseparable from a specific competence. This competence, functioning as a principle of relevance, leads its owner to discern and distinguish features that are ignored or treated as identical by other principles of construction and also to identify properties common to different realities, and therefore to declare equivalent the realities characterized by these properties, so generating classes defined with more or less rigour, such as styles (gothic, rococo), schools (impressionists, symbolists) or the manners of an artist. (This description would equally well apply to the habitus of the priest,[9] the journalist, the doctor,[10] the boxer[11] or the scientist: Kuhn refers, in *The Structure of Scientific Revolutions*, to the 'disciplinary matrix', 'a constellation of beliefs, values, techniques and so on, that is shared by a community.'[12])

Like the artistic field, each scientific universe has its specific *doxa*, a set of inseparably cognitive and evaluative presuppositions whose acceptance is implied in membership itself. These include the major obligatory pairs of opposites which, paradoxically, unite those whom they divide, since agents have to share a common acceptance of them to be able to fight over them, or through them, and so to produce position-takings which are immediately *recognized* as pertinent and meaningful by the very agents whom they oppose and who are

[9] C. Suaud, *La Vocation* (Paris: Éditions de Minuit, 1978).
[10] J. Cassell, *Expected Miracles: Surgeons at Work* (Philadelphia: Temple University Press, 1991).
[11] L. Wacquant, 'Corps et âme. Notes ethnographiques d'un apprenti boxeur', *Actes de la Recherche en Sciences Sociales*, no. 80 (1989), pp. 33–67.
[12] T. S. Kuhn, *The Structure of Scientific Revolutions*, 2nd edn (Chicago: University of Chicago Press, 1970), p. 182.

opposed to them. These pairs of specific opposites (epistemological, artistic, etc.) which are also social oppositions between complicit opponents within the field, define – in politics too – the space of legitimate discussion, excluding any attempt to produce an unforeseen position as absurd, eclectic or simply unthinkable (whether it be the absurd and misplaced intrusion of the 'naïf', the 'amateur' or the autodidact, or the major subversive innovation of the religious, artistic or even scientific heresiarch). The most fundamental and most deeply buried oppositions are the ones that are subverted or destroyed by the authors of major symbolic revolutions – like Manet, for example, who overturned the canonical oppositions of academic painting, between ancient and contemporary, 'sketch' and 'finished work'.

The consecrated oppositions eventually appear as inscribed in the nature of things, even when the slightest critical examination, especially when armed with knowledge of the field (constructed as such) very often forces one to discover that each of the opposing positions has no content beyond its relationship with the antagonistic position of which it is sometimes just the rationalized inversion. This is clearly the case with a number of pairs of opposites now current in the social sciences: individual and society, consensus and conflict, consent and constraint, or, in Anglo-American sociology, structure and agency. It is even more obviously true of divisions into 'schools', 'movements' or 'currents' – 'structuralism', 'modernism', 'postmodernism' – so many labels passing for concepts which have hardly any more autonomy with respect to oppositions between social positions than the divisions of the same kind which prevail in the literary or artistic fields (such as the division in the late nineteenth-century literary field between naturalism and symbolism).

The constituting disposition – at once arbitrary, or even displaced or derisory, from the point of view of another field, and necessary, and therefore imperatively demanded (for fear of vulgarity, ridicule, etc.), from the point of view of the specific legality of the field in question – is this tacit adherence to the *nomos*, that particular form of belief, *illusio*, which is demanded by scholastic fields and which presupposes suspension of the objectives of ordinary existence, in favour of new stakes, posited and produced by the game itself. As is shown by the scandal aroused by every challenge to the founding self-evidences, this primordial belief is much more deeply buried, more 'visceral' and, therefore, more difficult to uproot, than the explicit beliefs explicitly professed in the field (of religion, for example).

Philosophies of wisdom tend to reduce all kinds of *illusio*, even the 'purest', like *libido sciendi*, to simple illusions, which one has to abandon in order to attain the spiritual freedom with respect to all

worldly prizes which comes from the suspension of all forms of investment. That is also what Pascal does when he condemns as 'diversions'
the forms of 'lust' associated with the lower orders, those of the flesh
and of the mind, because they have the effect of distracting man from
the only true belief, the one which is engendered in the order of
charity.

Illusio understood as immediate adherence to the necessity of a
field is all the less likely to appear to consciousness because it is in a
sense removed from discussion: as the fundamental belief in the value
of the stakes of the dispute and in the presuppositions inscribed in
the very fact of disputing, it is the unexamined condition of the dispute. To undertake to discuss arguments, one has to believe that they
merit discussion and to believe, in any case, in the merits of the
dispute. *Illusio* does not belong to the order of explicit principles,
theses that are put forward and defended, but of action, routine,
things that are done, and that are done because they are things that
one does and that have always been done that way. All those who are
involved in the fields, whether champions of orthodoxy or heterodoxy,
share a tacit adherence to the same *doxa* which makes their competition possible and assigns its limits (the heretic remains a believer who
preaches a return to purer forms of the faith). It effectively forbids
questioning of the principles of belief, which would threaten the very
existence of the field. Participants have ultimately no answer to questions about the reasons for their membership in the game, their visceral
commitment to it; and the principles which may be invoked in such a
case are merely *post festum* rationalizations intended to justify an
unjustifiable investment, to themselves as much as to others.

Digression: Differentiation of powers and circuits of legitimation

As relatively autonomous fields become constituted, there is a shift
away from political undifferentiatedness and *mechanical solidarity*
between interchangeable powers (like the elders of clan units or the
'notables' of village society), or from a *division of the labour of
domination* reduced to a small number of specialized functions or
even a pair of antagonistic powers, such as warriors, *bellatores*, and
priests, *oratores*. Ceasing to be embodied in specialized persons or
institutions, power is differentiated and dispersed (this is probably
what Michel Foucault meant to suggest, no doubt in opposition to
the Marxist vision of the centralized, monolithic apparatus, with his
rather vague metaphor of 'capillarity'). It is realized and manifested
only through a whole set of fields linked by *organic solidarity*, which

means that they are both different and interdependent. More precisely, it is exercised, invisibly and anonymously, through the actions and reactions, apparently anarchic but in fact structurally constrained, of agents and institutions located in fields that are at once competitive and complementary, such as the economic field and the educational field, and engaged in circuits of legitimating exchanges which are ever longer and more complex and therefore symbolically ever more effective, but which also make ever more room, potentially at least, for conflicts of power and authority.

A kind of separation of powers, very different from that advocated by Montesquieu, is cast in reality in the form of the differentiation of microcosms and the actual or potential conflicts between the separate powers which results from this. On the one hand, the powers exercised in the various fields (especially those where a particular kind of cultural capital is at stake, like the medical field or the legal field) can no doubt be oppressive in a particular respect, and in their own domain, and therefore likely to provoke legitimate resistance, but they enjoy a relative autonomy vis-à-vis the political and economic powers, thereby offering the possibility of some freedom with regard to them. On the other hand, while it is true that those who occupy the dominant positions in the various fields are united by an objective solidarity based on the homology between their positions, they are also set against each other, within the field of power, by relations of competition and conflict, especially over the dominant principle of domination and the 'exchange rate' between the different kinds of capital which are the basis of the different kinds of power. It follows that the dominated can always take advantage of the conflicts between the powerful, who very often need their assistance in order to triumph. A number of historical confrontations regarded as exemplary moments in the 'class struggle' have in fact been merely the extension, through the logic of alliances with the dominated, of struggles among the dominant groups within the field of power – struggles which, because, for the purposes of legitimation or mobilization, they use strategies of symbolic universalization of particular interests, can nevertheless advance the idea of the universal and therefore at least formal recognition of the interests of the dominated.

Every advance in the differentiation of powers is a further protection against the imposition of a single, unilinear hierarchy based on a concentration of all powers in the hands of one person (as in Caesaro-papism) or one group, and, more generally, against *tyranny* understood as the intrusion of the powers associated with one field into the functioning of another: 'Tyranny consists in the desire of universal power beyond its scope. . . . Tyranny is the wish to have in one way what can only be had in another. We render different duties to different merits; the duty of love to the pleasant; the duty of fear to the strong; duty of belief to the learned.'[13] There is tyranny, for example, when political power or economic power intervenes in the scientific field or the literary field, either directly or through a more specific power, such as that of academies, publishers, committees or journalism (which is now tending ever more to widen its hold over the various fields, especially the political, intellectual, legal and scientific ones), to impose its hierarchies and repress the assertion of the specific principles of hierarchization.[14]

Tyrannical ambitions, which aim to absolutize one principle of vision and division and constitute it as the ultimate, unquestionable principle of all others, are, paradoxically, claims to legitimacy, albeit sometimes illogical ones. Thus force cannot assert itself as such, as brute violence, an arbitrariness that is what it is, without justification; and it is a fact of experience that it can only perpetuate itself under the colours of legitimacy, and that domination succeeds in imposing itself durably only in so far as it manages to secure recognition, which is nothing other than misrecognition of the arbitrariness of its principle. In other words, it wants to be justified (and therefore recognized, respected, honoured, considered), but its only chance of being so lies in declining to be exercised (every use of force with a view to obtaining its recognition can only supply a symbolically self-destructive reinforcement of its arbitrariness). It follows that powers based on (physical or economic) force can only obtain their legitimation through powers that cannot be suspected of obeying force; and that the legitimating efficacy of an act of recognition (homage, a mark of deference, a token of respect) varies with the degree of independence of the agent or institution that grants it (and also with the recognition that he or it enjoys). It is almost zero in the case of self-consecration (Napoleon seizing the crown from the hands of the Pope in order to crown himself) or self-celebration (an author supplying his own panegyric). It is weak when the acts of recognition are performed by mercenaries (a theatre *claque*, advertisers or propagandists), accomplices or even close associates, whose judgements are suspected of being imposed by a form of egoistic indulgence or emotional blindness, and when these acts enter into circuits of exchanges which are all the more transparent the more direct and short they are (the 'mutual back-scratching' of reviewers, for example). By contrast,

[13] Pascal, *Pensées*, 332.
[14] I have described this intrusion in the case of television in *Sur la télévision* (Paris: Liber-Raisons d'Agir, 1996).

the effect of legitimation is greatest when all real or visible relationship of material or symbolic interest between the agents or institutions concerned disappears and when the author of the act of recognition is himself recognized.

So force has to be expended in order to get force misrecognized and recognized and to produce the justified force called law. The symbolic efficacy of the labour of legitimation is closely linked to the degree of differentiation of this labour and therefore to the associated risk of diversion to other ends. The prince can obtain a truly effective legitimation service from his poets, painters or jurists only in so far as he grants them the (relative) autonomy which is the condition for independent judgement but which may also be the basis for critical questioning. For, while apparent autonomy or misrecognized dependence may have the same effects as real independence, the almost inevitable counterpart of symbolic efficacy, which requires a certain independence of the legitimator from the legitimated, is a corresponding risk that the legitimator will divert his delegated power of legitimation for his own benefit. Thus in twelfth-century Bologna the appearance of a body of professional jurists exposed the ambiguity of the relationship between temporal power and cultural power (as in other times between *bellatores* and *oratores*). As Kantorowicz has shown, the autonomizing of the legal field provided the prince with powers of a new type, which were more legitimate because they were based on the authority that the legal corps had won and asserted against him; but it was also the basis of the demands that the jurists made against him and of power struggles in which the holders of the monopoly of the legitimate manipulation of texts could invoke the specific authority of law against arbitrary princely power.

Likewise, the arts and literature can no doubt offer the dominant agents some very powerful instruments of legitimation, either directly, through the celebration they confer, or indirectly, especially through the cult they enjoy, which also consecrates its celebrants. But it can also happen that artists or writers are, directly or indirectly, at the origin of large-scale symbolic revolutions (like the bohemian lifestyle in the nineteenth century, or, nowadays, the subversive provocations of the feminist or homosexual movements), capable of shaking the deepest structures of the social order, such as family structures, through transformation of the fundamental principles of division of the vision of the world (such as the male/female opposition) and the corresponding challenges to the self-evidences of common sense.[15]

[15] R. S. Halvorsen and A. Prieur, 'Le droit à l'indifférence: le mariage homosexuel', *Actes de la Recherche en Sciences Sociales*, no. 113 (June 1996), pp. 6–15.

As the field of power becomes differentiated and as, correlatively, the circuits of legitimating exchanges become longer and more complex, so the cost in social energy expended on the labour of legitimation increases, as do the threats of crisis. The progress in symbolic efficacy which accompanies a growing complexity of the circuits of legitimation and, especially, the intervention of mechanisms as complex and disguised as those of the educational institution, is counterbalanced by the considerable increase in the possibilities of subversive diversion of the specific capital associated with membership of one or another of the fields arising from the process of differentiation (with, for example, all the factors of transformation linked to the educational system, from the individual and collective dissatisfaction engendered by the structural *déclassement* resulting from the 'devaluation' of diplomas and the mismatches between qualifications and jobs, to major subversive movements like that of 1968).

The professionals of discourse, who have the 'competence' (in both senses) to describe the world and to give shape and form (religious, legal, etc.) to experiences that are often difficult to express (unease, indignation, revolt) and to perform a kind of universalization of what they utter by the mere fact of making it public, thereby giving it a form of official recognition and the appearance of reason and *raison d'être* (with, for example, prophetic quasi-systematization), are structurally inclined towards a diversion of capital based on the absolutization of one kind of capital among others (technocracy, the 'republic of judges', theocracy, etc.).

A rationalist historicism

But the social sciences are not condemned to the pure (Pascalian) acknowledgement of original arbitrariness, albeit salutary and liberatory in its own right. They can also undertake to understand and explain their own genesis and, more generally, the genesis of scholastic fields, in other words the processes of emergence (or autonomization) from which they arose, as well as the genesis of the dispositions that were invented as the fields were constituted and which slowly install themselves in bodies in the course of the learning process. The specific task of these sciences is to ground, not in reason, but, so to speak, in history, in *historical reason*, the historical necessity or *raison d'être* of the separate, privileged microcosms in which statements about the world that aspire to universality are constructed. The knowledge thus obtained contains the possibility of a reflexive mastery of this dual history – individual and collective – and of the unwanted effects it may exert on thought.

If one accepts that scientific reason is a product of history and that it asserts itself ever more strongly with the growth of the relative autonomy of the scientific field with respect to external constraints and determinations, in other words as the field more strongly imposes its specific laws of functioning, especially as regards argument and critique, then one is led to reject both of the commonly accepted alternatives: 'logicist' absolutism, which claims to give *a priori* 'logical foundations' to scientific method, and 'historicist' or 'psychologistic' relativism, which, in the formulation that Quine gives of it, for example, holds that the failure of the attempt to reduce mathematics to logic leaves no other recourse than to 'naturalize epistemology' by referring it to psychology.[16]

Nor does one have to choose between the two terms of the new alternative symbolized nowadays by the names of Habermas and Foucault, themselves eponymous heroes of two movements called 'modern' and 'postmodern' – on one side, Habermas's juridico-discursive conception, which asserts the autonomous force of law and seeks to found democracy on legal institutionalization of the forms of communication which are necessary to the formation of rational will; on the other side, Foucault's analysis of power, which, observing the microstructures of domination and the strategies of struggle for power, leads to a rejection of universals and in particular of the search for any kind of universally acceptable morality.

Likewise, while one has to repudiate the objectivist illusion of the 'view from nowhere' (in Thomas Nagel's phrase), a pre-critical certainty which accepts without examination the objectivity of a non-objectified point of view, this is not done in order to fall into the illusion of the 'view from everywhere' that narcissistic reflexivity pursues in its 'postmodern' form, a critique of foundation which elides the question of the (social) foundation of critique, a 'deconstruction' which fails to 'deconstruct' the 'deconstructor'. In endless movement, startling and imperturbable, ungraspable, the rootless, free-floating (*atopos*) philosopher seeks, in accordance with the Nietzschian metaphor of the *dance*, to escape every localization, every fixed viewpoint of a motionless spectator, every objectivist perspective, claiming to be able to adopt an infinite number of viewpoints on the text to be

[16] Cf. W. V. O. Quine, 'Epistemology naturalized', in *Ontological Relativity and Other Essays* (New York: Columbia University Press, 1969).

'deconstructed', inaccessible as much to the author as to the critic. Unassailable, always a jump ahead, renouncing transcendence only in appearance, a master of the game of 'catcher caught', especially with the social sciences, which he has absorbed the better to challenge, to 'supersede' and to deny them, he is always confident of challenging the most radical challenges and, if nothing else is left to philosophy, of bearing witness that no one can better deconstruct philosophy than the philosopher himself.

What characterizes all these alternatives, which are simply the projection into the heaven of 'ideas' of the social divisions of the fields, is that they give the illusion that thought is trapped in a totally arbitrary way in a totally arbitrary dilemma. 'If I have to choose between two evils,' said Karl Kraus, 'I choose neither.' On either side, the effort of thought (and of thought about thought) encounters its limit in the fact that, suffering from a form of aristocratic *hubris*, it can only see itself as the solitary enterprise of a thinker who seeks his intellectual salvation only in his singular lucidity. And this is not the only common feature that these seemingly totally opposed theoretical visions owe to their common participation in the scholastic presuppositions. Thus, though it is difficult not to see the linguistic fetishism of the *lector* in the theory of 'communicative action', the legitimatory transfiguration of the scholastic relation to language, equally it is probably the typically scholastic fetishism of the autonomized text which leads a number of those who see themselves as 'postmodern' to confer the status of self-sufficient, self-engendered texts, amenable to purely internal critique, on all social realities and on the social world itself. This is true, for example, of one kind of feminist critique which tends to make the female body, the female condition or women's lower status a pure product of performative social construction and which, forgetting that it is not sufficient to change language or theory to change reality (the typical illusion of the *lector*) uncritically attributes political efficacy to textual critique. While it never does harm to point out that gender, nation or ethnicity or race are social constructs, it is naive, even dangerous, to suppose and suggest that one only has to 'deconstruct' these social artefacts, in a purely performative celebration of 'resistance', in order to *destroy* them. It amounts to ignoring that, while categorization by sex, race or nation is indeed a sexist, racist or nationalist 'invention', it is inscribed in the objectivity of institutions, that is to say, of things and bodies. As Max Weber pointed out long ago, there is no greater threat to a workers' movement, or any other, than 'objectives rooted in misrecognition of the real relationships'. And one may in any case doubt the reality of a resistance which ignores the resistance of 'reality'.

The dual face of scientific reason

While it forbids one to move fictitiously beyond the uncrossable limits of history, a realist vision of history leads one to examine how, and in what historical conditions, history can be made to yield some truths irreducible to history. We have to acknowledge that reason did not fall from heaven as a mysterious and forever inexplicable gift, and that it is therefore historical through and through; but we are not forced to conclude, as is often supposed, that it is reducible to history. It is in history, and in history alone, that we must seek the principle of the relative independence of reason from the history of which it is the product; or, more precisely, in the strictly historical, but entirely specific logic through which the exceptional universes in which the singular history of reason is fulfilled were established.

These universes based on *skholè* and on scholastic distance from necessity and urgency (particularly economic necessity) favour social exchanges in which social constraints take the form of logical constraints (and vice versa). If they are favourable to the development of reason, this is because, to put oneself forward there, one has to put forward reasons; to win there, one has to win with arguments, demonstrations or refutations. The 'pathological motives' that Kant referred to, and from which the agents engaged in the 'pure' universes of scholastic thought are in no way exempt (as is shown by plagiarism or the thefts of discoveries in the scientific universe), can only become effective in these universes on condition that they comply with the rules of methodical dialogue and generalized critique.

But we should make no mistake: we are as far here from the irenic vision, evoked by Habermas, of an intellectual exchange subject to the 'strength of the best argument' (or from Merton's description of the 'scientific community') as we are from the Darwinian or Nietzschian representation of the scientific world which, in the name of the slogan 'power = knowledge' into which Foucault's work is too often condensed, summarily reduces all sense relations (and scientific relations) to power relations and to struggles to advance interests. It is perfectly possible to assert the specificity and autonomy of scientific discourse without exceeding the limits of scientific observation and without resorting to the various kinds of *deus ex machina* that are traditionally invoked in such cases. Scientific fields, microcosms which, in a certain respect, are social worlds like others, with concentrations of power and capital, monopolies, power relations, selfish interests, conflicts, etc., are also, *in another respect*, exceptional, somewhat miraculous universes, in which the necessity of reason is instituted to varying degrees in the reality of structures and dispositions.

There are no transhistorical universals of communication, as Apel or Habermas suppose; but there are socially instituted and guaranteed forms of communication which, like those which *in fact* prevail in the scientific field, give their full efficacy to mechanisms of universal-ization such as the cross-controls which the logic of competition imposes more effectively than any plea for 'impartiality' or 'ethical neutrality'.

Thus, in its generic dimension the scientific field contradicts the hagiographic vision which celebrates science as an exception to the common laws of a general theory of fields or the economy of prac-tices. Scientific competition presupposes and produces a specific form of interest, which appears disinterested only in comparison with ordin-ary interests, in particular those for power and money, and which is oriented towards winning the monopoly of scientific authority, in which technical competence and symbolic power are inextricably com-bined. But, in its specific dimension, it differs from all other fields (more or less, depending on its degree of autonomy, which varies according to the speciality, the society and the period) in the organ-ized and regulated form that competition takes there, in the logical and experimental constraints to which it is subject, and the cognit-ive ends it pursues. As a consequence, rather like the 'ambiguous images' of Gestalt theory, it lends itself, because of its intrinsic dual-ity, to two simultaneous readings. The pursuit of the accumulation of knowledge is inseparably the quest for recognition and the desire to make a name for oneself; technical competence and scientific know-ledge function simultaneously as instruments of accumulation of symbolic capital; intellectual conflicts are always also power strug-gles, the polemics of reason are the contests of scientific rivalry, and so on.

Those who use the fact that a proposition is the outcome of a process of historical emergence to contest its truth content, or who, like Rorty,[17] argue that epistemic power relations are reducible to political power relations, that science differs from the other forms of knowledge not in epistemological terms but above all in its capacity to impose its definitions through rhetorical persuasion, and that, in a word, what determines the truth of a particular form of knowledge is power alone, which, by structuring the 'language games', orients our preferences towards certain metaphors rather than others, forget what is essential. It is certain that every would-be scientific proposition about the physical world is a construct, which asserts itself against

---

[17] R. Rorty, 'Feminism and pragmatism', *Radical Philosophy*, no. 59 (1991), pp. 3–14.

others, and that the different visions thereby confronted within the scientific fields owe some of their relative strength, even in the most autonomous fields, to the social strength of those who advocate them (or of their position) and to the symbolic efficacy of their rhetorical strategies. The fact remains that, despite everything, the struggle always takes place under the control of the constitutive norms of the field and solely with the weapons approved within the field, and that, claiming to apply to the properties of things themselves, their structures, their effects, etc., and therefore to have the status of truths, the propositions engaged in this struggle recognize one another tacitly or explicitly as amenable to the test of coherence and the verdict of experiment. So it is the simple observation of a scientific world in which the defence of reason is entrusted to a collective labour of critical confrontation placed under the control of the facts that forces one to adhere to a critical and reflexive realism which rejects both epistemic absolutism and irrationalist relativism.

Censorship of the field and scientific sublimation

There is little to be gained, beyond a few symbolic profits of dubious quality, in descending from the hagiographic vision to a 'reductionist' vision (sometimes called the 'strong programme', in the sociology of science) which, insisting on the indisputable fact that social universes are endlessly constructed by performative definitions and classifying operations, reduces the interests and strategies of knowledge to interests and strategies of power, thereby simply sweeping away one of the two inseparable faces of the reality of scholastic fields. That is why, after having clearly posited this *intrinsic duality* of the universe of science and of everything that partakes of it, one has to emphasize its specific dimension and show how the specific *drive* engendered by the field is led to *sublimate* itself in order to be fulfilled within the limits and under the constraint of the *censorship* of the field.

The anarchic confrontation of individual investments and interests is transformed into rational dialogue only to the extent that the field is sufficiently autonomous (and therefore equipped with sufficiently high entry barriers) to exclude the importation of non-specific weapons, especially political or economic ones, into the internal struggles – to the extent that the participants are constrained to use only instruments of discussion or proof corresponding to the scientific demands in the matter (such as the 'principle of charity'), and are therefore obliged to sublimate their *libido dominandi* into a *libido sciendi* that can only triumph by answering a demonstration with a refutation, one scientific fact with another scientific fact.

The constraints capable of favouring actions that tend to contribute to the progress of reason need not, in most cases, take the form of explicit rules. They are inscribed in the institutionalized procedures regulating entry into the game (selection and co-option); in the conditions of exchange (form and forum of discussion, legitimate problematic, etc.); in the mechanisms of the field, which, functioning as a market, attributes positive or negative sanctions to individual productions according to quite specific rules, irreducible to those governing the economic or political universes; and, above all, in the dispositions of the agents which are the product of this set of effects – the inclination and aptitude to perform the 'epistemological break', for example, being inscribed in the whole logic of the functioning of the autonomous field, capable of generating its own problems instead of receiving them ready-made from outside. (In the case of the social sciences, the establishment of the social conditions for the epistemological break and for autonomy is particularly necessary and particularly difficult. Because their object, and therefore what they say about it, is politically contentious – a fact which brings them into competition with all those who claim to speak with authority about the social world, writers, journalists, politicians, priests, etc. – they are particularly exposed to the danger of 'politicization'. It is always possible to import and impose external forces and forms into the field, which generate heteronomy and are capable of thwarting, neutralizing and sometimes annihilating the conquests of research freed from presuppositions.)

Thus, as the collectively accumulated scientific resources increase and, correlatively, the requirements for entry into the field are raised, *de jure* or *de facto* excluding aspirants who lack the necessary competence to compete effectively, the agents and institutions engaged in the competition tend ever more to have only the most formidable of their competitors for potential addressees or 'clients'. Their validity claims are forced to confront competing claims, also scientifically armed, to obtain recognition; the only chance for the authors of discoveries to be understood and recognized is by those of their peers who are both most competent and least prone towards indulgent complicities and therefore most inclined and qualified to engage the specific resources accumulated throughout the whole history of the field in a critique of these discoveries tending to advance reason through the power of refutations, corrections and additions.

The scientific field is an armed struggle among adversaries who possess weapons whose power and effectiveness rises with the scientific capital collectively accumulated in and by the field (and therefore, in the incorporated state, in each of the agents) and who agree at least to appeal to the verdict of experience, the 'real', as a kind of ultimate referee. This 'objective reality' to which everyone explicitly or tacitly refers is ultimately no more than what the researchers engaged in the field at a given moment agree to consider as such, and it only ever manifests itself in the field through the *representations* given of it by those who invoke its arbitration. This can also be true of other fields, such as the religious field or the political field, where, in particular, the adversaries fight to impose principles of vision and division of the social world, systems of classification, into classes, regions, nations, ethnic groups, etc., and never cease to call the social world to witness, asking it to confirm or disconfirm their diagnoses or prognoses, their visions or their forecasts. But the specificity of the scientific field stems from the fact that the competitors agree on the principles of verification of conformity to the 'real', common methods for validating theses and hypotheses, in short, on the tacit contract, inseparably political and cognitive, which founds and governs the *work of objectification*. Consequently, what clashes in the field are competing social constructions, representations (with all that this word implies of theatrical presentation, 'staging'), but *realistic representations*, which claim to be grounded in a 'reality' endowed with all the means of imposing its verdict through the arsenal of methods, instruments and experimental techniques collectively accumulated and implemented, under the constraint of the disciplines and censorship of the field and also through the invisible force of the orchestration of habitus.

Thus the field is the site of a regime of rationality set up in the form of rational constraints, which, objectified and manifested in a particular structure of social exchange, encounter the immediate complicity of the dispositions that researchers have largely acquired through experience of the disciplines of the 'scientific city'. It is these dispositions which enable them to construct the space of the specific possibles inscribed in the field (the problematic) in the form of a state of the argument, of the question, of knowledge, itself embodied in agents or institutions, remarkable figures, '-isms', etc. They are what enables them to operate the symbolic system offered by the field in accordance with the rules which define it and which they respect for a strength that is *both logical and social*. The experience of the transcendence of scientific objects, especially mathematical ones, that essentialist theories invoke is the particular form of *illusio* which arises in the relationship between agents possessing the habitus socially required by the field and symbolic systems capable of imposing

their demands on those who perceive them and operate them, and
endowed with an autonomy closely linked to that of the field (which
explains why the sense of transcendent necessity rises with the capital of accumulated resources and the qualifications demanded for
entry).

(Those who describe cultural objects, and especially mathematical
entities, as transcendent entities, pre-existing their apprehension (then
described, in the manner of the natural sciences, as a discovery),
forget that the constraining force of mathematical procedures (or of
the signs in which they are expressed) derives in part at least from the
fact that they are accepted, acquired and implemented in and through
durable, collective dispositions. The necessity and self-evidence of
these transcendent 'beings' only impress themselves on those who
have acquired the necessary aptitudes to 'receive' them, through a
long learning process (the social history of mysticism as described by
Jacques Maître shows that the same is true, for very similar reasons,
of experience of the supernatural 'beings' of religion, which also presupposes dispositions acquired, in part at least, in a field bearing a
specific tradition). Mathematical symbols – at once timeless and historical, transcendent and immanent – like religious symbols, paintings or poems, become live and active – but according to their specific
legality, which enforces itself as a system of demands and therefore
with a claim to exist according to a determinate mode of existence,
aesthetic, legal or mathematical, etc. – only in relation to a space of
agents inclined and able to bring this autonomous symbolic space
into active existence by making it operate in accordance with the
rules that define it.

Thus historicization frees one from the Platonic illusion of the
autonomy of the world of ideas (especially mathematical ones, but
also legal or literary ideas), a form of fetishism which is expressed in
almost identical forms in the various fields. This illusion is present in
the experience of *necessity* that arises from the always somewhat
miraculous encounter between a universe of symbols, operators and
rules, and an agent who has incorporated them and on whom they
impose themselves by imposing the uses that can be made of them
and therefore the sometimes unexpected products of their operation.
There is no 'beyond' to history and, even if it distresses those who
have transferred their nostalgia for the absolute onto works of art, literature and even science, the social sciences have to continue to seek
the principle of the existence of works of art, science and literature –
in their historical but also their transhistorical aspects – in the specific
logic of the scholastic fields, paradoxical worlds which are capable of
imposing and inspiring the most 'disinterested' interests.)

The anamnesis of origin

The social sciences, sciences without a foundation, forced to accept themselves as historical through and through, destroy every founding ambition and force one to accept things as they are, as entirely stemming from history. The insistence that everything is historical, including the common cognitive dispositions which, resulting from the constraints that the regularities of the world have brought to bear, for thousands of years, on a living being who was obliged to adapt to them in order to survive, make the world immediately knowable, does not mean, as is sometimes too hastily said, that one is professing a historicist or sociologistic reductionism. It means that one is refusing to replace God the creator of 'eternal verities and values', as Descartes put it, with the creative Subject, and giving back to history and to society what was given to a transcendence or a transcendent subject. More precisely, it means abandoning the mythology of the uncreated 'creator', of which Sartre provided the exemplary formulation, with the self-destructive notion of the 'original project',[18] an expression of the dream of being *causa sui* which goes hand in hand with a horror of genetic thought, and accepting that the true 'subject' of the most accomplished human works is none other than the field in which – that is, thanks to which and against which – they are accomplished (or, which almost amounts to the same thing, a particular position in the field, associated with a particular constellation of dispositions – which may partially be formed elsewhere than in the field). It is true to say, with André Gide, that 'art is born of constraint', but the constraint is that of the objective structure of the possibilities and impossibilities that are inscribed in a field or which, more precisely, arise in the relationship between a habitus and a field.

Thus, on the one hand, against the Platonist fetishism which runs through all scholastic thought, social science endeavours to establish the genealogy of the objective structures of the scholastic fields (and in particular the scientific field) and of the cognitive structures which are both the product and the condition of their functioning. It analyses the specific logic of the various social universes which generate symbolic systems claiming universal validity as well as the corresponding cognitive structures, and relates the supposedly absolute laws of logic to the immanent constraints of a field (or a 'form of life') and in particular to the socially regulated activity of discussion and justification of utterances. On the other hand, against relativistic reductionism, it shows that, while it does not differ in an absolute

---

[18] J.-P. Sartre, *Being and Nothingness* (London: Methuen, 1969), pp. 561ff.

way from the other fields in terms of the motivations engaged in it, the scientific field stands quite apart from them in terms of the constraints (for example, the principle of contradiction, implied in the necessity of submitting oneself to the test of controversy) which an agent has to accept in order to secure the triumph of his passions or interests, those of the censorship imposed by cross-control that is exercised through armed competition. The necessity is a quite specific one, itself arising from a quite specific history in the almost teleological logic of its unfolding.

The long process of historical emergence in the course of which the specific necessity of each field is asserted is not the continuous parthenogenesis of reason fertilizing itself, reducible (retrospectively) to a long chain of reasons, that is imagined by the intellectualist vision (and the history of ideas, especially in science and philosophy). But nor is it reducible to a pure and simple sequence of accidents, as Pascal sometimes suggests, in order to combat the arrogance of triumphant reason. It owes its specific, essentially sociological, logic to the fact that the actions that are produced in a field are doubly determined by the specific logic of the field: at each moment, the structure of the space of positions which results from the whole history of the field, when perceived by agents conditioned in their dispositions by the demands of that structure, appears to them as a space of possibles capable of orienting their expectations and their projects by its demands and even of determining them, negatively at least, by its constraints, so favouring actions that tend to contribute to the development of a more complex structure. Artist, writer or scientist, each one, when she sets about her work, is like a composer at her piano, which offers apparently unlimited possibilities to invention in writing – and in performance – but at the same time imposes the constraints and limits inherent in its structure (for example, the range of the keyboard), itself determined by its manufacture – constraints and limits which are also present in the dispositions of the artist, themselves dependent on the possibilities of the instrument, even if those dispositions are what reveals them and brings them to more or less complete existence.

The opacity of historical processes derives from the fact that human actions are the non-random and yet never rationally mastered product of countless self-obscure encounters between habitus marked by the history from which they arise and social universes (in particular, fields) in which they realize their potentialities, but, under the constraint of the structure of those universes, receiving from that dual necessity their specifically historical logic, intermediate between the logical reason of 'truths of reason' and the pure contingency of 'truths of fact', which cannot be deduced, but can be understood or even necessitated.

The objection will perhaps be raised at this point that, magically evading the antinomy between the descriptive and the normative, I am putting forward a *prescriptive description* of the scientific field, which, as an explanation of the truth of its functioning, provides a knowledge of the objective necessity of the field offering the possibility of freedom with respect to that necessity, and therefore of a practical ethics aimed at increasing that freedom. And indeed, there is no constative assertion about this field which cannot be read normatively. This is true of the observation that, in certain conditions, competition favours the progress of knowledge; or the observation that the definition of the stake of the scientific game is itself at stake in the scientific game, and that, consequently, in this game there are no judges who are not also parties (as is seen particularly well at the time of revolutionary breaks: who will be competent to judge a theory or a method calling into question the established definition of theoretical or methodological competence?). Does not this performative vision reintroduce a form of normativeness by positing that truth and objectivity are the forced product of a social mechanism of non-violent and but not disinterested struggle? By stating it, does not the 'subject' of this performative representation in some sense situate himself outside of the game, which he perceives as such, from an external, superior position, thereby asserting the possibility of a sovereign, totalizing, objective viewpoint, that of the neutral, impartial spectator?

One does not easily leave the spontaneously performative logic of language, which, as I have always insisted, helps to make (or make exist) what it says, especially through the inseparably cognitive and political constructive efficacy of classifications. And it cannot be denied that reflexive historico-sociological analysis tends to produce and impose, in a quite circular way, its own criteria of scientificity. But is it possible – without invoking a *deus ex machina* – to escape from a circle that is present in reality, and not just in the analysis? It is indeed the autonomization of the scientific field which makes possible the establishment of specific laws, laws which then contribute to the progress of reason and so to the autonomization of the field.

To complicate everything, how (supposing that it were really desirable) can one prevent the description of more advanced, more autonomous states of the scientific field from appearing as pregnant with a critique of less advanced states, especially of the field of the social sciences, within which it is engendered? It is certain that knowledge of the major tendencies of scientific development – a constant rise in the entry qualifications, growing homogeneity among the competitors, a declining gap between strategies of conservation and strategies of subversion, replacement of major periodic revolutions by multiple, more minor, permanent revolutions, freed from external political causes and effects, etc. – implies and induces a normative definition of the fundamental law of a truly scientific field, namely consensus on the legitimate objects of debate and on the legitimate means of regulating it. It is no less certain that this knowledge offers a real criterion for the difference between the false agreements of a religious, philosophical or political orthodoxy (or a false science), which are based on an *a priori* complicity and on socially pre-established forms of validation (*communis doctorum opinio*), and real disagreements, which can be called scientific because they are based on an agreement limited to the stake of the disagreement and can therefore lead to a real agreement, albeit necessarily provisional.

If there is a truth, it is that truth is a stake in struggles. And this is true in the scientific field itself. But the struggles that take place there have their own logic, which raises them from the infinite play of mirrors of radical perspectivism. The objectification of these struggles, and the model of the correspondence between the space of positions and the space of position-takings which reveals its logic, are the product of an effort armed with instruments of totalization and analysis (such as statistics) and oriented towards objectivity, the ultimate but endlessly retreating horizon of a set of collective practices which we can describe, with Bachelard, as 'a constant effort of desubjectivization'.

Reflexivity and twofold historicization

The adoption of critical reflexivity is inspired not by a purely theoretical intention which would be an end in itself, but by two convictions, confirmed by experience. First, the principle of the most serious errors or illusions of anthropological thought (which are found no less among specialists in the social sciences – historians, sociologists, ethnologists – than among philosophers), and in particular the vision of the agent as a conscious, rational, unconditioned individual (or 'subject'), lies in the social conditions of production of anthropological discourse, in other words in the structure and functioning of the fields in which discourse on 'humanity' is produced. Secondly, there can be thought about the social conditions of thought which offers thought the possibility of a genuine *freedom* with respect to those conditions.

To explore and make explicit all the commitments and procliv-
ities associated with the interests and habits of thought linked to
occupation of a position (to be won or defended) in a field are,
strictly speaking, infinite tasks. One would be falling into a form of
the scholastic illusion of the omnipotence of thought if one were to
believe it possible to take an absolute point of view on one's own
point of view. The imperative of reflexivity is not some kind of rather
futile point of honour, that of the thinker who would like to be able
to occupy a transcendent viewpoint with respect to the empirical
viewpoints of ordinary agents or his competitors in the scientific world,
radically and definitively separated, as if by an initiatory break, from
his own empirical viewpoint as an empirical agent, engaged in the
games and the stakes of his universe.

It is again their habits and ambitions of thought that lead some
philosophers to denounce the concern for reflexivity as the ambition
of an individual who seeks to attain a position of absolute knowledge
and to speak with the voice of an authoritarian reason, as the sole
possessor of the truth. In reality, reflexivity is incumbent upon all
those who are engaged in the scientific field; and it is achieved, through
the play of the competition which unites and divides them, when the
conditions are fulfilled for this competition to obey the imperatives of
rational polemics and for each participant to have an interest in sub-
ordinating his 'selfish' interests to the rules of dialogic confrontation.

Each individual conquest of reflexivity (such as the discovery of
the scholastic illusion) is destined by the logic of competition to become a weapon in the scientific struggle and so to become a necessity
for all those engaged in it. No one can forge weapons to be used
against his opponents without having those weapons immediately
used against him by them or by others. It is from this social logic, and
not from some illusory, sanctimonious deontology, that one can
expect progress towards greater reflexivity, imposed by the effects of
mutual objectification and not by a simple and more or less narcissistic turning of subjectivities upon themselves. The scientific statement
of the logic of the functioning of the scientific field can also help, by
making it more conscious and more systematic, to arm the mutual
surveillance within the field and so strengthen its efficacy (which does
not rule out cynical uses of the knowledge thereby offered).

To practise reflexivity means questioning the privilege of a knowing 'subject' arbitrarily excluded from the effort of objectification. It
means endeavouring to account for the empirical 'subject' of scientific practice in the terms of the objectivity constructed by the scientific 'subject' – in particular by situating him at a determinate point in
social space-time – and so acquiring a more acute awareness and a

greater mastery of the constraints that can be exerted on the scientific
'subject' through the links which bind him to the empirical subject,
his interests, drives, and presuppositions, and which he must break in
order to constitute himself. How can one fail to recognize that the
'choices' of the 'free' and 'disinterested' subject glorified by tradition
are never totally independent of the mechanics of the fields and therefore of the history of which it is the outcome and which remains
embedded in its structures and, through them, in the cognitive structures, principles of vision and division, concepts, theories and methods
applied, which are never totally independent of the position he occupies
within the field and the associated interests?

Nor can one be satisfied with seeking the conditions of possibility
and the limits of objective knowledge in the 'subject', as the classical
(Kantian) philosophy of knowledge recommends (and as ethnomethodology or 'constructivist' idealism still do today). One has to look
into the object constructed by science (the social space or the field) to
find the social conditions of possibility of the 'subject' and of his
work of constructing the object (including *skholè* and the whole heritage of problems, concepts, methods, etc.) and so to bring to light
the social limits of his act of objectification. It is thus possible to
renounce the absolutism of classical objectivism without falling into
relativism. Indeed, to every advance in knowledge of the social conditions of production of 'subjects' there corresponds an advance in
knowledge of the scientific object, and vice versa. This is never clearer
than when research applies itself to the scientific field itself (as with
the research whose findings I presented in *Homo Academicus*): it
then becomes obvious that the conditions of possibility of scientific
knowledge and those of its object are one and the same.

Thus, if the historical sciences destroy the illusion of the transcendence of a transhistorical, transpersonal reason, both in the classical
form that it took with Kant and the renovated form that Habermas
gives it when he locates the universal forms of reason in language,
they make it possible to extend and radicalize the critical intention of
Kantian rationalism and to give its full efficacy to the effort to rescue
reason from history by helping to give sociological weapons to the
free and generalized exercise of an epistemological critique of all by
all, deriving from the field itself, in other words from the conflictual
but regulated cooperation that competition imposes there.

There is no reason for despair – far from it – in the fact that the
so-called eternal verities and values have to be sought not from a
more or less skilfully secularized form of revelation but from that
very particular form of struggle in which each agent, in order to win,
can and must use the best weapons produced for and by the previous

state of the struggle, and where what is at stake is the capacity to tell the truth about the world – the very world in which the struggle takes place – and the referee is the sanction of reality, to which the supporters of different positions can and must refer themselves. In accepting this fact and in working to reveal the historical and social conditions, both individual and collective, of the production and reception of cultural works, together with the corresponding limits, the historical· sciences in no way seek to discredit these productions by reducing them to contingency or absurdity. Quite on the contrary, they seek to increase or reinforce the means of saving them from this fate by bringing to light the economic and social constraints which bear on these fields of cultural production. By turning the instruments of knowledge that they produce against themselves, and especially against the social universes in which they produce them, they equip themselves with the means of at least partially escaping from the economic and social determinisms that they reveal and of dispelling the threat of historicist relativization that they contain, not least for themselves.

Far from being a polemical denunciation aimed at devaluing reason, as is sometimes claimed, analysis of the conditions in which the work of reason is performed is a privileged instrument of the polemics of reason. By endeavouring to intensify awareness of the limits that thought owes to its social conditions of production and to destroy the illusion of the absence of limits or of freedom from all determinations which leaves thought defenceless against these determinations, it aims to offer the possibility of a real freedom with respect to the determinations that it reveals. Any advance in knowledge of the scientific field, with its power relations, its effects of domination, its tyrannies and its clienteles, also advances the theoretical and practical means of mastering the effects of the external constraints (such as those which now come through journalism) and of the internal constraints which pass on their efficacy (such as those of competition for celebrity, but also for grants, public or private contracts, etc.) and which may also, paradoxically, weaken the capacity for resistance to heteronomy.

Thus, paradoxically, while they seem now to provide the best weapons for an irrationalist denunciation of science disguised as a denunciation of scientism or positivism, social sciences uncompromisingly accepting the radical historicity of reason and tempered by the test of historicization could be the surest support for a historicist rationalism or a rationalist historicism. Once it has repudiated the illusory quest for an ontological foundation, for which anti-rationalist nihilism still betrays a nostalgia, the collective work of critical reflexivity should enable scientific reason to control itself ever more closely, in and through conflictual cooperation and mutual critique, and so to move progressively towards total independence of constraints and contingencies, a kind of *focus imaginarius*, to which the rationalist conviction aspires and by which it is measured.

The universality of strategies of universalization

It is no doubt true that logic is embedded in a social relationship of regulated debate, made possible by reference to common markers or, more precisely, in a rational exchange based on the adoption of the same point of view by all participants, which is constitutive of their membership of that universe and therefore both of the divergences and the convergences that are expressed there. But this does not mean that the 'ideal speech situation' in which all participants have equal chances to defend their position, to engage or continue the discussion, to put forward their feelings and judgements freely, to ask for explanations and justifications, establishes itself everywhere and always by its own force. And the same Grice who set out the 'cooperative principle' ('Make your contribution such as is required, at the stage at which it occurs, by the accepted purpose or direction of the talk exchange in which you are engaged')[19] observes that it is constantly flouted (one could say the same of the principle put forward by Habermas, according to which consensus must be attained by the sheer force of the arguments). In other words, Grice's maxim, far from being a sociological law accounting for the actual behaviour of real speakers really engaged in a conversation, is in fact a kind of implicit presupposition of all conversation, a specific variant of the principle of reciprocity, which, though it is constantly transgressed, can be invoked at any time, as a reminder of the tacitly accepted rule or an implicit reference to what a conversation has to be in order to be a real dialogue.

However, under the cover of saying what a thing really is, what it is in reality, one is always liable to say what it should be in order to be really what it is, and so to slide from the descriptive to the normative, from 'is' to 'ought-to-be'. We have to acknowledge the universality of the official recognition granted to the imperatives of universality, a kind of 'spiritual point of honour' of humanity – the imperatives of cognitive universality which require the negation of the subjective,

---

[19] H. P. Grice, 'Logic and conversation', in P. Cole and J. Morgan (eds), *Syntax and Semantics 3: Speech Acts* (New York: Academic Press, 1975), p. 45.

the personal, in favour of the transpersonal and the objective; imperatives of ethical universality which require the negation of egoism and particular interest in favour of disinterestedness and generosity. But we must also acknowledge the universality of the actual transgression of these norms. And analysis of essence has to give way to historical analysis, the only kind that is capable of describing the very process of which analysis of essence unwittingly records the result, that is to say, the movement whereby the 'ought-to-be' advances through the emergence of universes capable of practically imposing the norms of ethical and cognitive universality and really obtaining the sublimated behaviours corresponding to the logical and moral ideal.

If the universal does advance, this is because there are social microcosms which, in spite of their intrinsic ambiguity, linked to their enclosure in the privilege and satisfied egoism of a separation by status, are the site of struggles in which the prize is the universal and in which agents who, to differing degrees depending on their position and trajectory, have *a particular interest in the universal*, in reason, truth, virtue, engage themselves with weapons which are nothing other than the most universal conquests of the previous struggles. This is true of the legal field, the site of struggles in which the stakes are far from all and always being in accordance with law, but which, even when they aim to transform the rules of law (as is now the case in the area of commercial law), must take place *according to these rules*.[20]

Thus jurists, who by a collective labour over several centuries invented the State, have been able to institute, truly *ex nihilo*, a whole set of concepts, procedures and forms of organization aiming to serve the general interest, the public, the public interest, only in so far as, in so doing, they instituted themselves as holders or trustees of the powers associated with the exercise of State authority and could thus secure for themselves a form of private appropriation of public service, based on education and merit, and no longer on birth. In other words, the luminous rise of reason and the liberatory epic crowned by the French Revolution that is exalted in the Jacobin vision has a dark reverse side, the progressive rise of the holders of cultural capital, and in particular the jurists, who, from the medieval canonists to the advocates and professors of the nineteenth century or the technocrats of the present day, have managed, notably thanks

---

[20] Cf. Y. Dezalay and B. Garth, 'Merchants of law as moral entrepreneurs: constructing international justice out of the competition for transnational business disputes', *Law and Society Review*, 29, no. 1, pp. 27–64.

to the Revolution – one episode in a long, continuous struggle – to take the place of the old nobility and install themselves as a State nobility.

The ambiguity of the civilizing usurpation, a universalizing monopolization, is reproduced in each of the uses of law which implies that one should, in appearance at least, privilege deduction (from principles or precedents) over induction, 'pure' affirmation of the principles of universal ethics over realist (sociological, one might say) transaction with realities. And the extreme caution of jurists – especially at the highest levels – stems from the fact that they cannot forget that each judicial act contributes to the making of law by creating a precedent and that they in a sense endlessly bind themselves by their decisions and especially by the element of universal rationality in which they must dress them, by the seemingly deductive 'rationalizations' which they produce after the event in order to justify them but which can become the principle of decisions quite opposite to those that they have justified.

The unification and relative universalization associated with the rise of the State are inseparable from the monopolization by a few of the universal resources that it produces and procures (Weber, and Elias after him, ignored the process of the constitution of a State capital and the process of the monopolization of this capital by the State nobility which helped to produce it, or, more precisely, produced itself as such by producing it). But this *monopoly of the universal* can only be obtained at the cost of the (at least apparent) submission of those who hold it to the reasons of universality, and therefore to a universalist representation of domination. Those who, like Marx, reverse the official image that the State bureaucracy seeks to give of itself and describe the bureaucrats as usurpers of the universal, acting like private proprietors of public resources, are not wrong. But they ignore the very real effects of the obligatory reference to the values of neutrality and disinterested devotion to the public good which becomes more and more incumbent on State functionaries in the successive stages of the long labour of symbolic construction which leads to the invention and imposition of the official representation of the State as the site of universality and the service of the general interest.

Thus, political scandal, in the form of revelation by the press of an ethical transgression by an eminent personality, underlines the rule of devotion to the general interest, in other words, disinterestedness, which is required of all individuals designated to be the official incarnation of the group. As if the privilege of embodying the public interest implied renunciation of all that is protected by the privacy of private life, the publication of private information about so-called 'public' figures is tolerated (whereas, in the case of private individuals, it is condemned, to varying degrees depending on the legal tradition). This is especially so when it is discovered that, having committed themselves to the public interest, they have transgressed the frontier between the private and the public, in particular by using public resources for private purposes, so that the privacy of the private has in fact served to hide a private use of what is public.

There are universes which, like the political field and especially the bureaucratic field, more insistently demand at least external submission to the universal, even if one cannot ignore the gap between the official norm prescribing the obligation of disinterestedness and the reality of practice, with all the lapses from that obligation, all the cases of 'private use of public property', misappropriation of public goods and services, corruption or bribery, all the perks, concessions, privileges and other abuses in which advantage is derived from non-application or transgression of the rule. Because of their paradoxical logic, these universes (like the fields of cultural production) favour the appearance of disinterested dispositions, through the rewards they give to the *interest in disinterestedness*.

The universal is the object of an official recognition and the recognition universally given to the sacrificing of selfish interests (especially economic ones) universally favours the strategies of universalization, through the undeniable symbolic profits it provides. There is nothing that groups recognize and reward more unconditionally and demand more imperatively than the unconditional manifestation of respect for the group as a group (which is affirmed, in particular, in seemingly quite anodyne rituals of 'civic religion'), and they give social recognition even to the recognition (even if feigned and hypocritical) of the rule that is implied in strategies of universalization. The profits of universality are one of the major stakes in symbolic struggles, in which reference to the universal is the weapon par excellence. To fall into line with the rule, to 'regularize' (a *de facto* situation), is to try to put the group on one's side by declaring one's recognition of the rule of the group and therefore of the group itself; and submission to the order of the group is also the principle of all the strategies, sincere or hypocritical, tending to universalize practices which may have very non-universal principles, by applying the universal forms and formulae ('rationalizations'), by disguising and repressing private interests and profits, by invoking principles, reasons or motives which may be more or less fictitious but which imply renunciation of the arbitrary affirmation of the arbitrary – all behaviours which groups, in their realism, know how to recognize at their true value and to reward as 'pious hypocrisies'[21] and 'homage that vice pays to virtue'.

And one is tempted to say, contrary to the moralists who insist on pure intentions, that it is good that it should be so. No one can any longer believe that history is guided by reason; and if reason, and also the universal, moves forward at all, it is perhaps because there are profits in rationality and universality so that actions which advance reason and the universal advance at the same time the interests of those who perform them.

As soon as one ceases to deny the evidence of history and accepts that reason is not rooted in an ahistorical nature and that, as a human invention, it can only assert itself in social games capable of favouring its appearance and its exercise, one can arm oneself with a historical science of the historical conditions of its emergence to try to strengthen everything that, in each of the different fields, tends to favour the undivided rule of its specific logic, in other words independence from any kind of extrinsic power or authority – tradition, religion, the State, market forces. One might then, in this spirit, treat the realistic description of the scientific field as a kind of reasonable utopia of what a political field conforming to democratic reason might be like; or, more precisely, as a model which, by comparison with the observed reality, would indicate the principles of action aimed at promoting the equivalent, within the political field, of what is observed in the scientific field in its most autonomous forms, that is to say, a regulated competition, which would control itself, not through the intervention of a deontology – that alibi of a clear conscience, ritually invoked in conferences and consultative committees – but by its own immanent logic, through social mechanisms capable of forcing agents to behave 'rationally' and to sublimate their drives.

If one wants to go beyond preaching, then it is necessary to implement practically, by using the ordinary means of political action – creation of associations and movements, demonstrations, manifestoes, etc. – the *Realpolitik* of reason aimed at setting up or reinforcing, within the political field, the mechanisms capable of imposing the sanctions, as far as possible automatic ones, that would tend to discourage deviations from the democratic norm (such as the corruption of elected representatives) and to encourage or impose the appropriate behaviours; aimed also at favouring the setting up of non-distorted social structures of communication between the holders of power and the citizens, in particularly through a constant struggle for the independence of the media.

---

[21] *'pieuses hypocrisies'*, modelled on 'mensonges pieux', 'white lies'. *Trans.*

I realize that the 'moral philosophy' underlying this *Realpolitik* may be disenchanting, and I fear that all those who endlessly declare their faith in democratic dialogue, the ethics of communication and rational universalism will be quick to denounce the cynical realism of a description of how things really work, which, though it does not imply the slightest form of resignation, will be suspected of rationalizing what it states. In reality, if one is not, at best, to indulge in an irresponsible utopianism, which often has no other effect than to procure the short-lived euphoria of humanist hopes, almost always as brief as adolescence, and which produces effects quite as malign in the life of research as in political life, it is necessary, I think, to return to a 'realistic' vision of the universes in which the universal is generated. To be content, as one might be tempted, with giving the universal the status of a 'regulatory idea', capable of suggesting principles of action, would be to forget that there are universes in which it becomes a 'constitutive', immanent principle of regulation, such as the scientific field, and to a lesser extent the bureaucratic field and the juridical field; and that, more generally, as soon as principles claiming universal validity (those of democracy, for example) are stated and officially professed, there is no longer any social situation in which they cannot serve at least as symbolic weapons in struggles of interest or as instruments of critique for those who have a self-interest in truth and virtue (like, nowadays, all those, especially in the minor State nobility, whose interests are bound up with the universal advances associated with the State and with law).

All that is said here applies first and foremost to the State, which, like all the historical gains linked to the relatively autonomous history of the scholastic fields, is marked by a profound ambiguity. It can be described and treated simultaneously as a relay, no doubt a relatively autonomous one, of economic and political powers which have little interest in universal interests, and as a neutral body which, because it conserves, within its very structure, the trace of previous struggles, the gains of which it records and guarantees, is capable of acting as a kind of umpire, no doubt always somewhat biased, but ultimately less unfavourable to the interests of the dominated, and to what can be called justice, than what is exalted, under the false colours of liberty and liberalism, by the advocates of 'laisser-faire', in other words the brutal and tyrannical exercise of economic force.

4

Bodily Knowledge

～✧～

The question of the subject is raised by the very existence of sciences that take as their object what is customarily called the 'subject', that object for which there are objects – sciences that consequently engage presuppositions diametrically opposed to those defended by 'philosophies of the subject'. Even among specialists of the social sciences, there will always be those who will deny the right to objectify another subject and to produce its objective truth. And it would be naive to think that one can reassure the defenders of the sacred rights of subjectivity by giving guarantees of scientificity and pointing out that the assertions of the social sciences, which are based on a specific kind of labour armed with specially developed methods and tools and subject to collective control, have nothing in common with the peremptory verdicts of everyday existence, based on partial, self-interested intuition – gossip, insult, slander, rumour and flattery – which are common currency even in intellectual life. Quite the contrary. It is the scientific intention itself which is rejected as an unbearable violence, a tyrannical usurpation of the imprescriptible right to truth-telling that every 'creator' claims by definition for herself, especially when the object is none other than herself, in her singularity as an irreplaceable being, or for her peers (as is seen from the cries of affronted solidarity that are provoked by every attempt to subject writers, artists or philosophers to scientific inquiry in its ordinary form). And it can even happen, in some corners of the intellectual world, that those who show themselves most concerned for the spiritual dimension of the 'person', perhaps because they confuse the methodical procedures of objectification with the rhetorical strategies of polemics, pamphlets, or worse, defamation or slander, do not hesitate to see the propositions of the sociologist as 'denunciations', which they feel entitled and required to denounce, or verdicts that bear witness to a diabolical pretension to usurp a divine power and make the judgement of science the last judgement.

In fact, even if some of them sometimes forget it, choosing the easy option of retrospective trial, historians or sociologists simply aim to establish universal principles of explanation and understanding, valid for every 'subject', naturally including the agent who states them and who knows full well that he can be subjected to critique in the name of those principles. Their propositions, the expressions of the logic of a field subject to the impersonal dialectic of demonstration and refutation, are always exposed to the critique of their competitors and the test of reality, and when they apply to the scientific worlds themselves the whole movement of scientific thought is enacted through them, in and through this return upon itself.

Having said this, I am well aware that the very intention of objectively defining, through categories of thought that are necessarily categorical, and, worse, of explaining – and genetically, albeit with all the methodological and logical precautions of probabilistic reasoning and language (which are unfortunately often misunderstood) – is destined to be seen as especially scandalous when it applies to the scholastic worlds, in other words to people who see themselves as statutorily qualified to explain rather than be explained, to objectify rather than be subject to objectification, and who see no reason to delegate to another authority what they see as a discretionary power of symbolic life or death (which moreover they find it normal to exercise on a daily basis, without accepting the safety barriers of scientific discipline). It is not surprising that philosophers have always been in the front line of the battle against the scientific ambition of explaining when 'man' is in question, seeking to confine the 'sciences of man', in accordance with Dilthey's classic distinction, to 'understanding', which is seemingly more understanding of their freedom and their singularity, or 'hermeneutics', which, by virtue of the traditions linked to its religious origins, is more appropriate to the study of the sacred texts of scholastic production.[1]

---

[1] As A. Grünbaum shows, in a cruel critique of so-called 'hermeneutic' philosophies, it is, bizarrely, in the name of a narrowly positivist definition, founded on typically positivist distinctions between theory and empirical observation, reasons and causes, the mental and the physical, etc., and an often somewhat simple view of the natural

To find a way out of this interminable debate, one can simply start
out from a paradoxical observation, condensed by Pascal into an
admirable formula, which immediately points beyond the dilemma of
objectivism and subjectivism: 'By space the universe comprehends and
swallows me up like an atom; by thought I comprehend the world.'[2]
The world encompasses me, comprehends me as a thing among things,
but I, as a thing for which there are things, comprehend this world.
And I do so (must it be added?) *because* it encompasses and comprehends me; it is through this material inclusion – often unnoticed or
repressed – and what follows from it, the incorporation of social
structures in the form of dispositional structures, of objective chances
in the form of expectations or anticipations, that I acquire a practical
knowledge and control of the encompassing space (I know confusedly
what depends on me and what does not, what is 'for me' or 'not for
me' or 'not for people like me', what it is 'reasonable' for me to do,
to hope for and ask for). But I cannot comprehend this practical
comprehension unless I comprehend both what distinctively defines
it, as opposed to conscious, intellectual comprehension, and also the
conditions (linked to positions in social space) of these two forms of
comprehension.

The reader will have understood that I have tacitly expanded the
notion of space to include, as well as physical space, which Pascal is
thinking of, what I call social space, the locus of the coexistence of
social positions, mutually exclusive points, which, for the occupants,
are the basis of points of view. The 'I' that practically comprehends
physical space and social space (though the subject of the verb *comprehend*, it is not necessarily a 'subject' in the sense of philosophies
of mind, but rather a habitus, a system of dispositions) is comprehended, in a quite different sense, encompassed, inscribed, implicated
in that space. It occupies a position there which (from statistical
analyses of empirical correlations) we know is regularly associated
with position-takings (opinions, representations, judgements, etc.) on
the physical world and the social world.

From this paradoxical relationship of double inclusion flow all the
paradoxes which Pascal assembled under the heading of wretchedness and greatness, and which ought to be meditated on by all those

sciences that the advocates of hermeneutic particularism condemn the social sciences
to a special status that they do not seek and by the same token disqualify with the
shameful label of positivism any form of those sciences that refuses this status (cf.
A. Grünbaum, *The Foundations of Psychoanalysis: A Philosophical Critique* (Berkeley:
California University Press, 1984), pp. 1–94).
[2] Pascal, *Pensées*, 348.

who remain trapped in the scholastic dilemma of determinism and freedom: determined (wretchedness), man can know his determinations (greatness) and work to overcome them. These paradoxes all find their principle in the privilege of reflexivity: 'Man knows that he is wretched. He is therefore wretched, because he is so; but he is really great because he knows it.'[3] Or again: 'The weakness of man is far more evident in those who know it not than in those who know it.'[4] It is no doubt true that one cannot expect any greatness, at least in matters of thought, except through knowledge of 'wretchedness'. And perhaps, in accordance with the same, typically Pascalian dialectic of the reversal of values, sociology, a form of thought detested by 'thinkers' because it gives access to knowledge of the determinations which bear on them and therefore on their thought, is, more than the would-be radical breaks which often leave things unchanged, capable of offering them the possibility of escaping from one of the commonest forms of the wretchedness and weakness to which ignorance or the lofty refusal to know so often condemn thought.

Analysis situs

As a body and a biological individual, I am, in the way that things are, situated in a place; I occupy a position in physical space and social space. I am not *atopos*, placeless, as Plato said of Socrates, nor 'rootless and free-floating' as was rather too casually put by the man who is sometimes regarded as the one of the founders of the sociology of intellectuals, Karl Mannheim. Nor am I endowed, as in folk tales, with the physical and social ubiquity (which Flaubert dreamed of) that would enable me to be in several places and several times at once, to occupy simultaneously several physical and social positions. (Place, *topos*, can be defined absolutely, as the site where a thing or an agent 'takes place', exists, in short, as a localization, or relationally, topologically, as a position, a rank in an order.)

The idea of a separate individual is based, in a quite paradoxical way, on the naive apprehension of what, as Heidegger put it in a lecture in 1934, 'is perceived from outside', what is 'graspable and solid', that is, the body: 'Nothing is more familiar to us than the impression that man is an individual living being among others and that the skin is his boundary, that inwardness is the seat of experiences and that he has experiences in the same way that he has a stomach and that he is subject to various influences, to which he

---

[3] Pascal, *Pensées*, 416.
[4] Pascal, *Pensées*, 376.

responds.' This spontaneous materialism, the most naive kind, which only wants to know what it can 'handle' (*das Handgreifliche*, as Heidegger puts it), could explain the tendency to physicalism which, treating the body as a thing that can be measured, weighed and counted, aspires to turn the science of 'man' into a science of nature. But it could also explain, more paradoxically, both the 'personalist' belief in the uniqueness of the person – the basis of the scientifically disastrous opposition between the individual and society – and the inclination towards 'mentalism', thematized in Husserl's theory of intentionality as noesis, an act of consciousness, containing noemata, the contents of consciousness.

(If 'personalism' is the main obstacle to the construction of a scientific vision of the human being and one of the focuses of past and present resistance to the imposition of such a vision, this is no doubt because it is a condensed form of all the theoretical postures – mentalism, spiritualism, individualism, etc. – of the most common spontaneous philosophy, at least in societies of Christian tradition and in the most favoured regions of those societies. It is also because it encounters the immediate complicity of all those who, being concerned to think of themselves as unique 'creators' of singularity, are always ready to strike up new variations on the old conservative themes of the open and the closed, conformism and anti-conformism, or unknowingly to reinvent the opposition, constructed by Bergson against Durkheim, between '*orders* dictated by *impersonal* social requirements' and the '*appeals* made to the conscience of each of us by persons' – saints, geniuses and heroes.[5] The social sciences, having been initially built up, often at the cost of indisputably scientistic distortions, against the religious view of the world, found themselves constituted as a central bastion on the side of the Enlightenment – with, in particular, the sociology of religion, the heart of Durkheim's undertaking and of the resistance it aroused – in the political and religious struggle over the vision of 'humanity' and its destiny. And most of the polemics of which they are periodically the target simply extend the logic of political struggles into intellectual life. That is why one finds there all the themes of the old battles fought in the last century by writers like Barrès, Péguy or Maurras, but also Bergson, or by angry young reactionaries such as Agathon, the pseudonym of Henri Massis and Alfred de Tarde, against the 'scientism' of Taine and Renan and the 'New Sorbonne' of Durkheim and Seignobos.[6]

[5] H. Bergson, *The Two Sources of Morality and Religion*, tr. R. A. Audra and C. Brereton (Notre Dame, Ind.: University of Notre Dame Press, 1977), p. 84.
[6] Cf. F. K. Ringer, *Fields of Knowledge: Academic Culture in Comparative Perspective* (Cambridge: Cambridge University Press, 1992).

One would only have to change the names in order for any of the inexhaustible refrains on determinism and freedom, on the irreducibility of creative genius to all sociologistic explanations, or a *cri du cœur* like Paul Claudel's – 'At last I was leaving the repulsive world of a Taine or a Renan, of those horrible mechanisms governed by inflexible laws, which could moreover be known and taught' – to be attributable to one or another of those who now present themselves as the champions of human rights or the inspired prophets of the 'return of the subject'.)

The 'mentalist' vision, which is inseparable from belief in the dualism of mind and body, spirit and matter, originates from an almost anatomical and therefore typically scholastic viewpoint on the body from outside. (Just as the perspective vision was embodied in the *camera obscura* of Descartes's *Dioptrics*, this point of view is in a way materialized in the circular ampitheatre, around a dissecting table for anatomy lessons, to be seen at the University of Uppsala.) 'A man is a substance,' wrote Pascal, 'but if we dissect him, will he be the head, the heart, the stomach, the veins, each vein, each portion of a vein, the blood, each humour in the blood?'[7] This body-as-thing, known from outside as a mechanism, the limiting case of which is the body undergoing the mechanistic dismantling of dissection, the skull with the empty eye-sockets of pictorial vanities, and which is opposed to the inhabited and *forgotten* body, felt from inside as opening, energy, tension or desire, and also as strength, connivance and familiarity, is the product of the extension to the body of a spectator's relation to the world. Intellectualism, the scholastic spectator's theory of knowledge, is thus led to ask of the body, or about the body, problems of knowledge, like the Cartesian philosophers who, because they felt unable to account for the control exerted over the body and so have an intellectual knowledge of bodily action, were forced to attribute human action to divine intervention. The difficulty increases with speech: every speech act, as an incorporeal meaning expressed in material sounds, is nothing short of a miracle, a kind of transubstantiation.

On the other hand, the self-evidence of the isolated, distinguished body is what prevents the fact being realized that this body which indisputably functions as a principle of individuation (in as much as it localizes in space and time, separates, isolates, etc.), ratified and reinforced by the legal definition of the individual as an abstract, interchangeable being, without qualities, is also – as a real agent, that is to say, as a habitus, with its history, its incorporated properties – a

[7] Pascal, *Pensées*, 115.

principle of 'collectivization' (*Vergesellschaftung*), as Hegel puts it. Having the (biological) property of being open to the world, and therefore exposed to the world, and so capable of being conditioned by the world, shaped by the material and cultural conditions of existence in which it is placed from the beginning, it is subject to a process of socialization of which individuation is itself the product, with the singularity of the 'self' being fashioned in and by social relations. (One might also speak, as Strawson does, but perhaps in a slightly different sense, of 'collectivist subjectivism'.)[8]

The social space

Just as physical space, according to Strawson,[9] is defined by the reciprocal externality of positions (another way of referring to Leibniz's 'order of coexistences'), the social space is defined by the mutual exclusion, or *distinction*, of the positions which constitute it, that is, as a structure of juxtaposition of social positions (themselves defined, as we shall see, as positions in the structure of distribution of the various kinds of capital). Social agents, and also things in so far as they are appropriated by them and therefore constituted as *properties*, are situated in a place in social space, a distinct and distinctive place which can be characterized by the position it occupies relative to other places (above, below, between, etc.) and the distance (sometimes called 'respectful': *e longinquo reverentia*) that separates it from them. As such, they are amenable to an *analysis situs*, a social topology (the very one which provided the object for my book *Distinction*, and which, it can be seen, is very far from the misreading of that work – no doubt on the basis of the title alone and despite what is expressly stated within it – according to which the quest for distinction is the principle of all human behaviours).

Social space tends to be translated, with more or less distortion, into physical space, in the form of a certain arrangement of agents and properties. It follows that all the divisions and distinctions of social space (high/low, left/right, etc.) are really and symbolically expressed in physical space appropriated as reified social space (with, for example, the opposition between the smart areas – rue du Faubourg Saint-Honoré or Fifth Avenue – and the working-class areas or the suburbs). This space is defined by the more or less close

[8] P. F. Strawson, *Skepticism and Naturalism: Some Varieties* (London: Methuen, 1985).
[9] P. F. Strawson, *Individuals: An Essay in Descriptive Metaphysics* (London: Methuen, 1959).

correspondence between a certain order of coexistence (or distribution) of agents and a certain order of coexistence (or distribution) of properties. Everyone, therefore, is characterized by the place where he is more or less permanently domiciled (to be a 'vagrant', 'of no fixed abode', is to lack social existence; 'high society' occupies the high ground of the social world). He is also characterized also by the relative position – and therefore the *rarity, a source of material or symbolic revenues* – of his locations, both temporary (for example, places of honour and all the precedences of all protocols) and permanent (private and professional addresses, reserved places, unbeatable views, exclusive access, priority, etc.). Finally, he is characterized by the extent of the space he takes up and occupies (in law), through his properties (houses, land), which are more or less 'space-consuming'.

Comprehension

What is comprehended in the world is a body for which there is a world, which is included in the world but in a mode of inclusion irreducible to simple material and spatial inclusion. *Illusio* is that way of *being in* the world, of being occupied by the world, which means that an agent can be affected by something very distant, even absent, if it participates in the game in which he is engaged. The body is linked to a place by a direct relationship of contact, which is just one way among others of relating to the world. The agent is linked to a space, that of a field, proximity within which is not the same as proximity in physical space (even if, other things being equal, what is directly perceived always has a sort of practical privilege). It is because of the *illusio* which constitutes the field as the space of a game that thoughts and actions can be affected and modified without any physical contact or even any symbolic *interaction*, in particular in and through the relationship of *comprehension*. The world is comprehensible, immediately endowed with meaning, because the body, which, thanks to its senses and its brain, has the capacity to be present to what is outside itself, in the world, and to be impressed and durably modified by it, has been protractedly (from the beginning) exposed to its regularities. Having acquired from this exposure a system of dispositions attuned to these regularities, it is inclined and able to anticipate them practically in behaviours which engage a *corporeal knowledge* that provides a practical comprehension of the world quite different from the intentional act of conscious decoding that is normally designated by the idea of comprehension. In other words, if the agent has an immediate understanding of the familiar world, this is because the cognitive structures that he implements are the product of incorporation of the structures of the world in which he acts; the instruments of construction that he uses to know the world are constructed by the world. These practical principles of organization of the given are constructed from the experience of frequently encountered situations and can be revised and rejected in the event of repeated failure.

(I am well aware of the critique of 'dispositional' concepts, a ritual one which can therefore secure large symbolic profits at a small cost in reflection. But, in the particular case of anthropology, it is not clear how one could avoid recourse to such notions without denying the self-evidence of the facts: to speak of dispositions is simply to take note of a natural predisposition of human bodies, the only one, according to Hume – as read by Deleuze[10] – that a rigorous anthropology is entitled to assume, a *conditionability* in the sense of a natural capacity to acquire non-natural, arbitrary capacities. To deny the existence of acquired dispositions, in the case of living beings, is to deny the existence of learning in the sense of a selective, durable transformation of the body through the reinforcement or weakening of synaptic connections.[11])

To understand practical understanding, one has to move beyond the alternatives of thing and consciousness, mechanistic materialism and constructivist idealism. More precisely, one has to discard the mentalism and intellectualism which lead to a view of the practical relation to the world as a 'perception' and of that perception as a 'mental synthesis' – without ignoring the practical work of construction which, as Jacques Bouveresse observes, 'implements non-conceptual forms of organization'[12] that owe nothing to the intervention of language.

In other words, one has to construct a materialist theory which (in accordance with the wish that Marx expressed in the *Theses on Feuerbach*) is capable of taking back from idealism the 'active side' of practical knowledge that the materialist tradition has abandoned to it. This is precisely the function of the notion of habitus, which restores to the agent a generating, unifying, constructing, classifying power, while recalling that this capacity to construct social reality, itself socially constructed, is not that of a transcendental subject but of a socialized body, investing in its practice socially constructed

---

[10] G. Deleuze, *Empirisme et subjectivité* (Paris: PUF, 1953), p. 2.

[11] J.-P. Changeux, *L'Homme neuronal* (Paris: Fayard, 1983).

[12] J. Bouveresse, *La Demande philosophique. Que veut la philosophie et que peut-on vouloir d'elle?* (Paris: Éditions de l'Éclat, 1996), p. 36.

organizing principles that are acquired in the course of a situated and dated social experience.

Digression on scholastic blindness

If all these things that are so simple are ultimately so difficult to think, it is because the errors that are pushed aside, which have to be recalled at each stage in the analysis, come in pairs (one escapes from mechanism only through a constructivism that is immediately liable to fall into idealism), and because the opposing theses, which have to be rejected, are always ready to be reborn from their ashes, resurrected by polemical interests, because they correspond to opposing positions in the scientific field and in social space. It is also partly because we are haunted by a long theoretical tradition permanently supported and reactivated by the scholastic situation, which is perpetuated through a blend of reinvention and repetition and which is, for the most part, no more than a laborious theorization of the half-learned 'philosophy' of action. Twenty centuries of diffuse Platonism and of Christianized readings of the *Phaedo* incline us to see the body not as an instrument of knowledge but as a hindrance to knowledge, and to ignore the specificity of practical knowledge, which is treated either as a simple obstacle to knowledge or as incipient science.

The common root of the contradictions and paradoxes that routinely scholastic thought thinks it finds in a rigorous description of practical logics is nothing other than the philosophy of mind that such thought implies, which cannot conceive of spontaneity and creativity without the intervention of a creative intention, or finality without a conscious aiming at ends, regularity without observance of rules, signification in the absence of signifying intention. To make a further difficulty, this philosophy is embedded in ordinary language and its grammatical constructions ready-made for teleological description, and in the conventional forms of story-telling, like biography, historical narrative or the novel, which, in the eighteenth and nineteenth centuries, was, as Michel Butor points out, almost entirely identified with the narration of the adventures of an individual and almost always takes the form of strings of 'decisive individual actions, preceded by a voluntary deliberation, which determine one another'.[13]

The idea of 'voluntary deliberation', which has provided matter for so many dissertations, leads it to be assumed that every decision, conceived as a theoretical choice among theoretical possibles constituted

[13] M. Butor, *Répertoire*, vol. 2 (Paris: Éditions de Minuit, 1964), p. 214.

as such, presupposes two preliminary operations: first, drawing up a complete list of possible choices; secondly, determining the consequences of the different strategies and evaluating them comparatively. This totally unrealistic representation of ordinary action, which is more or less explicitly applied by economic theory and which is based on the idea that every action is preceded by a premeditated and explicit plan, is no doubt particularly typical of the scholastic vision, a knowledge that does not know itself, because it ignores the privilege which inclines its possessors to privilege the theoretical point of view, detached contemplation, withdrawn from practical concerns and, in Heidegger's phrase, 'unburdened of the self as being-in-the-world'.

Habitus and incorporation

One of the major functions of the notion of habitus is to dispel two complementary fallacies each of which originates from the scholastic vision: on the one hand, mechanism, which holds that action is the mechanical effect of the constraint of external causes; and, on the other, finalism, which, with rational action theory, holds that the agent acts freely, consciously, and, as some of the utilitarians say, 'with full understanding', the action being the product of a calculation of chances and profits. Against both of these theories, it has to be posited that social agents are endowed with habitus, inscribed in their bodies by past experiences. These systems of schemes of perception, appreciation and action enable them to perform acts of practical knowledge, based on the identification and recognition of conditional, conventional stimuli to which they are predisposed to react; and, without any explicit definition of ends or rational calculation of means, to generate appropriate and endlessly renewed strategies, but within the limits of the structural constraints of which they are the product and which define them.

The language of strategy, which one is forced to use in order to designate the sequences of actions objectively oriented towards an end that are observed in all fields, must not mislead us: the most effective strategies, especially in fields dominated by values of disinterestedness, are those which, being the product of dispositions shaped by the immanent necessity of the field, tend to adjust themselves spontaneously to that necessity, without express intention or calculation. In other words, the agent is never completely the subject of his practices: through the dispositions and the belief which are the basis of engagement in the game, all the presuppositions constituting the practical axiomatics of the field (the epistemic *doxa*, for example) find their way into the seemingly most lucid intentions.

The practical sense is what enables one to act as one 'should' (*ôs dei*, as Aristotle put it) without positing or executing a Kantian 'should', a rule of conduct. The dispositions that it actualizes – ways of being that result from a durable modification of the body through its upbringing – remain unnoticed until they appear in action, and even then, because of the self-evidence of their necessity and their immediate adaptation to the situation. The schemes of habitus, very generally applicable principles of vision and division which, being the product of incorporation of the structures and tendencies of the world, are at least roughly adjusted to them, make it possible to adapt endlessly to partially modified contexts, and to construct the situation as a complex whole endowed with meaning, in a practical operation of quasi-bodily *anticipation* of the immanent tendencies of the field and of the behaviours engendered by all isomorphic habitus, with which, as in a well-trained team or an orchestra, they are in immediate communication because they are spontaneously attuned to them.

(It is not unusual for the advocates of 'rational action theory' to claim allegiance alternately, in the same text, with the mechanist vision, which is implied in their recourse to models borrowed from physics, and with the teleological vision, each being rooted in the scholastic opposition between pure consciousness and the body-as-thing (I am thinking in particular of Jon Elster,[14] who has the merit of stating explicitly that he identifies rationality with conscious lucidity and that he regards any adjustment of desires to the possibilities that is secured by obscure psychological forces as a form of irrationality). It is thus possible for them to explain the rationality of practices, indifferently, by the hypothesis that agents act under the direct constraint of causes that the scientist is able to identify, or by the apparently quite opposite hypothesis that agents act with complete knowledge of the situation ('en connaissance de cause', as the phrase goes) and are capable of doing by themselves what the scientist does in their place in the mechanist hypothesis.

If it is so easy to slide from one to the other of these opposing positions, this is because external mechanical determinism, by causes, and intellectual determinism, by reasons – reasons of 'enlightened self-interest' – meet up and merge. What varies is the propensity of the scientist, a quasi-divine calculator, to lend, or not, to the agents his perfect knowledge of the causes or his clear awareness of the

[14] J. Elster, *Sour Grapes: Studies in the Subversion of Rationality* (Cambridge: Cambridge University Press, 1983).

reasons. For the founders of utilitarian theory, and especially Bentham, whose major work was entitled *Deontology*, the theory of the economy of pleasures was explicitly normative. In rational action theory it is equally so but believes it is descriptive: it presents a normative model of what the agent should be if he wants to be rational (in the scientist's sense) as a description of the explanatory principle of what he really does.[15] This is inevitable when one chooses to recognize no other principle of reasonable actions than rational intention, purpose, project, no other explanatory principle of the agent's actions than explanation by reasons or by causes which are efficient as reasons, enlightened self-interest (and the utility function) being, strictly speaking, nothing other than the agent's interest as it appears to an impartial observer, or, which amounts to the same thing, to an agent obeying 'perfectly prudent preferences',[16] in other words one who is perfectly informed.

This enlightened self-interest is clearly not so remote from the 'objective interest' which is invoked by an apparently radically opposed theoretical tradition and which underlies the idea of 'imputed class consciousness' (the basis of the equally fantastical notion of 'false consciousness') as expressed by Lukács: 'the thoughts and feelings which men would have in a particular situation if they were *able* to assess both the situation as a whole [that is, from a scholastic viewpoint...] and the interests arising from it in their impact on immediate action and on the whole structure of society.'[17] It can be seen that scholastic interests do not need to be enlightened interests in order to be the thing in the world best distributed among *scholars*.[18])

With a Heideggerian play on words, one might say that we are *disposed* because we are *exposed*. It is because the body is (to unequal degrees) exposed and endangered in the world, faced with the risk of emotion, lesion, suffering, sometimes death, and therefore obliged to take the world seriously (and nothing is more serious than emotion, which touches the depths of our organic being) that it is able to acquire dispositions that are themselves an openness to the

[15] Cf. J. Coleman, *Foundations of Social Theory* (Cambridge: Harvard University Press, 1991).
[16] R. H. Hare, 'Ethical theory and utilitarianism', in A. Sen and B. Williams (eds), *Utilitarianism and Beyond* (London and Cambridge: Cambridge University Press, 1977).
[17] G. Lukács, *History and Class Consciousness* (London: Merlin Press, 1971), p. 51.
[18] Alludes to Descartes's 'Common sense is the best distributed thing in the world, for everyone is convinced he is well supplied with it'; *scholars* here and elsewhere in English in the original. *Trans.*

world, that is, to the very structures of the social world of which they are the incorporated form.

The relation to the world is a relation of presence in the world, of being in the world, in the sense of belonging to the world, being possessed by it, in which neither the agent nor the object is posited as such. The degree to which the body is invested in this relation is no doubt one of the main determinants of the interest and attention that are involved in it and of the importance – measurable by their duration, intensity, etc. – of the bodily modifications that result from it. (This is what is forgotten by the intellectualist vision, a vision directly linked to the fact that scholastic universes treat the body and everything connected with it, in particular the urgency of the satisfaction of needs and physical violence, actual or potential, in such a way that the body is in a sense excluded from the game.)

We learn bodily. The social order inscribes itself in bodies through this permanent confrontation, which may be more or less dramatic but is always largely marked by affectivity and, more precisely, by affective transactions with the environment. One thinks, obviously, especially after the work of Michel Foucault, of the normalization exerted through the discipline of institutions. But it would be wrong to underestimate the pressure or oppression, continuous and often unnoticed, of the ordinary order of things, the conditionings imposed by the material conditions of existence, by the insidious injunctions and 'inert violence' (as Sartre puts it) of economic and social structures and of the mechanisms through which they are reproduced.

The most serious social injunctions are addressed not to the intellect but to the body, treated as a 'memory pad'. The essential part of the learning of masculinity and femininity tends to inscribe the difference between the sexes in bodies (especially through clothing), in the form of ways of walking, talking, standing, looking, sitting, etc. And rites of institution are simply the limiting case of all the explicit actions through which groups work to inculcate the social limits or, which amounts to the same thing, social classifications (the male/female division, for example), to naturalize them in the form of divisions in bodies, bodily *hexis*, dispositions, which are meant to be as durable as the indelible inscriptions of tattooing, and the collective principles of vision and division. As much in everyday pedagogic action ('sit up straight', 'hold your knife in your right hand') as in rites of institution, this psychosomatic action is often exerted through emotion and suffering, psychological or even physical, particularly the pain inflicted when applying distinctive signs – mutilation, scarification or tattoos – to the surface of the body itself. The passage in *The Penal Colony* in which Kafka recounts that all the letters of the law that a prisoner has broken are inscribed on his body 'radicalizes and literalizes with grotesque brutality', as E. L. Santner suggests,[19] the ruthless mnemotechnics that groups often resort to in order to naturalize arbitrariness and – another intuition of Kafka's (and Pascal's) – so confer on it the absurd and impenetrable necessity which is concealed, without a 'beyond', behind the most sacred institutions.

A logic in action

Misrecognition, or forgetting, of the relation of immanence to a world that is not perceived as a world, as an object placed before a self-conscious perceiving subject, as a spectacle or representation capable of being taken in with a single gaze, is no doubt the elementary, or original, form of the scholastic illusion. The principle of practical comprehension is not a knowing consciousness (a transcendental consciousness, as Husserl presents it, or even an existential *Dasein*, for Heidegger) but the practical sense of a habitus inhabited by the world it inhabits, *pre-occupied* by the world in which it actively intervenes, in an immediate relationship of involvement, tension and attention, which constructs the world and gives it meaning.

Habitus, a particular but constant way of entering into a relationship with the world which contains a knowledge enabling it to anticipate the course of the world, is immediately present, without any objectifying distance, in the world and the 'forth-coming' [*l'à venir*] that it contains (which distinguishes it from a *mens momentanea* without history). *Exposed to the world*, to sensation, feeling, suffering, etc., in other words engaged in the world, in play and at stake in the world, the body (well) disposed towards the world is, to the same extent, oriented towards the world and what immediately presents itself there to be seen, felt and expected: it is capable of mastering it by providing an adequate response, having a hold on it, using it (and not decoding it) as an instrument that is 'well in hand' (in the terms of Heidegger's famous analysis) and which, never considered as such, is run through, as if it were transparent, by the task that it enables the agent to perform and towards which it is oriented.

The agent engaged in practice knows the world but with a knowledge which, as Merleau-Ponty showed, is not set up in the relation of externality of a knowing consciousness. He knows it, in a sense, too well, without objectifying distance, takes it for granted, precisely

---

[19] E. L. Santner, *My Own Private Germany: Daniel Paul Schreber's Secret History of Modernity* (Princeton: Princeton University Press, 1996).

because he is caught up in it, bound up with it; he inhabits it like a garment [*un habit*] or a familiar habitat. He feels at home in the world because the world is also in him, in the form of habitus, a virtue made of necessity which implies a form of love of necessity, *amor fati*.

The action of practical sense is a kind of necessary coincidence – which gives it the appearance of pre-established harmony – between a habitus and a field (or a position in a field). Someone who has incorporated the structures of the field (or of a particular game) 'finds his place' there immediately, without having to deliberate, and brings out, without even thinking about it, 'things to be done' (business, *pragmata*) and to be done 'the right way', action plans inscribed like a watermark in the situation, as objective potentialities, urgencies, which orient his practice without being constituted as norms or imperatives clearly defined by and for consciousness and will. To be able to use a tool (or do a job), and to do it 'comfortably' – with a comfort that is both subjective and objective, and characterized as much by the efficiency and ease of the action as by the satisfaction and felicity of the agent – one has to have 'grown into it' through long use, sometimes methodical training, to have made one's own the ends inscribed in it as a tacit 'manual', in short, to have let oneself be used, even instrumentalized, by the instrument. It is on that condition that one can attain the *dexterity* that Hegel referred to, the knack that hits on the right result without having to calculate, doing exactly what needs to be done, as and when it needs to be done, without superfluous movements, with an economy of effort and a necessity that are both inwardly felt and externally perceptible. (One thinks of what Plato describes as *orthè doxa*, right opinion, the 'learned ignorance' that hits the mark, owing nothing to chance, by a kind of adjustment to the situation that is neither thought nor willed as such: 'This is the means which statesmen employ for their direction of states, and they have nothing more to do with wisdom than soothsayers and diviners; for these people utter many a true thing when inspired, but have no knowledge of anything they say.')[20]

In so far as it is the product of the incorporation of a *nomos*, of the principle of vision and division constitutive of a social order or a field, habitus generates practices immediately adjusted to that order, which are therefore perceived, by their author and also by others, as 'right', straight, adroit, adequate, without being in any way the product of obedience to an order in the sense of an imperative, to a norm or to legal rules. This practical, non-thetic intentionality, which has

[20] Plato, *Meno*, 99c.

nothing in common with a *cogitatio* (or a noesis) consciously oriented towards a *cogitatum* (a noema), is rooted in a posture, a way of bearing the body (a *hexis*), a durable way of being of the durably modified body which is engendered and perpetuated, while constantly changing (within limits), in a twofold relationship, structured and structuring, to the environment. Habitus constructs the world by a certain way of orienting itself towards it, of bringing to bear on it an attention which, like that of a jumper preparing to jump, is an active, constructive bodily tension towards the imminent forthcoming (*allodoxia*, the mistake we sometimes make when, waiting for someone, we seem to see that person in everyone who comes along, gives an accurate idea of this tension).

(Practical knowledge is very unequally demanded and necessary, but also very unequally adequate and adapted, depending on the situation and the realm of activity. In contrast to the scholastic universes, some universes, such as those of sport, music or dance, demand a practical engagement of the body and therefore a mobilization of the corporeal 'intelligence' capable of transforming, even inverting, the ordinary hierarchies. And one would need to collect methodically all the notes and observations which, dispersed here and there, especially in the didactics of these physical skills – sports, obviously, and more especially the martial arts, but also theatrical activities and the playing of musical instruments – would provide precious contributions to a science of this form of knowledge. Sports trainers seek effective ways of speaking to the body, in the situations, with which everyone is familiar, where one understands with an intellectual understanding the movement to make or not to make, without being able actually to do what one has understood, for lack of comprehension through the body.[21] Likewise a number of stage directors resort to pedagogic practices whose common feature is that they seek to induce a suspension of intellectual, discursive understanding and, in accordance with Pascal's model of the production of belief, to lead the actor, by a long series of exercises, to rediscover postures of the body which, being charged with mnemic experiences, are capable of stirring up thoughts, emotions and imagination.)

Just as habitus is not an instantaneous being, condemned to the Cartesian discontinuity of successive moments, but, in the language of Leibniz, a *vis insita* that is also a *lex insita*, a force endowed with a law, and therefore characterized by constants and constancies (often underlined by explicit principles of truth to self, *constantia sibi*, like

---

[21] Cf. L. Wacquant, 'Pugs at work: bodily capital and bodily labor among professional boxers', *Body and Society*, 1, no. 1 (Mar. 1996), pp. 65–94.

the imperatives of honour), equally it is not the isolated, egoistic calculating subject of the utilitarian tradition and the economists (and, coming after them, the 'methodological individualists'). It is the site of durable solidarities, loyalties that cannot be coerced because they are grounded in incorporated laws and bonds, those of the *esprit de corps* (of which family loyalty is a particular form), the visceral attachment of a socialized body to the social body that has made it and with which it is bound up. As such, habitus is the basis of an *implicit collusion* among all the agents who are products of similar conditions and conditionings, and also of a practical experience of the transcendence of the group, of its ways of being and doing, each agent finding in the conduct of all his peers the ratification and legitimation ('the done thing') of his own conduct, which, in return, ratifies and, if need be, rectifies, the conduct of the others. This *collusio*, an immediate agreement in ways of judging and acting which does not presuppose either the communication of consciousnesses, still less a contractual decision, is the basis of a practical mutual under-standing, the paradigm of which might be the one established between members of the same team, or, despite the antagonism, all the players engaged in a game.

The principle of the ordinary cohesion which is *esprit de corps* has its limiting case in the disciplinary training imposed by totalitarian regimes, with formalistic exercises and rituals or the wearing of a distinctive dress intended to symbolize the (social) body as unity and difference, but also to 'hold' the body by imposing a certain garb on it (the priest's cassock, for example, the permanent reminder of the ecclesiastical condition), or through great mass manifestations such as gymnastic displays or military parades. These strategies of mani-pulation aim to shape bodies so as to make each of them an embodi-ment of the group (*corpus corporatum in corpore corporato*, as the canonists put it) and to institute between the group and the body of each of its members a relation of 'somatic compliance', a subjection by suggestion which holds bodies and makes them function like a kind of collective automaton.

Habitus spontaneously orchestrated among themselves and pre-adjusted to the situations in which they operate and of which they are the product (a particular, but particularly frequent case) tend to produce sets of actions which, without any need for deliberate conspiracy or coordination, are roughly attuned to each other and in accordance with the interests of the agents concerned. The simplest example is that of the reproductive strategies which privileged famil-ies produce, without consultation or deliberation, that is, separately and often in subjective competition, and which have the effect of contributing (with the help of objective mechanisms such as the logic of the legal field or the educational field) to the reproduction of existing positions and the social order.

The orchestration of habitus which, being the product of the same conditions of existence and the same conditionings (with variants, corresponding to particular trajectories), spontaneously produce behaviours adapted to the objective conditions and tending to satisfy the shared individual interests, thus enables one, without appealing to conscious, deliberate acts and without involving any kind of functionalism, to account for the appearance of teleology which is often observed at the level of collectives and which is ordinarily ascribed to the 'collective will' (or consciousness, or even to a conspiracy of collective entities that are personalized and treated as subjects collectively determining their goals (the 'bourgeoisie', the 'dominant class', etc.). I am thinking for example of the strategies for the defence of the corporate body which, implemented blindly and on a strictly individual basis, by the teachers in French higher education, in a period of rapid expansion of student numbers, enabled them to reserve access to the highest positions in the education system to newcomers corresponding as closely as possible to the old principles of recruitment, that is, as little different as possible from the ideal of the male *agrégé* from the École Normale.[22] And it is again the orchestration of habitus which shows the way out of the paradoxes invented *ex nihilo* by utilitarian individualism, such as the 'free rider dilemma': the investment, the belief, the passion, the *amor fati*, which are inscribed in the relationship between habitus and the social world (or the field) of which it is the product mean that there are things that cannot be done in certain circumstances ('that's not done') and others that cannot *not* be done (the example par excellence being everything that is demanded by the principle *noblesse oblige*). Among these things are all kinds of behaviours which the utilitarian tradition cannot account for, such as loyalties and commitments to people and groups, and, more generally, all the behaviours of disinterestedness, the limiting case of which is *pro patria mori*, analysed by Kantorowicz, the sacrifice of the egoistic ego, an absolute challenge to all utilitarian calculators.

Coincidence

Phenomenological description, though indispensable in order to break with the scholastic vision of the ordinary vision of the world, and

---

[22] For lack of space to spell out here the subtlety, revealed by statistical analysis, of the strategies of substitution which were implemented, I refer the reader to *Homo Academicus* (Cambridge: Polity Press, 1988), esp. pp. 136–51.

while it comes close to the real, is liable to stand in the way of a full understanding of practical understanding and of practice itself, because it is totally ahistorical and antigenetic. One therefore has to return to the analysis of presence in the world, but historicizing it, in other words, raising the question of the social construction of the structures or schemes which the agent implements in order to construct the world (and which are excluded as much by a Kantian type of transcendental anthropology as by an eidetic analysis in the style of Husserl and Schutz, and, after them, ethnomethodology, or even the otherwise very enlightening analysis by Merleau-Ponty); and secondly one has to examine the question of the social conditions that have to be fulfilled to make possible the experience of the social world as self-evident which phenomenology describes without providing itself with the means of accounting for it.

The experience of a world that is 'taken for granted' presupposes agreement between the dispositions of the agents and the expectations or demands immanent in the world into which they are inserted. This perfect coincidence of practical schemes and objective structures is only possible in the particular case in which the schemes applied to the world are the product of the world to which they are applied, that is, in the ordinary experience of the familiar world (as opposed to foreign or exotic worlds). The conditions for such an immediate mastery remain the same when one moves away from experience of the common-sense world, which presupposes mastery of instruments of knowledge accessible to all and capable of being acquired through ordinary practice of the world – up to a certain point, at least – into experience of the scholastic worlds and the objects produced there, such as works of art, literature or science, which are not immediately accessible to the untutored eye.

The indisputable charm of stable and relatively undifferentiated societies, the sites par excellence, according to Hegel, who had a very acute intuition of it, of concrete liberty as 'being at home' (*bei sich sein*) in what is,[23] arises from the quasi-perfect coincidence between habitus and habitat, between the schemes of the mythic vision of the world and the structure of domestic space, for example, organized according to the same oppositions,[24] or between expectations and the objective chances of realizing them. In differentiated societies themselves, a whole series of social mechanisms tend to ensure the adjustment of dispositions to positions, thereby offering those who benefit

[23] Cf. B. Bourgeois, *Hegel à Francfort ou Judaïsme, Christianisme, Hégélianisme* (Paris: Vrin, 1970), p. 9.
[24] P. Bourdieu, 'The Kabyle house or the world reversed', in *The Logic of Practice* (Cambridge: Polity Press, 1990), pp. 271–83.

from them an enchanted (or mystified) experience of the social world. Thus it can be observed that, in very different social universes (employers, the episcopacy, professors, etc.), the structure of the space of agents distributed according to the characteristics capable of characterizing habitus (social origin, education, qualifications, etc.) that are attached to the social person corresponds fairly closely to the structure of the space of positions or posts (companies, bishoprics, faculties or disciplines, etc.) distributed according to their specific characteristics (for companies, for example, turnover, number of employees, age, legal status).

Thus, because habitus is, as its name suggests, a product of a history, the instruments of construction of the social that it invests in practical knowledge of the world and in action are socially constructed, in other words structured by the world that they structure. It follows from this that practical knowledge is doubly informed by the world that it informs: it is constrained by the objective structure of the configuration of properties that the world presents to it; and it is also structured through the schemes, resulting from incorporation of the structures of the world, that it applies in selecting and constructing these objective properties. In other words, action is neither 'purely reactive', in Weber's phrase, nor purely conscious and calculated. Through the cognitive and motivating structures that it brings into play (which always depend, in part, on the field, acting as a field of forces, of which it is the product), habitus plays its part in determining the things to be done, or not to be done, the urgencies, etc., which trigger action. Thus, to account for the differential impact of an event like the crisis of May 1968, as recorded by statistics relating to very different areas of practice, one is led to assume the existence of a general disposition which can be characterized as sensitivity to order (or disorder) and which varies depending on social conditions and the associated social conditionings. It is this disposition which means that objective changes to which others remain insensitive (economic crisis, administrative measures, etc.) can be translated, for some agents, into modifications of behaviour in various areas of practice (and even in fertility strategies[25]).

One could thus extend a proposition of Gilbert Ryle's to the explanation of human behaviours: just as one should not say that a window broke because a stone hit it, but that it broke, when the stone hit it, *because* it was breakable, similarly, as can be seen with particular clarity when an insignificant, apparently fortuitous event unleashes

---

[25] Cf. P. Bourdieu and A. Darbel, 'La fin d'un malthusianisme', in Darras, *Le Partage des bénéfices* (Paris: Éditions de Minuit, 1966).

enormous consequences that are bound to appear disproportionate to all those who have different habitus, one should not say that a historical event determined a behaviour but that it had this determining effect because a habitus capable of being affected by that event conferred that power upon it. Attribution theory establishes that the causes which a person attributes to an experience (and which, as the theory does not say, depend on his or her habitus) are one of the major determinants of the action she will perform in response to that experience (for example, in the case of a battered wife, going back to her husband in conditions that her counsellors judge intolerable). This must not lead us to say (as Sartre does, for example) that the agents choose (in 'bad faith') what determines them, since, while we can say that they determine themselves inasmuch as they construct the situations that determine them, it is clear that they have not chosen the principle of their choice, that is, their habitus, and that the schemes of construction they apply to the world have themselves been constructed by the world.

One can also say, following the same logic, that habitus helps to determine what transforms it. If it is accepted that the principle of the transformation of habitus lies in the gap, experienced as a positive or negative surprise, between expectations and experience, one must suppose that the extent of this gap and the significance attributed to it depend on habitus: one person's disappointment may be another's unexpected satisfaction, with the corresponding effects of reinforcement or inhibition.

Dispositions do not lead in a determinate way to a determinate action; they are revealed and fulfilled only in appropriate circumstances and in the relationship with a situation. They may therefore always remain in a virtual state, like a soldier's courage in the absence of war. Each of them can manifest itself in different, even opposite, practices, depending on the situation. For example, the same aristocratic disposition of bishops of noble origin may be expressed in apparently opposite practices in different historical contexts, in Meaux, a small provincial town, in the 1930s and in Saint-Denis, a 'red suburb', in the 1960s.[26] Having said this, the existence of a disposition (as a *lex insita*) is a basis for predicting that, in all conceivable circumstances of a particular type, a particular set of agents will behave in a particular way.

---

[26] Cf. P. Bourdieu and M. de St Martin, 'La Sainte famille. L'épiscopat français dans le champ du pouvoir', *Actes de la Recherche en Sciences Sociales*, no. 44–5 (1982), pp. 2–53, where it can be seen that bishops of aristocratic origin, who previously conformed to the role in its most traditional form, can, notably at Saint-Denis, adopt entirely progressive positions, in particular on immigration. *Trans.*

Habitus as a system of dispositions to be and to do is a potentiality, a desire to be which, in a certain way, seeks to create the conditions of its fulfilment, and therefore to create the conditions most favourable to what it is. In the absence of any major upheaval (a change of position, for example), the conditions of its formation are also the conditions of its realization. But, in any case, the agent does what is in his power to make possible the actualization of the potentialities inscribed in his body in the form of capacities and dispositions shaped by conditions of existence. And a number of behaviours can be understood as efforts to maintain or produce a state of the social world or of a field that is capable of giving to some acquired disposition – knowledge of an ancient or modern language, for example – the possibility and opportunity of being actualized. This is one of the major principles (with the available means of realization) of everyday choices as regards objects or persons. Guided by one's sympathies and antipathies, affections and aversions, tastes and distastes, one makes for oneself an environment in which one feels 'at home' and in which one can achieve that fulfilment of one's desire to be which one identifies with happiness. And we do indeed observe (in the form of a significant statistical relationship) a striking agreement between the characteristics of agents' dispositions (and social positions) and those of the objects with which they surround themselves – houses, furniture, household equipment, etc – or of the people with whom they most durably associate – spouses, friends and connections.

The paradoxes of the distribution of happiness, of which La Fontaine supplied the principle in his fable of the cobbler and the financier, are fairly easily explained. Since the desire for fulfilment is roughly measured by its chances of realization, the degree of inner satisfaction that the various agents experience does not depend as much as one might think on their effective power in the sense of an abstract, universal capacity to satisfy needs and desires abstractly defined for an indifferent agent; rather, it depends on the degree to which the mode of functioning of the social world or the field in which they are inserted enables his habitus to come into its own.

The encounter of two histories

The principle of action is therefore neither a subject confronting the world as an object in a relation of pure knowledge nor a 'milieu' exerting a form of mechanical causality on the agent; it is neither in the material or symbolic end of the action nor in the constraints of the field. It lies in the complicity between two states of the social, between history in bodies and history in things, or, more precisely, between the history objectified in the form of structures and mechanisms (those of the social space or of fields) and the history incarnated in bodies in the form of habitus, a complicity which is the basis of a relation of quasi-magical participation between these two realizations of history. Habitus, the product of a historical acquisition, is what enables the legacy of history to be appropriated. Just as the letter escapes from the state of a dead letter only through the act of reading which presupposes an acquired aptitude for reading and deciphering, so the history objectified in instruments, monuments, works, techniques, etc. can become activated and active history only if it is taken in hand by agents who, because of their previous *investments*, are inclined to be *interested* in it and endowed with the aptitudes needed to reactivate it.

It is in the relationship between habitus and the field, between the feel for the game and the game itself, that the stakes of the game are generated and ends are constituted which are not posited as such, objective potentialities which, although they do not exist outside that relationship, impose themselves, within it, with absolute necessity and self-evidence. The game presents itself to someone caught up in it, absorbed in it, as a transcendent universe, imposing its own ends and norms unconditionally. There is nothing sacred except to the sense of the sacred, but this sense encounters the sacred as a full transcendence, and the *illusio* is an illusion or 'diversion' only for someone who perceives the game from the outside, from the scholastic standpoint of an 'impartial spectator'.

This having been said, the correspondence that is observed between positions and position-takings never has a mechanical or inevitable character. In a field, for example, it is only established through the practical strategies of agents endowed with different habitus and quantities of specific capital, and therefore with unequal mastery of the specific forces of production bequeathed by all the previous generations and capable of perceiving the space of positions as more or less wide spaces of possibles in which the things that offer themselves to them as 'to be done' present themselves more or less compellingly. (To those who would attribute this observation to some kind of 'determinist' preconception, I would only like to indicate the endlessly renewed astonishment I have many times experienced at the necessity that the logic of my research led me to discover – not to exculpate myself from some unpardonable crime against freedom, but to encourage those who are indignant at such determination in the uncovering of determinisms to abandon the language of metaphysical denunciation or moral condemnation and to situate themselves, if appropriate, on the terrain of scientific refutation.)

The body is in the social world but the social world is in the body (in the form of *hexis* and *eidos*). The very structures of the world are present in the structures (or, to put it better, the cognitive schemes) that agents implement in order to understand it. When the same history pervades both habitus and habitat, dispositions and position, the king and his court, the boss and his firm, the bishop and his diocese, history communicates in a sense to itself, gives back to itself its own reflection. The doxic relation to the native world is a relationship of belonging and possession in which the body possessed by history appropriates immediately the things inhabited by the same history. Only when the heritage has taken over the inheritor can the inheritor take over the heritage. And this appropriation of the inheritor by the heritage, the precondition for the appropriation of the heritage by the inheritor (which has nothing inevitable about it), takes place under the combined effect of the conditionings inscribed in the position of inheritor and the pedagogic action of his predecessors, themselves possessed possessors.

The inherited inheritor, appropriated by his heritage, does not need to *want*, in the sense of deliberating, choosing and consciously deciding, in order to do what is appropriate, what corresponds to the interests of the heritage, its conservation and its increase. He may not strictly speaking know what he says or does and yet do and say nothing that is not appropriate to the demands of perpetuation of the heritage. (This is no doubt what explains the role given to professional heredity, especially through the procedures, largely obscure to themselves, of co-option to corporate bodies: the inherited and therefore immediately attuned habitus, and the corporeal constraint exercised through it, are the surest guarantee of direct and total adherence to the often implicit demands of these institutions. The reproductive strategies which it engenders are one of the mediations through which the social order fulfils its tendency to persevere in its being, in a word, its *conatus*.)

Louis XIV is so completely identified with the position he occupies in the field of gravitation of which he is the sun that it would be as futile to try to determine which of the actions occurring in the field is or is not the product of his will as it would be, in a concert, to try to distinguish what is done by the conductor and what by the players. His very will to dominate is a product of the field that it dominates and which makes everything turn to his advantage: 'The people thus enmeshed held each other fast in this situation, however grudgingly they bore it. Pressure from those of lower rank or less privileged forced the more favoured to maintain their advantages, and conversely the pressure from above compelled those on whom it weighed to escape it by emulation, forcing them too into the competition for status.'[27]

Thus, a State which has become the symbol of absolutism and which, even for the monarch himself ('L'État, c'est moi'), who has most direct interest in this representation, presents, in the highest degree, the appearances of an 'Apparatus' in fact masks a field of struggles in which the holder of 'absolute power' must engage at least enough to maintain and exploit the divisions and so mobilize for his own benefit the energy generated by the balance of tensions. The principle of the perpetual movement which stirs the field does not lie in some motionless prime mover – here, the Sun King – but in the struggle itself, which is produced by the constitutive structures of the field and tends to reproduce its structures and hierarchies. It is in the actions and reactions of the agents: they have no choice but to struggle to maintain or improve their position, that is, to conserve or increase the specific capital which is only generated in this field; and so they help to bring to bear on all the others the constraints, often experienced as unbearable, which arise from the competition (unless, of course, they exclude themselves from the game, in a heroic renunciation which, from the point of view of the *illusio*, is social death and therefore an unthinkable option). In short, no one can benefit from the game, not even those who dominate it, without taking part in the game and being taken in by the game. Hence there would be no game without players' (visceral, corporeal) commitment to the game, without the interest taken in the game as such which is the source of the different, even opposite, interests of the various players, the wills and ambitions which drive them and which, being produced by the game, depend on the positions they occupy within it.

Thus, objectified history becomes activated and active only if the more or less institutionalized position, with the more or less codified programme of action that it contains, finds – like a garment, a tool, a book or a house – someone who sees in it enough of themselves to take it up and make it their own, and by the same token to be taken up by it. The café waiter is not playing at being a waiter, as Sartre would have it.[28] When he puts on his black trousers and white jacket, which might have been designed to express a democratic and quasi-bureaucratic version of the devoted dignity of the servant of an aristocratic household, and performs the ceremonial of eagerness and

[27] N. Elias, *The Court Society* (Oxford: Blackwell, 1983), p. 88. One could, *mutatis mutandis*, replace Louis XIV and his court with Sartre and the French intellectual field in the 1950s.
[28] J.-P. Sartre, *Being and Nothingness*, (London: Methuen, 1969), p. 59.

attention, which may be a strategy to cover up delay or an omission, or to pass off mediocre fare, he is not making himself a thing (or an 'in-itself'). His body, which contains a history, *espouses* his job, in other words a history, a tradition, which he has never seen except incarnated in bodies, or more precisely, in the uniforms inhabited by a certain habitus that are called waiters. This does not mean he has learned to be a waiter by imitating waiters, constituted as explicit models. He enters into the character of the waiter not as an actor playing a part, but rather as a child imitates his father and, without even needing to 'pretend', adopts a way of using the mouth when talking or of swinging his shoulders when walking which seems to him constitutive of the social being of the accomplished adult. It cannot even be said that he takes himself for a waiter; he is too completely taken up by the job to which he was socio-logically destined – for example, as the son of a small shopkeeper who must earn enough to set up his own business. By contrast, one only has to put a student in his position (as was sometimes seen after May '68, in some 'avant-garde' restaurants) to see him signal in countless ways the distance he means to keep, precisely by affecting to play it as a *role*, from a job which does not correspond to the (socially constituted) idea he has of his being, that is, of his social destiny, a job for which he does not feel made, and in which, as the Sartrian café-goer puts it, he does not intend to 'be imprisoned'.

For proof that the intellectual distances himself no more than the waiter from his post and from what defines him as an intellectual, that is, the scholastic illusion of distance from all positions, one only has to read *as an anthropological document* the analysis with which Sartre extends and 'universalizes' the famous description: 'In vain do I fulfil the functions of a café waiter. I can be one only in the neutralized mode, as the actor is Hamlet, by mechanically making the *typical gestures* of my state and by aiming at myself as an imaginary café waiter through these gestures taken as an "analogue". What I attempt to realize is a being-in-itself of the café waiter, as if it were not in my power to confer their value and their urgency upon the duties and the rights of my position, as if it were not my free choice to get up each morning at five o'clock or to remain in bed, even though it meant getting fired. As if from the very fact that I sustain this role in existence I did not transcend it on every side, as if I did not constitute myself as a *beyond* of my condition. Yet there is no doubt that I *am* in a sense a café waiter – otherwise could I not just as well call myself a diplomat or a reporter?'[29]

[29] Ibid., p. 60.

One could dwell on every word of this almost miraculous product of the social unconscious which, with the aid of the double game allowed by an exemplary use of the phenomenological 'I' and of an 'understanding' identification with the other (Sartre made much use of it) projects an intellectual's consciousness into a café waiter's practice, or into the imaginary analogue of this practice, producing a kind of social chimera, a monster with a waiter's body and a philosopher's head. No doubt one needs to have the freedom to stay in bed without being fired to be able to see the person who gets up at five to sweep the floors and start up the coffee pot before the customers arrive as freeing himself (freely?) from the freedom to stay in bed, at the cost of being fired. The logic seen here, that of identification with a phantasm, is the one which has enabled others, presenting the 'intellectual' relation to the working-class condition as the working-class relation to that condition, to produce a worker entirely engaged in 'struggles' or, alternately, by simple inversion, as in myths, a worker desperately resigned to being only what he is, his 'being-in-itself' as a worker, lacking the freedom that comes from being able to count among one's possibles positions like those of diplomat or journalist.

The dialectic of positions and dispositions

In cases of more or less perfect coincidence between 'vocation' and 'mission', between the 'collective expectations', as Mauss puts it, inscribed, most often implicitly, in the position and the expectations or hopes buried in dispositions, between the objective structures and the cognitive structures through which they are perceived, it would be futile to seek to distinguish, in most cases, the aspects of practice that derive from the effect of positions and those that are the product of the dispositions which the agents bring into them – dispositions which govern their whole relation to the world, in particular their perception and appreciation of the position, therefore their way of holding it and so the very 'reality' of that position.

There is action, there is history, structures are conserved or transformed, only because there are agents who cannot be reduced to what common sense, and after it 'methodological individualism', put under the heading of individuals; agents who, as socialized bodies, are endowed with a set of dispositions implying both the propensity and the aptitude to enter into the game and to play it with more or less success.

Only recourse to dispositions can – short of the disastrous hypothesis of rational calculation of all the ramifications of action – account for the immediate understanding that agents obtain of the world by applying to it forms of knowledge derived from the history and structure of the very world to which they apply them; it alone can account for the feeling of self-evidence which, paradoxically, masks the particular (but relatively frequent) conditions which make it possible, even from those who describe it best, like Husserl or Schutz.

But the cases of adjustment of dispositions to situations additionally provide one of the most striking illustrations of the inanity of the preconstructed opposition between the individual and society or the individual and the collective. If this half-learned opposition withstands refutations so well, this is because it is sustained by the purely social force of routine thinking and automatic language; by the logic of the academic oppositions which underlie the subjects of dissertations and lectures (Tarde, or Weber, versus Durkheim, methodological individualism versus holism, RATS – rational action theorists – against CATS – collective action theorists, etc.); by the literary-philosophical tradition of libertarian dissidence against social powers and especially the State; and above all by the potency of the underlying political oppositions (liberalism against socialism, capitalism against collectivism) which unthinking and unscrupulous 'theorists' eagerly adopt in a sometimes barely euphemized form.[30]

The notion of habitus makes it possible to escape from this deadly dilemma and, by the same token, to move beyond the opposition between the realism which hypostatizes the social in an entity such as the Durkheimian 'collective consciousness', a false solution to a real problem, and radical nominalism, for which 'social realities' are just words. It is in each agent, and therefore in the individuated state, that there exist supra-individual dispositions capable of functioning in an orchestrated or, one could say, collective way (the notion of habitus makes it possible, as has been seen, to account for collective social processes, endowed with a kind of objective finality – like the tendency of dominant groups to ensure their own perpetuation – without appealing to personified collectives positing their own ends, or the mechanical aggregation of the rational actions of individual agents, or a central consciousness or will, capable of imposing itself through a discipline).

Because the social is also instituted in biological individuals, there is, in each biological individual, something of the collective, and

---

[30] Thus, in an exemplary text, François Bourricaud described the academic world as divided into two camps whose very names, 'totalitarian realism' and 'individualistic liberalism', make it clear that the logic in which he thinks them is at least as political as it is scientific (cf. F. Bourricaud, 'Contre le sociologisme: une critique et des propositions', *Revue Française de Science Politique*, supplement 1975, pp. 583–603).

therefore properties valid for a whole class of agents – which statistics can bring to light. Habitus understood as an individual or a socialized biological body, or as the social, biologically individuated through incarnation in a body, is collective, or transindividual – and so it is possible to construct classes of habitus, which can be statistically characterized. As such it is able to intervene effectively in a social world or a field to which it is generically adjusted.

But the collectivization of the biological individual performed by socialization does not sweep away all the anthropological properties linked to the biological support. And one also has to take note of all that the incorporated social – for example, cultural capital in its incorporated state – owes to the fact that it is linked to the biological individual and therefore dependent on the weaknesses and failings of the body – declining faculties, especially of memory, or the possible impairment of the heir to the throne, or death. And also everything that it owes to the specific logic of the functioning of the organism, which is not that of a simple mechanism but of a structure based on the integration of increasingly complex levels of organization, and which has to be brought into the equation to account for some of the most characteristic properties of habitus, like the tendency towards the generalization and systematicity of its dispositions.

The relationship between dispositions and positions does not always take the form of the quasi-miraculous and therefore mostly unremarked adjustment that is seen when habitus are the product of stable structures, the very ones in which they are actualized. In this case, because the agents are led to live in a world that is not radically different from the one that shaped their primary habitus, there is an unproblematic agreement between the position and the dispositions of its occupant, between the heritage and the inheritor, the post and its holder. In particular because of the structural transformations which abolish or modify certain positions, and also because of their inter- or intragenerational mobility, the homology between the space of positions and the space of dispositions is never perfect and there are always some agents 'out on a limb', displaced, out of place and ill at ease. The discordance, as in the case of the 'gentlemen of Port-Royal', may be the source of a disposition towards lucidity and critique which leads them to refuse to accept as self-evident the expectations and demands of the post. The dialectic between dispositions and positions is seen most clearly in the case of positions situated in zones of uncertainty in social space, such as still ill-defined occupations, as regards both the conditions of access and the conditions of exercise (youth leader, cultural organizer, public relations consultant, etc.). Because these posts, ill-defined and ill-guaranteed but open and 'full of potential' as the phrase goes, leave their occupants the possibility of defining them by bringing in the embodied necessity which is constitutive of their habitus, their future depends on what is made of them by their occupants, or at least those of them who, in the struggles within the 'profession' and in confrontations with neighbouring and rival professions, manage to impose the definition of the profession most favourable to what they are.

But the effects of the dialectic between the inclinations inscribed in habitus and the demands implied in the definition of the post are no less strong in the most regulated and rigidified sectors of the social structure, such as the oldest and most codified professions of public service. Thus, far from being a mechanical product of bureaucratic organization, some of the most characteristic features of the conduct of lower-rank civil servants, such as the tendency to formalism, fetishistic attachment to punctuality or rigid adherence to regulations, are the manifestation, in a situation particularly conducive to their actualization, of a system of dispositions which is also expressed outside the bureaucratic situation, in all areas of practice, and which would be sufficient to predispose the members of the petite bourgeoisie to the virtues demanded by the bureaucratic order and exalted by the ideology of 'public service': probity, attention to detail, punctiliousness and the propensity to moral indignation. The tendency of the bureaucratic field, a relatively autonomous space of relations (of power and struggle) among explicitly constituted and codified positions (defined in terms of *rank*, authority, etc.), to 'degenerate' into a 'total institution' demanding complete, mechanical identification of the 'functionary' with his function and with strict, literal application of the rules of law, regulations, directives, circulars, etc., is not linked mechanically to the morphological effects that size and number can exert upon structures (with, for example, the constraints imposed on communication); it can only take place in so far as it encounters the complicity of dispositions.

The further one moves away from the ordinary functioning of fields towards limits, which are perhaps never reached, where, with the disappearance of all struggle and all resistance to domination, the space of play rigidifies and shrinks into a 'total institution', in Goffman's sense, or – in a rigorous sense this time – an *apparatus*, the more the institution tends to consecrate agents who give everything to the institution (the Party, the Church, the Company, etc.) and who perform this *oblation* all the more easily the less capital they have outside the institution (the holders of 'in-house qualifications', for example), and therefore the less *freedom* with respect to it and to the specific capital and profits that it offers. The *apparatchik*, who owes everything to the apparatus, is the apparatus personified, ready to give everything to the apparatus that has given him all he has. He can be safely entrusted with the highest responsibilities because he can do nothing to advance his own interests that does not thereby satisfy the expectations of the apparatus. Like the oblate, he is predisposed to defend the institution, with absolute conviction, against the threats posed by the heretical deviations of those whom a capital acquired outside the institution authorizes and inclines to distance themselves from the internal beliefs and hierarchies.

Mismatches, discordance and misfirings

The fact that the responses habitus generates without calculation or project generally appear as adapted, coherent and immediately intelligible should not lead one to see them as a kind of infallible instinct, capable of producing responses miraculously adjusted to all situations. The adjustment, in advance, of habitus to the objective conditions is a *particular case*, no doubt particularly frequent (in the universes familiar to us), but it should not be treated as a universal rule.

(It is no doubt on the basis of the particular case of adjustment between habitus and structure that critics have often seen a principle of repetition and conservation in a concept, habitus, which originally forced itself upon me as the only way to understand the *mismatches* which were observed, in an economy like that of Algeria in the 1960s (and still today in many 'developing' countries), between the objective structures and the incorporated structures, between the economic institutions imported and imposed by colonization (or nowadays by the constraints of the market) and economic dispositions brought to them by agents formed in the precapitalist world. This quasi-experimental situation had the effect of showing up in negative form – through all the behaviours which were then described as lapses from 'rationality' and as 'resistance to modernity', and often attributed to mysterious cultural factors, such as Islam – the hidden conditions of the functioning of economic institutions, that is, the economic dispositions which agents have to possess in order for the economic structures to work harmoniously, so harmoniously that this essential condition of their functioning passes unnoticed, as in societies where economic institutions and dispositions have developed at the same rate.

I was thus led to question the universality of so-called rational economic dispositions and, by the same token, to address the question of the *economic conditions* – and cultural conditions – of access to these dispositions, a question which, paradoxically, economists fail to address, thereby accepting notions such as rational action or preferences, which are in fact economically determined and socially shaped, as ahistorical universals. Curiously, we can look to Bergson for a reminder of a historical self-evidence that the dehistoricization associated with familiarity leads one to forget: 'It takes centuries of culture to produce a utilitarian such as John Stuart Mill',[31] that is, what economists who invoke the founder of utilitarianism regard as a universal nature. The same would be true of everything that an unreflexive rationalism inscribes in reason. Logic is the unconscious of a society that has invented logic. Logical action as defined by Pareto, or rational action as understood by Weber, is an action which, having the same meaning for the agent who performs it and for the agent who observes it, has no exterior, no excess of meaning, except that it is unaware of the historical and social conditions of this perfect self-transparency.)

Habitus is not necessarily adapted to its situation nor necessarily coherent. It has degrees of integration – which correspond in particular to degrees of 'crystallization' of the status occupied. Thus it can be observed that to contradictory positions, which tend to exert structural 'double binds' on their occupants, there often correspond destabilized habitus, torn by contradiction and internal division, generating suffering. Moreover, even if dispositions may waste away or weaken through lack of use (linked, in particular, to a change in social position or condition), or as a result of heightened consciousness associated with an effort of transformation (such as the correction of accents, manners, etc.), there is an inertia (or *hysteresis*) of habitus which have a spontaneous tendency (based in biology) to perpetuate structures corresponding to their conditions of production. As a result, it can happen that, in what might be called the Don Quixote effect, dispositions are out of line with the field and with the 'collective expectations' which are constitutive of its normality. This is the case, in particular, when a field undergoes a major crisis and its regularities (even its rules) are profoundly changed. In contrast to what happens in situations of concordance when the self-evidence linked to adjustment renders invisible the habitus which makes it possible, the relatively autonomous principle of legality and regularity that habitus constitutes then appears very clearly.

But, more generally, the diversity of conditions, the corresponding diversity of habitus and the multiplicity of intra- and intergenerational movements of ascent or decline mean that habitus may, in many cases,

---

[31] Bergson, *The Two Sources of Morality and Religion*, p. 122.

be confronted with conditions of actualization different from those in which they were produced. This is true in particular whenever agents perpetuate dispositions made obsolete by transformations of the objective conditions (social ageing), or occupy positions demanding dispositions different from those they derive from their conditions of origin, whether durably, in the case of *parvenus*, or temporarily, like the most deprived agents when faced with situations governed by the dominant norms, like certain economic or cultural markets.

Habitus change constantly in response to new experiences. Dispositions are subject to a kind of permanent revision, but one which is never radical, because it works on the basis of the premises established in the previous state. They are characterized by a combination of constancy and variation which varies according to the individual and his degree of flexibility or rigidity. If (to borrow Piaget's distinction relating to intelligence), accommodation has the upper hand, then one finds rigid, self-enclosed, overintegrated habitus (as in old people); if adaptation predominates, habitus dissolves into the opportunism of a kind of *mens momentanea*, incapable of encountering the world and of having an integrated sense of self.

In situations of crisis or sudden change, especially those seen at the time of abrupt encounters between civilizations linked to the colonial situation or too-rapid movements in social space, agents often have difficulty in holding together the dispositions associated with different states or stages, and some of them, often those who were best adapted to the previous state of the game, have difficulty in adjusting to the new established order. Their dispositions become dysfunctional and the efforts they may make to perpetuate them help to plunge them deeper into failure. This was the case with the inheritors of 'great families' whom I observed in Béarn in the 1960s: driven by old dispositions and encouraged to do so by protective mothers clinging to a disappearing way of life, they condemned themselves to celibacy and a kind of social death.[32] It was also the case with the elect of the elite schools who, again in the 1960s, perpetuated, contrary to all reason, an image of academic achievement, especially with regard to the doctoral thesis, which condemned them to give way to newcomers, often academically less qualified, who were able to adopt the new, less demanding canons of academic performance or deviate from the 'royal road' into faster tracks (opting for the CNRS, the École des Hautes Études or the new disciplines).[33] And

[32] P. Bourdieu, 'Célibat et condition paysanne', *Études Rurales*, 5–6, (Apr.–Sept. 1962), pp. 32–136; 'Reproduction interdite', *Études Rurales*, no. 113–14, (Jan.–June 1989), pp. 15–36.

[33] P. Bourdieu, *Homo Academicus*.

history would provide countless examples of aristocracies, unwilling or unable to derogate (*noblesse oblige*), who allowed their privilege to turn into a handicap in the competition with less advantaged social groups.

In a more general way, habitus has its 'blips', critical moments when it misfires or is out of phase: the relationship of immediate adaptation is suspended, in an instant of hesitation into which there may slip a form of reflection which has nothing in common with that of the scholastic thinker and which, through the sketched movements of the body (for example, the one which, like a tennis player re-enacting a missed shot, takes stock with a glance or a gesture of the effects of the movement performed or the gap between it and what should have been done), remains turned towards practice and not towards the agent who performs it.

Must we surrender to habits of thought which, like the dichotomy of the conscious and the unconscious, lead one to ask the question of the relative weight, in the determination of practices, of the dispositions of habitus or of conscious will? Leibniz supplied a rare answer, in *The Monadology*, which has the virtue of making a place, a major one, for 'practical reason': 'Men act like beasts insofar as the sequences of their perceptions are based only on the principle of memory, like empirical physicians who have a simple practice without theory. We are all mere empirics in three-fourths of our actions.'[34] But, in reality, it is not easy to make the division, and a number of those who have reflected on what it means to follow a rule have observed that there is no rule, however precise and explicit (like legal or mathematical rules), that can provide for all the possible conditions of its execution and which does not, therefore, inevitably leave some degree of play or scope for interpretation, which is handed over to the strategies of habitus (a fact which ought to create some problems for those who postulate that regulated, rational behaviours are necessarily the result of the will to submit to explicit, recognized rules). Conversely, the improvisations of the pianist or the so-called freestyle figures of the gymnast are never performed without a certain presence of mind, as we say, a certain form of thought or even of *practical reflection*, the reflection in situation and in action which is necessary to evaluate instantly the action or posture just produced and to correct a wrong position of the body, to recover an imperfect movement (the same being true, *a fortiori*, of the behaviours of learning).

[34] W. G. Leibniz, 'The monadology', §28, in *Philosophical Papers and Letters*, ed. L. L. Loemker (Dordrecht and Boston: D. Reidel, 1956), p. 645.

Moreover, the degree to which one can abandon oneself to the automatisms of practical sense obviously varies with the situation and the area of activity, but also with the position occupied in social space: it is likely that those who are 'in their right place' in the social world can abandon or entrust themselves more, and more completely, to their dispositions (this is the 'ease' of the well-born) than those who occupy awkward positions, such as the *parvenus* and the *déclassés*; and the latter are more likely to bring to consciousness that which, for others, is taken for granted, because they are forced to keep watch on themselves and consciously correct the 'first movements' of a habitus that generates inappropriate or misplaced behaviours.

5

Symbolic Violence and Political Struggles

~∞~

Acquisition of the primary habitus within the family is very far from being a mechanical process of simple inculcation, analogous to the imprinting of a 'character' imposed by constraint.[1] The same is true of the acquisition of the specific dispositions demanded by a field, which takes place in the relationship between the primary dispositions, more or less remote from what the field calls for, and the constraints inscribed in the structure of the field: the work of specific socialization tends to favour the transformation of the original libido, that is, of the socialized affects constituted in the domestic field, as one or another form of specific libido, in particular through the transference of this libido onto agents or institutions belonging to the field (for example, for the religious field, major symbolic figures such as Christ or the Virgin, in their various historical representations).

Libido and *illusio*

New entrants bring in dispositions previously constituted within a socially situated family group, which are therefore more or less adjusted in advance (especially as a result of self-selection, experienced

---

[1] It is probably because some people have understood the notion of habitus in terms of a mechanistic representation of learning that they have seen it as a social variant of what is understood by 'character', a socially constituted destiny, fixed and frozen once and for all, for life.

as a 'vocation', or of occupational heredity) to the explicit or implicit requirements of the field, its pressures or demands, and more or less 'sensitive' to the signs of recognition and consecration calling for a matching recognition of the order which grants them. It is only through a whole series of imperceptible transactions, half-conscious compromises and psychological operations (projection, identification, transference, sublimation, etc.), socially encouraged, supported, channelled and even organized, that these dispositions are little by little transformed into specific dispositions, after all the infinitesimal adjustments needed in order either to 'rise to the challenge' or to 'back down', which accompany the infinitesimal or abrupt redirections of a social trajectory. In this process of transmutation, rites of institution, and especially those of the educational system, such as the initiatory tests of preparation and selection, which are quite similar in their logic to those of archaic societies, play a determinant role in favouring initial investment in the game.

One can equally well say that agents take advantage of the possibilities offered by a field to express and satisfy their drives and their desires, in some cases their neurosis, or that fields use the agents' drives by forcing them to subject or sublimate themselves in order to adapt to their structures and to the ends that are immanent within them. In fact, the two effects are observed in each case, no doubt in unequal proportions, depending on the field and the agent, and, from this point of view, one could describe each singular form of a specific habitus (of the artist, writer, or scientist, for example) as a kind of 'compromise formation' (in Freud's sense).

The process of transformation through which one becomes a miner, a farmer, a priest, a musician, a teacher or an employer is long, continuous and imperceptible, and, even when it is sanctioned by rites of institution (such as, in the case of the academic nobility, the long preparatory separation and the magic trial of the competitive examination), it normally excludes sudden, radical conversions. It starts in childhood, sometimes even before birth (since, as is particularly clear in what are sometimes called 'dynasties' – of musicians, entrepreneurs, academics, etc. – it involves the socially elaborated *desire* of the father or mother and sometimes a whole lineage). It generally carries on without crises or conflicts – though this does not mean without psychological or physical suffering, which, as a series of *tests*, is part of the conditions of development of the *illusio*; and it is never possible, in any case, to determine who, the agent or the institution, really chose; whether it is the good pupil who chooses the school or the school that chooses him, because everything in his *docile* behaviour shows that he chooses it.

The initial form of *illusio* is investment in the domestic space, the site of a complex process of socialization of the sexual and sexualization of the social. And sociology and psychology should combine their efforts (but this would require them to overcome their mutual suspicion) to analyse the genesis of investment in a field of social relations, thus constituted as an object of interest and preoccupation, in which the child is increasingly implicated and which constitutes the paradigm and also the principle of investment in the social game. How does the transition, described by Freud, occur, leading from a narcissistic organization of the libido, in which the child takes himself (or his own body) as an object of desire, to another state in which he orients himself towards another person, thus entering the world of 'object relations', in the form of the original social microcosm and the protagonists of the drama that is played out there?

One may suppose that, to obtain the sacrifice of 'self-love' in favour of a quite other object of investment and so to inculcate the durable disposition to invest in the social game which is one of the prerequisites of all learning, pedagogic work in its elementary form relies on one of the motors which will be at the origin of all subsequent investments: the *search for recognition*. Happy immersion, without distance or divided loyalties, in the family field may be described either as an extreme form of fulfilment or as an absolute form of alienation. Absorbed in the love of others, the child can only discover others as such on condition that he discovers himself as a 'subject' for whom there are 'objects' whose particularity is that they can take him as their 'object'. In fact, he is continuously led to take the point of view of others on himself, to adopt their point of view so as to discover and evaluate in advance how he will be seen and defined by them. His being is a being-perceived, condemned to be defined as it 'really' is by the perception of others.

Such might be the anthropological root of the ambiguity of symbolic capital – glory, honour, credit, reputation, fame – the principle of an egoistic quest for satisfactions of *amour propre* which is, at the same time, a fascinated pursuit of the approval of others: 'The greatest baseness of man is the pursuit of glory. But that is the greatest mark of his excellence; for whatever possessions he may have on earth, whatever health and essential comfort, he is not satisfied if he has not the esteem of men.'[2] Symbolic capital enables forms of domination which imply dependence on those who can be dominated by it, since it only exists through the esteem, recognition, belief, credit, confidence of others, and can only be perpetuated so long as it succeeds in obtaining belief in its existence.

[2] Pascal, *Pensées*, 404.

Initial pedagogic action, especially when it aims to develop suscept-ibility to a particular form of symbolic capital, finds its mainspring in this original relationship of symbolic dependence: 'Glory. – Admira-tion spoils all from infancy. Ah! How well said! Ah! How well done! How well-behaved he is! etc. The children of Port-Royal, who do not receive this stimulus of envy and glory, fall into carelessness.'[3] The work of socialization of drives is based on a permanent transaction in which the child makes renunciations and sacrifices in exchange for testimonies of recognition, consideration and admiration ('How well-behaved he is!'), sometimes expressly solicited ('Look at me, Daddy!'). This exchange, involving the whole person of the two partners, espe-cially the child of course, but also the parents, is highly charged with affectivity. The child incorporates the social in the form of affects, socially coloured and qualified, and paternal injunctions, prescrip-tions or condemnations no doubt tend to exert an 'Oedipus effect' (to use Popper's phrase)[4] when they come, as in a case analysed by Francine Pariente,[5] from a *polytechnicien* father, consigned by his very success to the status of an inaccessible and inimitable figure. But the social effects of the family *fatum*, in other words the set of posit-ive or negative verdicts pronounced on the child, performative state-ments of the being of the child which bring about what they state, or, more subtly and insidiously, the whole set of *silent censures* imposed by the very logic of the domestic order as a moral order, would not be so powerful or so dramatic if they were not charged with desire and, through repression, buried in the deepest level of the body where they are recorded in the form of guilts, phobias, or, in a word, pas-sion.[6] (Because, in the present state of the division of labour between the sexes, symbolic prizes such as honour, glory or celebrity are still offered mainly to men, boys are the privileged recipients of the ped-agogic action aimed at sharpening sensitivity to these prizes; they are especially encouraged to acquire the disposition to enter into the original *illusio* of which the family universe is the site, and are there-fore more susceptible to the charm of the social games which are socially reserved for them and in which the prizes are one or another of the various possible forms of domination.)[7]

---

[3] Pascal, *Pensées*, 151.
[4] K. Popper, *The Poverty of Historicism*, 2nd edn (London: Routledge and Kegan Paul, 1961), p. 13.
[5] Francine Pariente, oral communication.
[6] The testimony by Fritz Zorn, *Mars*, tr. Robert and Rita Kimer (London: Picador, 1982), can be read as an exemplary document for a socio-analysis of one kind of bourgeois upbringing.
[7] This analysis of the genesis of *illusio* is developed more fully in P. Bourdieu, *Male Domination* (Cambridge: Polity Press, forthcoming). *Trans.*

Bodily constraint

Analysis of the learning and acquisition of dispositions leads to the specifically historical principle of the political order. From the discovery that at the origin of law there is nothing other than arbitrariness and usurpation, that it is impossible to found law in reason and right, and that the Constitution – no doubt what most resembles, in the political order, a Cartesian primary foundation – is merely a founding fiction designed to disguise the act of lawless violence which is the basis of the establishment of law, Pascal draws a typically Machiavellian conclusion: since the people cannot be made to understand the liberatory truth about the social order (*veritatem qua liberetur*), because that truth could only threaten or ruin that order, the people must be 'deceived', not allowed to see 'the fact of usurpation', the inaugural violence in which law is rooted, by 'making it appear as authoritative, eternal'.[8]

In fact there is no need for such intentional mystification, as is still believed by those who attribute submission to law and the maintenance of the symbolic order to a deliberately organized action of propaganda or to the (no doubt significant) efficacy of the 'ideological State apparatuses' working for the dominant class. Indeed, Pascal himself also notes that 'custom makes all authority' and constantly reminds us that the social order is merely the order of bodies: the habituation to custom and law that law and custom produce by their very existence and persistence is largely sufficient, without any deliberate intervention, to impose a recognition of the law based on misrecognition of the arbitrariness which underlies it. The authority that the State is able to exercise no doubt derives reinforcement from the 'august apparel' that it deploys, especially through the judicial apparatus; but the obedience it obtains results for the most part from the docile dispositions that it inculcates through the very order that it establishes (and also, more specifically, through schooling). It follows that the most fundamental problems of political philosophy can only be posed and truly resolved by means of a return to the mundane observations of the sociology of learning and upbringing.

In contrast to a command, an action on a machine or a robot, which acts in mechanical ways, amenable to physical analysis, an order takes effect only through the person who executes it; which does not mean that it necessarily presupposes a conscious and deliberate choice on the part of the executant, implying for example the possibility of disobedience. Most of the time, it can rely on what

---

[8] Pascal, *Pensées*, 294.

Pascal calls 'the automaton' within us, in other words dispositions prepared to recognize it practically – which gives it its 'automatic' appearance and can incline one to interpret it in mechanistic terms. Symbolic force, that of a performative utterance, and especially of an order, is a form of power which is exercised on bodies, directly, and as if by magic, without any physical constraint; but the magic works only on the basis of previously constituted dispositions, which it 'triggers' like springs. It is therefore only an apparent exception to the law of the conservation of energy (or capital): it has its conditions of possibility, and its (in an expanded sense of the term) economic equivalent in the immense preparatory work that is needed to bring about a durable transformation of bodies and to produce the permanent dispositions that symbolic action reawakens and reactivates. (This transformative action is all the more powerful because it is, for the most part, exercised invisibly and insidiously through familiarization with a symbolically structured physical world and through early and prolonged experience of interactions informed by the structures of domination.)

Produced by the incorporation of a social structure in the form of a quasi-natural disposition that often has all the appearances of innateness, habitus is the *vis insita*, the potential energy, the dormant force, from which symbolic violence, and especially that exercised through performatives, derives its mysterious efficacy. It is also the origin of that particular form of symbolic efficacy, 'influence' (that of a person – 'a bad influence' – a thought, an author, etc.), which is often invoked as a tautological explanation and which loses all its mystery as soon as its quasi-magical effects are related to the conditions of production of the dispositions which predisposed certain agents to undergo it.

In a general way, the efficacy of external necessities depends upon the efficacy of an internal necessity. Thus, being the result of the inscription of a relation of domination into the body, dispositions are the true principle of the acts of practical knowledge and recognition of the magical frontier between the dominant and the dominated, which the magic of symbolic power only serves to trigger off. The practical recognition through which the dominated, often unwittingly, contribute to their own domination by tacitly accepting, in advance, the limits imposed on them, often takes the form of *bodily emotion* (shame, timidity, anxiety, guilt), often associated with the impression of *regressing* towards archaic relationships, those of childhood and the family. It is betrayed in visible manifestations, such as blushing, inarticulacy, clumsiness, trembling, all ways of submitting, however reluctantly, to the dominant judgement, sometimes in internal conflict and 'self-division', the subterranean complicity that a body slipping away from the directives of consciousness and will maintains with the violence of the censures inherent in the social structures.

All this appears with particular clarity in this description, taken from James Baldwin, of the mediations through which a black child learns and understands the difference between whites and blacks and the limits assigned to the latter: 'Long before the black child perceives this difference, and even longer before he understands it, he has begun to react to it, he has begun to be controlled by it. Every effort made by the child's elders to prepare him for a fate from which they cannot protect him causes him secretly, in terror, to begin to wait, without knowing that he is doing so, his mysterious and inexorable punishment. He must be "good", not only to please his parents and not only to avoid being punished by them; behind their authority stands another, nameless and impersonal, infinitely harder to please, and bottomlessly cruel. And this filters into the child's consciousness through his parents' tone of voice as he is being exhorted, punished, or loved; in the sudden, uncontrollable note of fear heard in his mother's or his father's voice when he has strayed beyond some particular boundary. He does not know what the boundary is, and he can get no explanation of it, which is terrifying enough, but the fear he hears in the voices of his elders is more frightening still.'[9]

Symbolic violence is the coercion which is set up only through the consent that the dominated cannot fail to give to the dominator (and therefore to the domination) when their understanding of the situation and relation can only use instruments of knowledge that they have in common with the dominator, which, being merely the incorporated form of the structure of the relation of domination, make this relation appear as natural; or, in other words, when the schemes they implement in order to perceive and evaluate themselves or to perceive and evaluate the dominators (high/low, male/female, white/black, etc.) are the product of the incorporation of the (thus naturalized) classifications of which their social being is the product.

To understand this particular form of domination one has to move beyond the false choice between constraint through *forces* and consent to *reasons*, between mechanical coercion and voluntary, free, deliberate submission. The effect of symbolic domination (sexual, ethnic, cultural, linguistic, etc.) is exerted not in the pure logic of knowing consciousnesses but in the obscurity of the dispositions of habitus, in which are embedded the schemes of perception and appreciation which, below the level of the decisions of the conscious

---

[9] J. Baldwin, *The Fire Next Time* (New York: Vintage International, 1993), p. 26.

mind and the controls of the will, are the basis of a relationship of practical knowledge and recognition that is profoundly obscure to itself. And so, for example, the paradoxical logic of male domination, the form par excellence of symbolic domination, and of female submission, of which it can be said, without contradiction, that it is both *spontaneous and extorted*, can only be understood if one takes note of the *durable effects* that the social order exerts on women, in other words of the dispositions spontaneously attuned to that order which it imposes on them.

Symbolic power is exerted only with the collaboration of those who undergo it because they help to *construct* it as such. But nothing would be more dangerous than to stop short at this observation (as idealist constructivism, in its ethnomethodological or other forms, does). This submission is in no way a 'voluntary servitude' and this complicity is not granted by a conscious, deliberate act; it is itself the effect of a power, which is durably inscribed in the bodies of the dominated, in the form of schemes of perception and dispositions (to respect, admire, love, etc.), in other words, beliefs which make one *sensitive* to certain public manifestations, such as public representations of power. It is these dispositions, in other words more or less what Pascal puts under the heading of 'imagination', which, he goes on to say, dispense 'reputation' and 'glory', give 'respect and veneration to persons, works, laws, and the great'. They are what gives the 'red robes', 'ermine', 'palaces' and 'fleurs-de-lis' of magistrates, the 'cassocks' and the 'mules' of physicians, the 'square caps' and 'too wide robes' of doctors the authority they exert on us;[10] but producing them required the prolonged action of countless powers which still govern us through them. And Pascal points out clearly, to invite us to neutralize them, that the effects of 'imagination' produced by the 'august apparel' and 'such authentic show' that necessarily accompanies the exercise of these powers (the examples he gives are all of 'charges or offices' held by the nobility of University or State) refer back to custom, in other words to education and the training of the body.

We are very far from the language of the 'imaginary' which is sometimes used nowadays, somewhat recklessly,[11] and which has nothing in common, despite the verbal coincidence, with what Pascal puts under the heading of 'imagination' (or 'opinion'), that is to say, both the support and the effect in bodies of symbolic violence. This submission, which the body can moreover reproduce by miming it,

[10] Pascal, *Pensées*, 82.
[11] By Cornelius Castoriadis, for example. *Trans.*

is not an act of consciousness aiming at a mental correlate, a simple mental representation (the ideas that one 'forms') capable of being combated by the sheer 'intrinsic force' of true ideas, or even what is ordinarily put under the heading of 'ideology', but a tacit and practical belief made possible by the habituation which arises from the training of the body. And another effect of the scholastic illusion is seen when people describe resistance to domination in the language of consciousness – as does the whole Marxist tradition and also the feminist theorists who, giving way to habits of thought, expect political liberation to come from the 'raising of consciousness' – ignoring the extraordinary inertia which results from the inscription of social structures in bodies, for lack of a dispositional theory of practices. While making things explicit can help, only a thoroughgoing process of countertraining, involving repeated exercises, can, like an athlete's training, durably transform habitus.

Symbolic power

Domination, even when based on naked force, that of arms or money, always has a symbolic dimension, and acts of submission, of obedience, are acts of knowledge and recognition which, as such, implement cognitive structures capable of being applied to all the things of the world, and in particular to social structures. These *structuring structures* are historically constituted forms, arbitrary in Saussure's and Mauss's sense, and it is possible to retrace their social genesis. Generalizing Durkheim's hypothesis that the 'primitive forms of classification' correspond to the structures of groups, one can seek their principle in the effect of the 'automatic' incorporation of social structures, reinforced by the action of the State, which, in differentiated societies, is able to inculcate universally, over its whole territory, a common principle of vision and division, identical or similar cognitive and evaluative structures. The State is consequently the foundation of a 'logical conformism' and a 'moral conformism' (the phrases are Durkheim's), an immediate, prereflexive consensus on the meaning of the world, which is the basis of the experience of the world as the 'common-sense world'. It follows that the theory of knowledge of the social world is a fundamental dimension of political theory; and that, on condition that one 'suspends' the 'suspension' of the political dimension which the claim to perceive the universal essence of the 'original experience of the social' leads them to perform, one can make use of phenomenological analyses of the 'natural attitude', that is, of the primary experience of the social world as self-evident, natural, taken for granted, to emphasize the extraordinary *acceptance* that the established order manages to obtain, no doubt to varying degrees depending on the social formation and on the phase (organic or critical) it is in, with different political effects depending on the foundations of that order and the principles of its perpetuation. This reminder is all the more necessary because the methodological voluntarism and optimism which define the populist vision of the 'people' as a site of subversion or, at least, of 'resistance' concur in setting aside realistic observations with the sometimes apocalyptic pessimism of the conservative vision of the 'masses' as a blind, brute force of subversion.

Phenomenological analysis, so perfectly 'neutralized' politically that one can read it without drawing any political conclusions, has the virtue of making visible all that is still granted to the established order by the most *para-doxal*, the seemingly most *critical* political experience, the one most resolved to perform the '*epokhè* of the natural attitude', as Schutz put it (in other words to suspend the suspension of doubt as to the possibility that the social world could be other than it is which is implied in the experience of the world as 'taken for granted'). Because dispositions are the product of the incorporation of objective structures and because expectations always tend to adjust themselves to chances, the instituted order always tends to appear, even to the most disadvantaged, if not as self-evident, natural, at least as more necessary, more self-evident than might be thought from the standpoint of those who, not having been brought up in such pitiless conditions, can only find them spontaneously unbearable and revolting. Phenomenological analysis, reread in this way (like, in a quite different register, Spinoza's analysis of *obsequium*, that 'constant will' produced by 'the conditioning through which the State shapes us for its use and which enables it to be conserved'), has the virtue of recalling what is most particularly ignored or repressed, especially in universes in which people tend to think of themselves as free of conformisms and beliefs, namely the relation of often insurmountable *submission* which binds all social agents, whether they like it or not, to the social world of which they are, for better or worse, the products. And if one needs to emphasize this truth very strongly, albeit with the exaggeration needed to awaken people from their doxic slumber by 'twisting the stick in the opposite direction', this is not done, of course, in order to deny the existence of strategies of *resistance*, individual or collective, ordinary or extraordinary, or to exclude the possibility of a differential sociological analysis of relations to the social world, or, more precisely of variations in the extent of the realm of *doxa* – relative to the realm of orthodox or heterodox opinions, expressed, constituted and articulated – depending on the society (and especially its degree of homogeneity and their organic or critical state) and depending on the position occupied in that society.

But, even in the most differentiated societies and those most subject to change, the presuppositions of *doxa* – those, for example, which underlie the choice of formulae of politeness – cannot be reduced to a set of formal, universal 'theses' like those set out by Schutz: 'In the natural attitude, I take for granted that fellow-men exist, that they act on me as I upon them, that – at least to a certain extent – communication and mutual understanding among us can be established, and that this is done with the help of some system of signs and symbols within the frame of some social organization and some social institutions – none of them of my own making.'[12] It would not be difficult to show that what is tacitly imposed on recognition by the 'inert violence' of the social order goes far beyond these few general, ahistorical anthropological propositions – as is shown by the countless manifestations (unease or silent shame) of submission before the legitimate culture and language. The primordial political belief is a particular viewpoint, that of the dominant, which presents and imposes itself as a universal viewpoint. It is the viewpoint of those who directly or indirectly dominate the State and who, through the State, have established their viewpoint as the universal viewpoint, after struggles against rival views. What today presents itself as self-evident, established, settled once and for all, beyond discussion, has not always been so and only gradually imposed itself as such. It is historical evolution which tends to abolish history, in particular by relegating to the past, to the unconscious, all the 'lateral possibles' which have been excluded; it thus comes to be forgotten that the 'natural attitude' that the phenomenologists refer to, that is, the primary experience of the world as self-evident, is a *socially constructed relationship*, as are the perceptual schemes that make it possible.

The phenomenologists, who have made this primary experience explicit, and the ethnomethodologists, who have set out to describe it, do not give themselves the means of accounting for it. While they are right to recall, in opposition to the mechanist vision, that social agents construct social reality, they fail to address the question of the social construction of the principles of construction of that reality which agents implement in the individual and also collective work of construction, and to consider the contribution of the State to that construction. In relatively undifferentiated societies, it is through the whole spatial and temporal organization of social life, and also through

---

[12] A. Schutz, *Collected Papers*, vol. 1: *The Problem of Social Reality* (The Hague, Boston, London: Martinus Nijhoff, 1962), p. 145.

rites of institution establishing definitive differences between those who have undergone the rite (for example, circumcision) and those who have not (for example, women) that the common principles of vision and division (the paradigm of which is the male–female opposition) are instituted in bodies. In modern societies, the State makes a decisive contribution towards the production and reproduction of the instruments of construction of social reality. As an organizational structure and as an authority regulating practices, it exerts a permanent action of formation of durable dispositions, through all the constraints and disciplines that it imposes uniformly on all agents. In particular, in reality and in people's minds it imposes all the fundamental principles of classification – sex, age, 'competence', etc. – through the imposition of divisions into social categories – such as active/inactive – which are the product of the application of cognitive 'categories', which are thus reified and naturalized. It is the source of the symbolic efficacy of all the rites of institution, those which are at the basis of the family, for example, and also those which are performed through the functioning of the educational system, which, between those it selects and those it eliminates, sets up durable and often definitive symbolic differences, universally recognized within the area of its authority.

The construction of the State is thus accompanied by the construction of a kind of common historical transcendental which, after a long process of incorporation, becomes immanent to all its 'subjects'. Through the structuring it imposes on practices, the State institutes and inculcates common symbolic forms of thought, social frames of perception, understanding or memory, State forms of classification or, more precisely, practical schemes of perception, appreciation and action. (When, as here and elsewhere in this text, I give numerous equivalent formulations, I am trying to help to demolish the false frontiers between artificially separated theoretical universes, for example, the neo-Kantian philosophy of symbolic forms proposed by Cassirer and the Durkheimian sociology of the primitive forms of classification – and to secure the means of cumulating the insights of each while increasing the chances of being understood.)

The State thereby creates the conditions for an immediate orchestration of habitus which is itself the foundation for a consensus on this set of shared self-evidences which constitute common sense. For example, the major rhythms of the social calendar, especially that of school holidays, which determines the great 'seasonal migrations' of contemporary societies, guarantee both common objective referents and harmonized subjective principles of division, thereby ensuring, beyond the irreducibility of lived experience of time, 'internal experiences of time' that are sufficiently concordant to make social life possible. Another example: the division of the academic world into disciplines is embedded in the form of disciplinary habitus generating an agreement between specialists which is responsible even for their disagreements and the form in which they express them and which also leads to all kinds of limitations and blindnesses in practices and representations, and distortions in relations with the representatives of other disciplines.

But fully to understand the immediate submission secured by the State order, one has to break with the intellectualism of the Kantian tradition and see that cognitive structures are not forms of consciousness but dispositions of the body, practical schemes, and that the obedience we give to State injunctions cannot be understood either as mechanical submission to force or as conscious consent to an order. The social world is full of *calls to order* which function as such only for individuals who are predisposed to notice them, and which, as a red light causes braking, trigger deep-rooted bodily dispositions without passing through consciousness and calculation. Submission to the established order is the product of the agreement between the cognitive structures that collective history (phylogenesis) and individual history (ontogenesis) has inscribed in bodies and the objective structures of the world to which they are applied. The self-evidence of the injunctions of the State imposes itself so powerfully because the State has imposed the cognitive structures through which it is perceived.

But we have to move beyond the neo-Kantian tradition, even in its Durkheimian form, on another point. Symbolic structuralism, by privileging the *opus operatum* (like Lévi-Strauss or Foucault in *The Order of Things*), no doubt condemns itself to ignore the active dimension of symbolic production, especially in the field of myth, that is, the question of the *modus operandi*, the 'generative grammar' in Chomsky's terms, and above all of its genesis, and therefore its relationship with particular social conditions of production. But it has the immense merit of seeking to extract the coherence of symbolic systems, considered as such. This coherence is one of the major principles of their specific *efficacy*, as is clearly seen in the case of law, where it is deliberately sought, but also in the case of myth or religion. The symbolic order is based on the imposition on all agents of structuring structures which derive part of their consistency and resistance to the fact that they are, in appearance at least, coherent and systematic, and that they are adjusted to the objective structures of the social world (this is true, for example, of the opposition between the male and the female, which is bound up with the tight network of all the oppositions of the mythico-ritual system, itself inscribed in bodies and in things). This immediate, tacit agreement (quite different from an explicit contract) is the basis of the relation of doxic submission which binds us to the established order with all the bonds of the unconscious, that is, of a history that is unaware of itself as such. Recognition of legitimacy is not, as Weber supposed, a free act of lucid consciousness: it is rooted in the immediate agreement between the incorporated structures, turned into practical schemes, such as those which organize temporal rhythms (for example the quite arbitrary division into *hours* of the school timetable), and the objective structures.

The doxic submission of the dominated to the objective structures of a social order of which their cognitive structures are the product – a real mystery so long as one remains enclosed in the intellectualist tradition of philosophies of mind – is thus clarified. In the notion of 'false consciousness' which some Marxists invoke to explain the effect of symbolic domination, it is the word 'consciousness' which is excessive; and to speak of 'ideology' is to place in the order of *representations*, capable of being transformed by the intellectual conversion that is called the 'awakening of consciousness', what belongs to the order of *beliefs*, that is, at the deepest level of bodily dispositions.

(When one is trying to account for symbolic power and the specifically symbolic dimension of State power, Marxist thought is more of a hindrance than a help. One can, by contrast, make use of the decisive contribution which Max Weber made in his writings on religion to the theory of symbolic systems, by reintroducing specialized agents and their specific interests. While, like Marx, Weber is less interested in the structure of symbolic systems (which he does not, moreover, call by this name) than in their function, he has the merit of drawing attention to the producers of these special products (religious agents, in the case which concerns him) and to their *interactions* (conflict, competition, etc.). Unlike the Marxists who, even if one can point to a text by Engels about the corps of jurists, tend to ignore the existence of specialized agents of production, he points out that to understand religion it is not sufficient to study religious symbolic forms, like Cassirer or Durkheim, or even the immanent structure of the religious message or the mythological corpus, like the structuralists: he focuses on the producers of the religious message, the specific interests which motivate them, and the strategies they use in their struggles, such as excommunication.

Applying, by a new break, the structuralist mode of thought (which is quite alien to Max Weber) not only to works and the relations between works (like symbolic structuralism) but also to the relations between the producers of symbolic goods, one can then construct as such not only the structure of symbolic productions, or, more precisely, the *space of symbolic position-takings* in a given area of practice (for example, religious messages), but also the structure of the system of the agents who produce them (for example, priests, prophets and sorcerers), or, more precisely, the *space of the positions* that they occupy (what I call the religious field, for example) in the competition among them. One then has the means of understanding these symbolic productions, as regards their function, their structure and their genesis, on the basis of the – empirically confirmed – homology between these two spaces.)

It is the prereflexive agreement between the objective structures and the incorporated structures, and not the efficacy of the deliberate propaganda of apparatuses or the free recognition of legitimacy by the citizens, which explains the – ultimately astonishing – ease with which, throughout history and apart from a few crisis situations, the dominant impose their domination: 'Nothing appears more surprising to those who consider human affairs with a philosophical eye than the easiness with which the many are governed by the few and the implicit submission with which men resign their own sentiments and passions to those of their rulers. When we inquire by what means this wonder is effected, we shall find that, as force is always on the side of the governed, the governors have nothing to support them but opinion. It is, therefore, on opinion only that government is founded, and this maxim extends to the most despotic and most military governments as well as to the most free and most popular.'[13]

Hume's astonishment brings up the fundamental question of all political philosophy, a question that is paradoxically masked when people pose a scholastic problem that is never really posed as such in ordinary existence, that of legitimacy. For the problem is that, for the most part, the established order is not a problem; outside crisis situations, the question of the legitimacy of the State does not arise. The State does not necessarily need to give orders and to exert physical coercion, or disciplinary constraint, to produce an ordered social world, so long as it is able to produce incorporated cognitive structures attuned to the objective structures and so secure doxic submission to the established order.

(Faced with this so typically Pascalian reversal of the vision of the half-learned, who misplace their astonishments, how can one not quote Pascal? 'The people have very sound opinions . . . The half-learned

---

[13] D. Hume, 'Of the first principles of government' (1758), in *Political Essays*, ed. K. Haakonssen (Cambridge: Cambridge University Press, 1994), pp. 16–19.

laugh at it, and glory in showing thereby the folly of the world; but, for a reason these men cannot grasp, the people are right.' And true philosophy makes light of the philosophy of 'those who stand half-way', who 'pretend to be wise' by mocking the people on the grounds that they are not sufficiently astonished at so many things so worthy of astonishment. Failing to consider 'the reason of the effects' which provoke their astonishment, they help to divert attention from realities more worthy of astonishment, such as 'the implicit submission with which men revoke their feelings and passions in favour of their leaders' (or, in the language of 1968, the docility with which they sacrifice their 'desires' to the 'repressive' demands of the 'dominant' order). A number of seemingly radical reflections on politics and power are indeed rooted in the revolts of aesthete adolescents, who sow their wild oats by denouncing the constraints of the social order, most often identified with the family – Gide's 'Families, I hate you' – or with the State – with the 'leftist' themes of 'repression' which 'self-evidently' inspired French philosophers post-1968. They are only one manifestation among others of that 'impatience with limits' that Claudel referred to, which does not predispose one to enter into a realistic and attentive (which does not mean resigned) understanding of social constraints. And one might read as a programme of scientific and political work Pascal's celebrated text on 'the reason of effects': 'Continual alternation of pro and con. We have, then, shown that man is foolish, by the estimation he makes of things which are not essential; and all these opinions are destroyed. We have next shown that all these opinions are very sound and that thus, since all these vanities are well founded [we are here very close to Durkheim's definition of religion as "well-founded delirium"], the people are not so foolish as is said. And so we have destroyed the opinion which destroyed that of the people. But we must now destroy this last proposition and show that it remains always true that the people are foolish, though their opinions are sound: because they do not perceive the truth where it is, and, as they place it where it is not, their opinions are always very false and very unsound.'[14])

Twofold naturalization and its effects

The passions of the dominated habitus (whether dominated in terms of sex, culture or language), a somatized social relationship, the law of the social body converted into the law of the body, are not of a

[14] Pascal, *Pensées*, 328.

kind that can be suspended by a simple effort of will, founded on a liberatory awakening of consciousness. A person who fights his timidity feels betrayed by his body, which recognizes paralyzing taboos or calls to order, where someone else, the product of different conditions, would see stimulating incitements or injunctions. It is quite illusory to think that symbolic violence can be overcome solely with the weapons of consciousness and will. The conditions of its efficacy are durably inscribed in bodies in the form of dispositions which, especially in the case of kinship relations and social relations conceived on this model, are expressed and experienced in the logic of feeling or duty, often merged in the experience of respect, affective devotion or love, and which can survive long after the disappearance of their social conditions of production.

Hence also the 'foolishness' of all religious, ethical or political stances consisting in expecting a genuine transformation of relations of domination (or of the dispositions which are, partly at least, a product of them) from a simple 'conversion of minds' (of the dominant or the dominated), produced by rational preaching and education, or, as *maîtres à penser* sometimes like to think, from a vast collective logotherapy which it falls to the intellectuals to organize. We know the futility of all actions which seek to use only the weapons of logical or empirical refutation in combating this or that form of racism – whether of ethnicity, class or sex – which in fact thrives on discourses capable of flattering the associated dispositions and beliefs (often relatively indeterminate, amenable to multiple verbal formulations, and obscure to themselves) by giving the sense or the illusion of expressing them. Habitus is not destiny; but symbolic action cannot, on its own, without transformation of the conditions of the production and transformation of dispositions, extirpate bodily beliefs, which are passions and drives that remain totally indifferent to the injunctions or condemnations of humanistic universalism (itself, moreover, rooted in dispositions and beliefs).

Consider, for example, nationalist passion, which can be found in different forms in the occupants of the two opposing positions of a relation of domination: Irish Protestants and Catholics, English-speaking or French-speaking Canadians, etc. The 'primary truth' to which the protagonists cling, and which it would be too easy to see as a 'primary error', a mere illusion of passion and blindness, is that nation, 'race', or 'identity', in the current phrase, is inscribed in things – in the form of objective structures, *de facto* separation, economic or spatial, etc. – and in bodies – in the form of tastes and distastes, likes and dislikes, which are sometimes called visceral. Objective (and objectivist) critique can easily denounce the naturalized vision of the region or nation, with its 'natural' frontiers and its 'linguistic' or other units, and show that all these substantial entities are merely social constructs, historical artefacts, often resulting from historical struggles similar to those they are supposed to have settled, not perceived as such but rather, and wrongly, as natural data.

But the critique of essentialist nationalism (the limiting case of which is racism), as well as often being an easy way of asserting one's distance from common passions, remains perfectly ineffective (and therefore likely to be legitimately suspected of having other motivations). Though denounced, condemned and stigmatized, the deadly passions of all racisms (of ethnicity, sex or class) perpetuate themselves because they are bound to the body in the form of dispositions and also because the relation of domination of which they are the product perpetuates itself in objectivity, continuously reinforcing the propensity to accept it, which, except in the case of a critical break (that performed by the 'reactive' nationalism of dominated peoples, for example), is no less strong among the dominated than the dominant.

If I have little by little come to shun the use of the word 'ideology', this is not only because of its polysemy and the resulting ambiguities. It is above all because, by evoking the order of ideas, and of action by ideas and on ideas, it inclines one to forget one of the most powerful mechanisms of the maintenance of the symbolic order, the *two-fold naturalization* which results from the inscription of the social in things and in bodies (as much those of the dominant as of the dominated – whether in terms of sex, ethnicity, social position or any other discriminating factor), with the resulting effects of symbolic violence. As is underlined by ordinary-language notions such as 'natural distinction' or 'gift', the work of legitimation of the established order is extraordinarily facilitated by the fact that it goes on almost automatically in the reality of the social world.

The processes which produce and reproduce the social order, both in things, museums for example, or in objective mechanisms such as those which tend to reserve access to those most endowed with inherited cultural capital, and in bodies, through the mechanisms which ensure the hereditary transmission of dispositions and the forgetting of it, offer to perception an abundance of tangible self-evidences, indisputable at first sight, which strongly tend to give to an illusory representation all the appearances of being grounded in reality. In short, the social order itself largely produces its own sociodicy. It follows that one only has to let the objective mechanisms do their work, which may be work upon oneself, in order, unwittingly, to grant the social order its ratification. And those who rush to the aid of the symbolic order threatened by crisis or critique need only point to the self-evidences of common sense, in other words the vision of itself that, except in extraordinary circumstances, the social world manages to impose. As a half-wise epigrammatist might put it, the established order is so well defended because one only has to be stupid in order to defend it. (This is, for example, what provides the almost insurmountable social strength of the doxosophers and their opinion polls, based on a not-even-conscious decision to let themselves be guided, in choosing and formulating their questions, in drawing up their categories or in interpreting their findings, by the mental habits and self-evidences of 'common sense'.)

Social science, which is obliged to make a critical break with primary self-evidences, has no better weapon for doing so than historicization, which, at least in the order of theory, makes it possible to neutralize the effects of naturalization, and in particular amnesia of the individual and collective genesis of a 'given' that gives itself with all the appearance of nature and asks to be taken at face value, taken for granted. But – and this is what makes anthropological inquiry so difficult – the effect of naturalization also applies to thought itself: the incorporation of the scholastic order can, as has been seen, impose presuppositions and limitations on thought which, being embedded in the body, are beyond the reach of consciousness.

In ordinary existence, the classifying operations through which agents construct the social world tend to be forgotten as such as they realize themselves in the social units which they produce – family, tribe, nation, etc. – and which have all the appearances of things (such as transcendence and resistance). In the same way, in the fields of cultural production, the concepts that we use – power, prestige, work, society – and the classifications that we engage explicitly (in definitions or notions) or implicitly (in particular through divisions into disciplines or specialities) use us as much as we use them, and 'automation' is a specific form of repression that consigns the very instruments of thought to the unconscious. Only historical critique, the major weapon of reflexiveness, can free thought from the constraints exerted on it when, surrendering to the routines of the automaton, it treats reified historical constructs as things. It is clear how damaging it is to reject historicization, a rejection which, for many thinkers, is constitutive of philosophy itself and which gives free rein to the historical mechanisms that it claims to ignore.

Practical sense and political labour

Thus, one cannot really describe the relationship between agents and the world except by placing at the centre the body and the process of incorporation, which both physicalist objectivism and marginalist subjectivism ignore. The structures of the social space (or of fields) shape bodies by inculcating in them, through the conditionings associated with a position in that space, the cognitive structures that these conditionings apply to them. More precisely, the social world, because it is an object of knowledge for those who are included in it, is, in part, the reified or incorporated product of all the different (and rival) acts of knowledge of which it is the object. But these position-takings on the world depend for their content and their symbolic force on the position that their producers occupy within it, and only an *analysis situs* can make it possible to construct these points of view as such, that is, as partial views each from a point (*situs*) in social space. Moreover, these determinate points of view are themselves determinant: to varying degrees, they play a part in making, unmaking and remaking the space, in the struggle of points of view, perspectives, classifications (consider, for example, the struggle over distributions, or, more precisely, over 'equality in distributions', *en tais dianomais*, in the phrase Aristotle used to define distributive justice).

So the social space cannot be reduced to a simple 'awareness context' in the interactionist sense, a universe of points of view reflecting each other *ad infinitum*.[15] It is the relatively stable site of the coexistence of points of view, in the dual sense of positions in the distribution of capital (economic, informational, social, etc.) and of the corresponding powers, but also of *practical reactions* to or representations of that space, produced from these points through habitus that are structured, and doubly informed, by the structure of the space and by the structure of the schemes of perception that are applied to it.

Points of view, in the sense of structured and structuring position-takings on the social space or on a particular field, are by definition different and competing. To explain why all fields are the site of competitions and conflicts, there is no need to invoke a selfish or aggressive 'human nature' or a 'will to power'. As well as the investment in the stakes that defines participation in the game and which, being common to all the players, sets them against and in competition with each other, it is the very structure of the field, that is, the structure of the (unequal) distribution of the various kinds of capital, which, by generating the rarity of certain positions and the corresponding profits, favours strategies aimed at destroying or reducing that rarity, through

---

[15] B. G. Glaser and A. Strauss, *Awareness of Dying* (Chicago: Aldine, 1965), pp. 274–85.

the appropriation of rare positions, or conserving it, through the defence of those positions.

The social space, that is, the structure of distributions, is both the basis of antagonistic position-takings on that space, which means, in particular, on the distribution, and a stake in struggles and confrontation between the points of view (which, one must endlessly repeat in order to escape from the scholastic illusion, are not necessarily representations, explicit, verbal position-takings). These struggles to impose the legitimate vision and representation of the space, the ortho-doxy, which in the political field often resort to prophecy or forecasting [*prévision*], aim to impose principles of vision and division – ethnic group, region, nation, class, etc. – which, through the effect of self-fulfilling prophecy, can help to make groups exist. They have the inevitable effect, especially when they are instituted in a political field (in contrast, for example, to the hidden struggles between the sexes in archaic societies), of bringing a more or less extensive part of the *doxa* to the level of explicit statement, that is, of constituted opinion – without ever, even in the most critical situations of the most critical social universes, reaching the total uncovering that is pursued by social science, that is, the complete suspension of doxic submission to the established order.

Each agent has a practical, bodily knowledge of her present and potential position in the social space, a 'sense of one's place' as Goffman puts it, converted into a *sense of placement* which governs her experience of the place occupied, defined absolutely and above all relationally as a rank, and the way to behave in order to keep it ('pulling rank') and to keep within it ('knowing one's place', etc.). The practical knowledge conferred by this sense of position takes the form of emotion (the unease of someone who is out of place, or the ease that comes from being in one's place), and it is expressed in behaviours such as avoidance or unconscious adjustments such as the correction of one's accent (in the presence of a person of higher rank) or, in situations of bilingualism, the choice of the language appropriate to the situation. It is this practical knowledge that orients interventions in the symbolic struggles of everyday life which contribute to the construction of the social world, less visibly but just as effectively as the theoretical struggles that take place within the specialized fields, especially the political, bureaucratic, juridical and scientific ones, that is, in the order of symbolic, mostly discursive, representations.

But, as a practical sense, this sense of present and potential placement is, as has been seen, capable of being made explicit in several ways. Hence the relative independence, with respect to position, of explicit position-taking, verbally stated opinion, opening the way for the specifically political action of *representation* – the work of the spokesperson who brings the supposed existence of a group to the level of verbal or indeed theatrical representation and who can help to make it exist by making it appear as the person who speaks (with a single voice) in its name, or even by making it visible as such by calling upon it to manifest itself in a public exhibition, a march or procession, or, in modern times, a demonstration, and so to declare its existence, its strength (linked to number) and its will, before the eyes of all.[16]

The sense of one's place is a practical sense (having nothing in common with what is generally referred to as 'class consciousness'), a practical knowledge that does not know itself, a 'learned ignorance' (*docta ignorantia*) which, as such, may be the victim of that particular form of misrecognition, *allodoxia*, consisting in mistakenly recognizing oneself in a particular form of representation and public enunciation of the *doxa*. The knowledge supplied by incorporation of the necessity of the social world, especially in the form of the sense of limits, is quite real, like the submission which it implies and which is sometimes expressed in the imperative statements of resignation: 'That's not for us' (or 'not for the likes of us') or, more simply, 'It's too expensive' (for us). It even contains (as I tried to show when questioning Algerian workers about the causes of unemployment) the rudiments of explicit statement or even explanation.[17] And it does not exclude – why would one suppose the contrary? – forms of resistance, either passive and internal, or active and sometimes collective, with, in particular, all the strategies aimed at escaping the most unpleasant forms of labour and exploitation (going slow, working to rule, sabotage). But it remains open to symbolic hijacking, forced as it is to entrust itself to spokespersons, the exclusive agents of the ontological leap presupposed by the move from *praxis* to *logos*, from practical sense to discourse, from practical vision to representation, that is, access to the order of specifically political opinion.

Political struggle is a (practical and theoretical) cognitive struggle for the power to impose the legitimate vision of the social world, or, more precisely, for the recognition, accumulated in the form of a symbolic capital of notoriety and respectability, which gives the authority to impose the legitimate knowledge of the *sense* of the social world, its present meaning and the direction in which it is going and should go. The work of 'worldmaking', which, as Nelson Goodman

---

[16] P. Champagne, *Faire l'opinion* (Paris: Éditions de Minuit, 1990).

[17] P. Bourdieu, *Travail et travailleurs en Algérie* (Paris and The Hague: Mouton, 1964), pp. 303ff. and *Algeria 1960: Essays*, tr. R. Nice (Cambridge: Cambridge University Press, 1979).

observes, consists in 'setting apart and putting together, often at the same time',[18] tends, when the social world is involved, to construct and impose the principles of division likely to conserve or transform this world by transforming the vision of its divisions and therefore of the groups which compose it and of their relations. It is in a sense a politics of perception aimed at maintaining or subverting the order of things by transforming or conserving the categories through which it is perceived, the words in which it is expressed. The effort to inform and orient the perception and the effort to make explicit the practical experience of the world go hand in hand, since one of the stakes in the symbolic struggle is the power of knowledge, that is, power over the incorporated instruments of knowledge, the schemes of perception and appreciation of the social world, the principles of division, which, at a given moment, determine the vision of the world (rich/poor, white/black, national/foreign, etc.), and the power to make see and make believe that this power implies.

By its very existence, the institution of the State as the holder of the monopoly of legitimate symbolic violence sets a limit on the symbolic struggle of all against all for this monopoly (that is, for the right to impose one's own principle of vision), thereby removing a certain number of divisions and principles of division from this struggle. But, at the same time, it makes the State itself one of the major stakes in the struggle for symbolic power. The State is the site par excellence of the imposition of the *nomos*, the official and effective principle of construction of the world, with, for example, all the acts of consecration and accreditation which ratify, legalize, legitimize, 'regularize' situations or acts of union (marriage, various contracts, etc.) or separation (divorce, breach of contract), which are thus raised from the status of pure contingent fact, unofficial or even disguised (a 'relationship'), to the status of official fact, known and recognized by all, published and public.

The form par excellence of the socially instituted and officially recognized symbolic power of construction is the legal authority, law being the objectification of the dominant vision recognized as legitimate, or, to put it another way, of the legitimate vision of the world, the ortho-doxy, guaranteed by the State. An exemplary manifestation of this State power of consecration of the established order is the *verdict*, a legitimate exercise of the power to say what is and to make exist what it states, in a performative utterance that is universally recognized (as opposed to an insult, for example); or again, the *birth certificate*, another creative statement, analogous to that performed

[18] N. Goodman, *Ways of Worldmaking* (Hassocks: Harvester Press, 1978), p. 7.

by a divine *intuitus originarius*, which, like Mallarmé's poet, fixes names, puts an end to argument about the way of naming by assigning an 'identity' (the identity card) or sometimes even a *title*, the principle of the constitution of a corporate body.

But while the State reserves for its directly mandated agents this power of legitimate distribution and redistribution of identities through the consecration of persons or things (with deeds of ownership, for example), it may delegate derived forms of it, such as the *certificate*, academic or medical, of aptitude, incapacity, invalidity, etc., a recognized social power giving legitimate access, entitlement, to advantages or privileges, or the *diagnosis*, a clinical act of scientific identification which may be endowed with legal efficacy through the prescription and play a part in the social distribution of privileges, by establishing a social frontier, the one which distinguishes a category of beneficiaries. (Here one should pause to reflect on the sociological observation – for example, the one I am transcribing here – which, though it claims the status of an experimental procedure, is liable to be seen as a ratification, an approbation, in other words a surreptitiously performative statement which, under the appearance of simply saying what is, tends additionally and tacitly to say what ought to be. This ambiguity is particularly clear in statistical observations: these record – using State categories, in the case of official statistics – distributions which themselves merely register the result of struggles for the determination of the legitimate distribution: where Social Security is concerned, for example, for the definition or redefinition of legitimate disability.)

Thus the social world is both the product and the stake of inseparably cognitive and political symbolic struggles over knowledge and recognition, in which each pursues not only the imposition of an advantageous representation of himself or herself, with the strategies of 'presentation of self' so admirably analysed by Goffman, but also the power to impose as legitimate the principles of construction of social reality most favourable to his or her social being (individual and collective, with, for example, struggles over the boundaries of groups) and to the accumulation of a symbolic capital of recognition. These struggles take place both in the order of everyday existence and within the fields of cultural production, which, even if they are not oriented towards this sole end, like the political field, contribute to the production and imposition of principles of construction and evaluation of social reality.

The specifically political action of legitimation is always carried out on the basis of the fundamental given of original acceptance of the world as it is, and the work of the guardians of the symbolic order, whose interests are bound up with common sense, consists in trying to restore the initial self-evidences of *doxa*. By contrast, the political action of subversion aims to liberate the potential capacity for refusal which is neutralized by misrecognition, by performing, aided by a crisis, a critical unveiling of the founding violence that is masked by the adjustment between the order of things and the order of bodies.

The symbolic work needed in order to break out of the silent self-evidence of *doxa* and to state and denounce the arbitrariness that it conceals presupposes instruments of expression and criticism which, like the other forms of capital, are unequally distributed. As a consequence, there is every reason to think that it would not be possible without the intervention of professional practitioners of the work of making explicit, who, in certain historical conjunctures, may make themselves the *spokespersons* of the dominated on the base of partial solidarities and *de facto* alliances springing from the homology between a dominated position in this or that field of cultural production and the position of the dominated in the social space. A solidarity of this kind, which is not without ambiguity, can bring about – with, for example, the defrocked priests of the millenarian movements of the Middle Ages, or the intellectuals ('proletaroid', as Weber calls them, or others) of the revolutionary movements of modern times – the *transfer of cultural capital* which enables the dominated to achieve a collective mobilization and subversive action against the established order; with, in return, the risk of hijacking which is contained in the imperfect correspondence between the interests of the dominated and those of the dominated-dominant who make themselves the spokespersons of their demands or their revolts, on the basis of a partial analogy between different experiences of domination.

The twofold truth

One cannot remain satisfied with the objectivist vision, which leads to physicalism, and for which there is a social world in itself, to be treated as a thing, with the scientist being able to treat the necessarily partial (in both senses) points of the view of the agents as simple illusions. Nor can one be satisfied with the subjectivist or marginalist vision, for which the social world is merely the product of the aggregation of all representations and all wills. Social science cannot be reduced to an objectification incapable of giving its due place to the effort of agents to construct their subjective representation of themselves and the world, sometimes against all the objective data; and it cannot be reduced to a recording of spontaneous sociologies and folk theories – which are already too present in scientific discourse, smuggling themselves in.

In fact, the social world is an object of knowledge for those who belong to it and who, comprehended within it, comprehend it, and produce it, but from the point of view they occupy within it. One therefore cannot exclude the *percipere* and the *percipi*, the knowing and the being-known, the recognizing and the being-recognized, which are the source of the struggles for recognition, and for symbolic power, that is, the power to impose the principles of division, knowledge and recognition. But nor can one ignore the fact that, in these truly political struggles to modify the world by modifying the representations of the world, the agents take up positions which, far from being interchangeable, as phenomenist perspectivism would have it, always depend, in reality, on their position in the social world of which they are the product but which they help to produce.

Since one cannot be content either with the primary vision or with the vision to which the work of objectification gives access, one can only strive to *hold together*, so as to integrate them, both the point of view of the agents who are caught up in the object and the point of view on this point of view which the work of analysis enables one to reach by relating position-takings to the positions from which they are taken. No doubt because the epistemological break always presupposes a social separation which, especially when it is ignored, can inspire a form of initiate's contempt for common knowledge, treated as an obstacle to be destroyed and not as an object to be understood, there is a strong temptation – and many social scientists fall into it – to stop short at the objectivist phase and the partial view of the 'half-learned', who, carried away by the wicked pleasure of disenchanting, fail to bring into their analysis the primary vision, Pascal's 'sound truth of the people', against which their constructions are built. The result is that the resistances that scientific objectification often provokes, which are felt and expressed with particular intensity in academic worlds, anxious to defend the monopoly of their own understanding, are not all or always entirely unjustified.

Social games are *in any case* very difficult to describe in their twofold truth. Those who are caught up in them have little interest in seeing the game objectified, and those who are not are often ill-placed to experience and feel everything that can only be learned and understood when one takes part in the game – so that their descriptions, which fail to evoke the enchanted experience of the believer, are likely to strike the participants as both trivial and sacrilegious. The 'half-learned', eager to demystify and denounce, do not realize that those they seek to disabuse, or unmask, both know and resist the truth they claim to reveal. They cannot understand, or take into account, the games of self-deception which make it possible to perpetuate an illusion for oneself and to safeguard a bearable form of 'subjective truth' in the face of calls to reality and to realism, and often with the complicity of the institution (the latter – the university, for example, for all its love of classifications and hierarchies – always offers compensatory satisfactions and consolation prizes that tend to blur the perception and evaluation of self and others).

But the defences that individuals put up against the discovery of their truth are as nothing beside the collective systems of defence used to mask the most fundamental mechanisms of the social order, those that govern the economy of symbolic exchanges. Thus the most indisputable discoveries, such as the existence of a strong correlation between social origin and academic success or between level of education and visits to museums, or between gender and the probability of access to the most prestigious positions in the scientific and artistic universes, may be rejected as scandalous untruths to be countered with examples presented as irrefutable ('my *concierge*'s son is at university', or 'I know children of *polytechniciens* who are total failures') or denials which surface, like Freudian slips, in distinguished conversation or in essays aspiring to some seriousness, and the canonical form of which was supplied by a senior member of the most distinguished bourgeoisie: 'Education, sir, is innate.' In as much as his work of objectifying and unveiling often leads him to produce the *negation of a denegation*, the sociologist must expect to see his discoveries both swept aside as trivial observations that have been known for all eternity, and violently contested, by the same people, as notorious errors with no other basis than polemical malevolence or envious resentment.

When this has been said, he must not use these resistances, which are very similar to those encountered in psychoanalysis, though more powerful because they are supported by collective mechanisms, as a reason for forgetting that the work of repression and the more or less fantastical constructions that it produces are part of the truth, with the same status as what they seek to disguise. If one recalls, as Husserl does, that 'the arche-original earth does not move', this is not an invitation to repudiate the work of Copernicus in order simply to replace it with the directly experienced truth (as is done by some ethnomethodologists and other constructivist advocates of 'sociologies of freedom', immediately applauded by all those who pine for the 'return of the subject' and the eagerly awaited end of the 'social' and the social sciences). It is simply an invitation to hold together the findings of objectification and the equally clear fact of primary experience, which, by definition, excludes objectification. More precisely, it is a question of accepting the permanent obligation of doing what is necessary in order to objectify the scholastic point of view, which enables the objectifying subject to take a point of view on the point of view of the agents engaged in practice, and to adopt a strange point of view, absolutely inaccessible within practice: the dual, bifocal point of view which, having reappropriated its experience as an empirical 'subject', comprehended in the world and also capable of comprehending the fact of implication and all that is implicit within it, endeavours to include in the (inevitably scholastic) theoretical reconstruction the truth of those who have neither the interest, nor the leisure, nor the necessary instruments to reappropriate the objective and subjective truth of what they are and what they do.

Case study 1: The twofold truth of the gift

This dual view is never, perhaps, more necessary than in the case of the experience of the gift, which cannot fail to strike one by its ambiguity. On the one hand, it is experienced (or intended) as a refusal of self-interest and egoistic calculation, and an exaltation of gratuitous, unrequited generosity. On the other hand, it never entirely excludes awareness of the logic of exchange or even confession of the repressed impulses and, intermittently, the denunciation of another, denied, truth of generous exchange – its constraining and costly character. This leads to the question of the *dual truth* of the gift and of the social conditions that make possible what can be described (somewhat inadequately) as an individual and collective self-deception.

The model I put forward in *Outline of a Theory of Practice* and *The Logic of Practice*[19] takes note of and accounts for the gap between the two truths and, in parallel with this, between the vision that Lévi-Strauss, thinking of Mauss, calls 'phenomenological' (in a rather peculiar sense) and the structural or structuralist approach. It is the lapse of time between the gift and the countergift that makes it possible to mask the contradiction between the experienced (or desired) truth of the gift as a generous, gratuitous, unrequited act, and the truth that emerges from the model, which makes it a stage in

---

[19] *Outline of a Theory of Practice* (Cambridge: Cambridge University Press, 1977) and *The Logic of Practice* (Cambridge: Polity Press, 1990).

a relationship of exchange that transcends singular acts of exchange. In other words, the interval that makes it possible to experience the objective exchange as a discontinuous series of free and generous acts is what makes gift exchange viable and acceptable by facilitating and favouring self-deception, a lie told to oneself, as the condition of the coexistence of recognition and misrecognition of the logic of the exchange.

But it is clear that individual self-deception is only possible because it is supported by a collective self-deception. The gift is one of those social acts whose social logic cannot become 'common knowledge', as economists put it (information is called 'common knowledge' when everyone knows that everyone else knows . . . that everyone has it). More precisely, it cannot be made public and become 'public know-ledge', an official truth, publicly proclaimed (like the great mottoes of the Republic, for example). This collective self-deception is only possible because the *repression* from which it is arises (whose prac-tical condition of possibility is indeed the lapse of time) is inscribed, as an *illusio*, at the foundation of the economy of symbolic goods. This anti-economic economy (using the restricted modern sense of 'economic') is based on the denial (*Verneinung*) of interest and calcula-tion, or, more precisely, on a collective labour devoted to maintain-ing misrecognition with a view to perpetuating a collective faith in the value of the universal, which is simply a form of individual and collective bad faith (in the Sartrian sense of lying to oneself). In other words, it is based on a permanent investment in institutions that, like gift exchange, produce and reproduce trust, and, more profoundly, trust in the fact that trust, that is, generosity, private or civic virtue, will be rewarded. No one is really unaware of the logic of exchange (it constantly surfaces in explicit form, when for example someone wonders whether a present will be judged sufficient), but no one fails to comply with the rule of the game, which is to act as if one did not know the rule. We might coin the term *common miscognition*[20] to designate this game in which everyone knows – and does not want to know – that everyone knows – and does not want to know – the true nature of the exchange.

If social agents can appear as both deceiving and deceived, if they can appear to deceive others and deceive themselves about their (gener-ous) 'intentions', this is because their deception (which can also be said, in a sense, to deceive no one) is sure to encounter the complicity both of the direct addressees of their act and of third parties who observe it. This is because all of them have always been immersed in

---

[20] In English in the original. *Trans.*

a social universe in which gift exchange is *instituted* in the form of an economy of symbolic goods. This quite distinctive economy is based both on specific objective structures and on internalized, embodied structures, *dispositions*, which the objective structures presuppose and which they produce by providing the conditions for their realization. Concretely, this means that the gift as a generous act is only possible for social agents who have acquired – in social universes in which they are expected, recognized and rewarded – generous dispositions adjusted to the objective structures of an economy capable of providing rewards (not only in the form of countergifts) and recognition, in other words a *market*, if such an apparently reductive term is permitted.

This market in symbolic goods presents itself in the form of a system of objective probabilities of profit (positive or negative), or, to use Marcel Mauss's phrase, a set of 'collective expectations' that can be counted on and that have to be reckoned with.[21] In such a social universe, the giver knows that his generous act has every chance of being recognized as such (rather than being seen as a naivety or an absurdity, a 'folly') and of obtaining the recognition (in the form of a countergift or gratitude) from the beneficiary – in particular because all the other agents operating in that world and shaped by its necessity also expect things to be so.

In other words, at the basis of generous action, of the (apparent) inaugural gift in a series of exchanges, there is not the conscious intention (calculating or not) of an isolated individual, but that *disposition* of habitus which is generosity, and which tends, without explicit and express intention, towards the conservation and increase of symbolic capital. Like the sense of honour (which can be the starting point for a series of murders obeying the same logic as gift exchange), this disposition is acquired either by being deliberately taught (as in the case of the young nobleman cited by Norbert Elias: when the son brings back, unspent, the purse of gold coins his father had given him, the father throws it out of the window before his eyes), or through early and prolonged exposure to social worlds in which it is the undisputed law of behaviour. For someone endowed with dispositions attuned to the logic of the economy of symbolic goods, generous conduct is not the product of a choice made by free will and virtue, a free decision made at the end of a deliberation that allows for the possibility of behaving differently; it presents itself as 'the only thing to do'.

---

[21] Cf. M. Mauss, *Œuvres* (Paris: Éditions de Minuit, 1974), vol. 2, p. 117: 'We are together in society in order to expect, together, this or that result.'

Only if one brackets off the *institution* – and the labour, especially the pedagogic labour, of which it is the product – and forgets that both the giver and the receiver are prepared, by the whole labour of socialization, to enter into generous exchange without intention or calculation of profit, to know and recognize the gift for what it is, in its twofold truth, can one bring up the subtle and insoluble paradoxes of an ethical casuistics. If one adopts the standpoint of a philosophy of mind, asking about the intentional meaning of the gift, and performs a kind of 'examination of conscience', seeking to know whether the gift, conceived as the free decision of an isolated individual, is a real gift, is really a gift, or (which amounts to the same thing) whether it conforms to the essence of a gift, to what a gift has to be – then this is indeed sufficient to raise insurmountable antinomies that force one to conclude that a gratuitous gift is impossible.

But if some writers can go so far as to say that the intention of giving destroys the gift, cancelling it out as a gift, that is, as a disinterested act, this is because, succumbing to a particularly acute form of the scholastic bias, and the intellectualist error that accompanies it, they are seeing the two agents involved in the gift as calculators who assign themselves the subjective project of doing what they are objectively doing (according to Lévi-Strauss's model), that is, an exchange obeying the logic of reciprocity. To put it another way, such an analysis puts into the minds of the agents the model that science has had to construct in order to account for their practice (here, the model of gift exchange). This amounts to producing a kind of theoretical monster, impossible in practice: the self-destructive experience of a generous, gratuitous gift that contains the conscious aim of obtaining the countergift, which is posited as a possible end.[22]

---

[22] Through the question of the true gift, the gift that is truly a gift (like, elsewhere, the question of the true observance of the rule, which requires one to go beyond the rule), Jacques Derrida formulates in new terms the old Kantian question of duty and the possibility of detecting some 'secret impulse of amour-propre' behind the greatest sacrifice, the one that is supposed to be performed out of pure duty when it is only performed in a way that 'conforms to duty'. (Such questionings are historically attested in the Byzantine *salos* who lived in the fear that his most saintly actions might be inspired by the symbolic profits associated with saintliness, cf. G. Dagron, 'L'homme sans honneur ou le saint scandaleux', *Annales ESC* (July–Aug. 1990), pp. 929–39.) As soon as every generous action that springs from a generous disposition is rejected as merely 'conforming to generosity', inevitably one denies the possibility of disinterested action, just as Kant, in the name of a similar philosophy of mind or intention, cannot conceive of a single action conforming to duty that cannot be suspected of obeying 'pathological' determinations (cf. J. Derrida, *Passions* (Paris: Galilée, 1993), pp. 87–9; on the – true – gift as 'duty beyond duty', 'law' and 'necessity without duty', see J. Derrida, *Donner le temps*, vol. 1: *La fausse monnaie* (Paris: Galilée, 1991), p. 197).

Thus, it is not possible to reach an adequate understanding of the gift without leaving behind both the philosophy of mind which makes a conscious intention the principle of every action, and the economism which knows no other economy than that of rational calculation and interest reduced to economic interest. Among the consequences of the process through which the economic field was constituted as such, one of the most pernicious, from the point of view of knowledge, is the tacit acceptance of a certain number of principles of division, the emergence of which is correlative with the social construction of the economic field as a separate universe (on the basis of the axiom 'business is business'), as the opposition between passions and interests – principles which, because they impose themselves unexamined, on all those who are immersed, from birth, in the 'icy waters' of the economic economy, tend to govern the science of economics, which itself sprang from that separation.[23] (It is probably because they – sometimes unwittingly – accept this *historically founded* opposition, which is explicitly stated in Pareto's founding distinction between logical actions and non-logical actions, 'residues' or 'derivations', that economists tend to specialize in analysis of behaviour motivated by interest alone: 'Many economists . . .' wrote P. A. Samuelson, 'would separate economics from sociology upon the basis of rational or irrational behavior.'[24])

The gift economy, in contrast to the economy in which equivalent values are exchanged, is based on a denial of the economic (in the narrow sense), on a refusal of the logic of the maximization of economic profit, that is to say, of the spirit of calculation and the exclusive pursuit of material (as opposed to symbolic) interest, a refusal that is inscribed in the objectivity of institutions and in dispositions. It is organized with a view to the accumulation of symbolic capital (a capital of recognition, honour, nobility, etc.) which is brought about in particular through the transmutation of economic capital achieved through the alchemy of symbolic exchanges (exchange of gifts, words, challenges and ripostes, murders, etc.) and only available to agents endowed with dispositions adjusted to the logic of 'disinterestedness'.

The economy of fair exchange is the product of a symbolic revolution that took place progressively, in European societies, with, for example, all the imperceptible processes of unveiling and 'disambiguation' of

---

[23] On the separation which occurred, in the seventeenth and eighteenth centuries, between passions and interests, or exclusively economic motives, see A. Hirschman, *The Passions and the Interests* (Princeton: Princeton University Press, 1977).

[24] P. A. Samuelson, *Foundations of Economic Analysis* (Cambridge: Harvard University Press, 1947), p. 90.

which the 'vocabulary of Indo-European institutions', analysed by Benveniste, conserves the trace, and which led from ransom (of a prisoner) to purchase, from the prize (for a notable action) to the wage, from moral recognition (gratitude) to recognizance, from belief to credit, from moral obligation to legally enforceable agreement.[25] This 'great and venerable revolution', as Marcel Mauss called it, was able to break away from the gift economy, which, he observes, 'was ultimately, at the time, anti-economic', only by progressively suspending the collective denial of the economic foundations of human existence (except in certain reserved sectors: religion, art, the family), so making possible the emergence of pure interest and the generalization of calculation and the spirit of calculation (assisted by the invention of wage labour and the use of money).

The possibility that then opens up of subjecting every kind of activity to the logic of calculation ('in business there's no room for sentiment') tends to legitimate this, so to speak, *official cynicism* which is particularly flaunted in law (with, for example, contracts providing for the most pessimistic and disreputable eventualities) and in economic theory (which, at the beginning, helped to create this economy, just as jurists' treatises on the State, which are often read as treatises of political philosophy, helped to create the State they seemingly describe). This economy, which turns out to be remarkably economical since, in particular, it makes it possible to dispense with the effects of the ambiguity of practices and the 'transaction costs' that weigh so heavily on the economy of symbolic goods (one only has to think of the difference between a personalized gift, which becomes a personal message, and a cheque for the equivalent amount), leads to the legitimation of the use of calculation even in the most sacred areas (purchase of indulgences, or the prayer wheel . . .) and the generalization of the *calculating disposition*, the perfect antithesis of the generous disposition, which comes hand in hand with the development of an economic and social order characterized, as Weber puts it, by calculability and predictability.

The particular difficulty we have in thinking about gifts is due to the fact that as the gift economy has tended to shrink to an island in the ocean of the fair-exchange economy, its meaning has changed (the tendency of some colonial ethnography to see it as no more than a form of credit being simply the limiting case of the propensity to ethnocentric reduction, the effects of which are still to be seen in the most reflexive-seeming analyses). Within an economic universe based

[25] E. Benveniste, *Indo-European Language and Society* (London: Faber, 1973).

on the opposition between passion and interest (or *amour fou* and the marriage of convenience), between things that are free and things that have a price-tag, the gift loses its real meaning as an act situated beyond the opposition between constraint and freedom, individual choice and collective pressure, disinterestedness and self-interest, and becomes a simple rational investment strategy directed towards the accumulation of social capital, with institutions such as public relations and company gifts, or a kind of ethical feat that is impossible to achieve because it is measured against the ideal of the true gift, understood as a perfectly gratuitous and gracious act performed without obligation or expectation, without reason or goal, for nothing.

If one is really to break away from the ethnocentric vision that underlies the questions of economism, and of scholastic philosophy, one would have to examine how the logic of gift exchange leads to the establishment of durable relationships that economic theories based on an ahistorical anthropology cannot comprehend. It is remarkable that economists who rediscover the gift[26] forget, as ever, to pose the question of the economic conditions of these 'anti-economic' acts (in the narrow sense of 'economic') and ignore the specific logic of the economy of symbolic exchanges that makes them possible. Thus, to explain 'how cooperation can arise' between individuals who are presumed to be (by nature) egoistic, 'how reciprocity gives rise to cooperation' between individuals who are held *ex hypothesi* to be 'motivated by their self-interest alone', the 'economics of conventions', an empty intersection between economics and sociology, can only invoke 'convention', a conceptual artefact that no doubt owes its success among economists to the fact that, like Tycho Brahe's attempt to salvage the Ptolemaic model of the universe with conceptual patchwork, it avoids a radical change of paradigm ('a regularity is a convention if everyone complies with it and if everyone expects others to do the same'; 'a convention is the result of an inner deliberation, balancing rules of moral action against instrumental rules of action'). This ad hoc invention cannot really account for social cohesion, either in gift economies – where it is never based entirely upon the orchestration of habitus but always makes room for elementary forms of contract – or in equal-exchange economies, where, although it depends heavily on the constraints of contract, it is also based to a large extent on the orchestration of habitus and on an adjustment

---

[26] Cf. P. Batifoulier, L. Cordonnier and Y. Zenou, 'L'emprunt de la théorie économique à la tradition sociologique, le cas du don contre-don', *Revue Économique*, 5 (Sept. 1992), pp. 917–46.

between the objective structures and the cognitive structures (or dispositions) that ensures the concordance of individual anticipations and 'collective expectations'.

The ambiguity of an economy oriented towards the accumulation of symbolic capital lies in the fact that communication, unduly privileged by the structuralist approach, is one of the channels of domination. The gift is expressed in the language of obligation. It is obligatory, it creates obligations, it obliges; it sets up a legitimate domination. Among other reasons, this is because it brings in the factor of time, by constituting the interval between gift and countergift (or murder and revenge) as a *collective expectation* of the countergift or gratitude or, more clearly, as recognized, legitimate domination, as submission that is accepted or loved. This is put well by La Rochefoucauld, whose position on the cusp between the equal-exchange economy and the gift economy gives him (like Pascal) an extreme lucidity about the subtleties of symbolic exchange, which structuralist ethnology is unaware of: 'Overmuch eagerness to discharge an obligation is a kind of ingratitude.'

Eagerness, normally a sign of submission, is here a sign of impatience with dependence, and therefore virtually an ingratitude, because of the haste it expresses, a haste to acquit a debt, to be quits, to be free to quit (without being forced, like some *khammès* – sharecroppers – in Kabyle society, into shameful flight), to shed an obligation, a recognition of debt. It is a haste to reduce the gap of time which distinguishes the generous exchange of gifts from the harsh exchange of equivalents and which means that one is bound so long as one feels bound to respond; a haste to cancel out the obligation that takes effect with the initial act of generosity and can only grow as recognition of debt, which can always be acquitted, turns into internalized gratitude, incorporated recognition, inscribed in the body itself in the form of passion, love, submission, respect, an unrepayable and, as people often say, everlasting debt.

Symbolic power relations are power relations that are set up and perpetuated through knowledge and recognition, which does not mean through intentional acts of consciousness. In order for symbolic domination to be set up, the dominated have to share with the dominant the schemes of perception and appreciation through which they are perceived by them and through which they perceive them; they have to see themselves as they are seen. In other words, their knowledge and recognition have to be rooted in practical dispositions of acceptance and submission, which, because they do not pass through deliberation and decision, escape the dilemma of consent or constraint.

Here we are at the heart of the transmutation that is the basis of symbolic power, a power that is created, accumulated and perpetuated through communication, through symbolic exchange. Because it brings matters to the level of knowledge and recognition (which implies that it can only occur between agents capable of communicating and understanding each other, therefore endowed with the same cognitive schemes and inclined to communicate and consequently to recognize each other as legitimate interlocutors, equal in honour, to agree to talk, to be 'on speaking terms'), communication converts brute power relations, which are always uncertain and liable to be suspended, into durable relations of symbolic power through which a person is bound and feels bound. It transfigures economic capital into symbolic capital, economic domination into personal dependence (in paternalism, etc.), even into devotion, (filial) piety or love. Generosity is possessive, and perhaps all the more so when, as in affective exchanges (between parents and children, or even between lovers) it is and appears most sincerely generous. 'It is unjust that men should attach themselves to me, even though they do it with pleasure and voluntarily. I should deceive those in whom I had created this desire; for I am not the end of any, and I have not the wherewithal to satisfy them. Am I not about to die? And thus the object of their attachment will die. Therefore, as I would be blamable in causing a falsehood to be believed, though I should employ gentle persuasion, though it should be believed with pleasure, and though it should give me pleasure; even so I am blameable in making myself loved.'[27] (The crises of the gift economy, which are always particularly tragic, coincide with the breaking of enchantment that reduces the logic of symbolic exchange to the order of economic exchange: 'After all we've done for you ...')

Here too, time plays a decisive role. The inaugural act that institutes communication (by addressing words, offering a gift, issuing an invitation or a challenge, etc.) always entails a kind of intrusion or even a calling into question (hence the interrogative precautions that tend to accompany it, as Bally observed: 'May I ask you the time?'). In addition, it always inevitably contains the potentiality of a hold, a bond. It is true that, contrary to what the structuralists' mechanical model would suggest, it implies uncertainty and therefore a temporal opening: one can always choose not to reply to the interpellation, invitation or challenge or not to reply immediately, to defer and to leave the other party in expectation. But non-response is still a response and it is not so easy to shrug off the initial calling into question,

[27] Pascal, *Pensées*, 471.

which acts as a kind of *fatum*, a destiny. The meaning of a positive response (repartee, countergift, riposte) is no doubt unequivocal as an affirmation and recognition of equality in honour that can be taken as the starting point for a long series of exchanges; by contrast, absence of response is essentially ambiguous and can always be interpreted, by the initiator or by others, either as a refusal to respond and a kind of snub or as an evasion attributable to impotence or cowardice, entailing dishonour.

The exotic or extra-ordinary character of the objects to which analyses of exchange have been applied, such as potlatch, has indeed caused it to be forgotten that the seemingly most gratuitous and least costly relations of exchange, such as expressions of concern, kindness, consideration or advice, not to mention acts of generosity that cannot be repaid, such as charity, when they are set up in conditions of lasting asymmetry (in particular because they link people separated by an unbridgeable economic or social gulf) and when they exclude the possibility of an equivalent in return, the very hope of an active reciprocity, which is the condition of possibility of genuine autonomy, are likely to create lasting relations of dependence, euphemized variants of enslavement for debt in archaic societies. For they tend to become inscribed in the body itself in the form of belief, trust, affection and passion, and any attempt to transform them through consciousness and will comes up against the stubborn resistance of affects and the tenacious injunctions of guilt.

Although there is apparently every difference in the world between them, the structuralist ethnologist who makes exchange the creative principle of the social bond and the neo-marginalist economist who desperately seeks the specifically economic principles of cooperation between agents reduced to the state of isolated atoms are united in ignoring the economic and social conditions in which historical agents are produced and reproduced, endowed (by their upbringing) with durable dispositions that make them able and inclined to enter into exchanges, equal or unequal, that give rise to durable relations of dependence. Whether it is the *philia* which, in the ideal vision at least, governs domestic relations, or the trust accorded to a person or an institution (a well-reputed trademark, for example), these relations of 'trust' or 'credit' are not necessarily grounded in and set up by rational economic calculation (as is sometimes supposed by those who seek to explain the trust placed in long-established companies by the length of the critical tests they have had to overcome), and they can always be ascribed to the durable domination that symbolic violence secures.

One would need to analyse here all the forms of necessarily ostentatious *redistribution* through which individuals (almost always the richest ones, naturally, as with the Greek munificence ('evergetism') analysed by Paul Veyne,[28] or royal or princely largesse) or institutions, companies (with their great foundations) or the State itself tend to set up asymmetrical relations of dependence of recognition–gratitude based on the credit granted to beneficence. One would also need to analyse the long process through which symbolic power, the accumulation of which initially benefited one individual, as in potlatch, gradually ceases to be the basis of personal power (through the personal appropriation of a clientele, distribution of gifts, livings, honours, grace and favours, as in the period of absolute monarchy) and becomes the basis of an impersonal State authority, through the bureaucratic redistribution which, although in principle it obeys the rule 'the State makes no presents' (to private individuals), never completely excludes – with corruption – forms of personal appropriation and patronage. Thus, through redistribution, taxation enters into a cycle of symbolic production in which economic capital is transformed into symbolic capital. As in potlatch, redistribution is necessary in order to secure the recognition of the distribution. While, as the official reading insists, it obviously tends to correct the inequalities of the distribution, it also and more importantly tends to produce recognition of the legitimacy of the State – one of the many things the opponents of the Welfare State forget in their short-term calculations.

What is underlined through gift exchange, a collective hypocrisy in and through which society pays homage to its dream of virtue and disinterestedness, is the fact that virtue is a political matter, that it is not and cannot be abandoned, with no other resource than a vague 'deontology', to the singular, isolated efforts of individual minds and wills or the examinations of conscience of a confessor's casuistics. The cult of individual success, preferably economic, that has accompanied the expansion of neoliberalism has tended – in a period when, to make it easier to 'blame the victims', there is a greater tendency than ever to pose political problems in moral terms – to obscure the need for collective investment in the institutions that produce the economic and social conditions for virtue, or, to put it another way, that cause the civic virtues of disinterestedness and devotion – a gift to the group – to be encouraged and rewarded by the group. The purely speculative and typically scholastic question of whether generosity and disinterestedness are possible should give way to the political question of the means that have to be implemented in order to create universes in which, as in gift economies, agents and groups would

---

[28] P. Veyne, *Le Pain et le cirque: sociologie historique d'un pluralisme politique* (Paris: Éditions du Seuil, 1976), pp. 185–373.

have an interest in disinterestedness and generosity, or, rather, could acquire a durable disposition to respect these universally respected forms of respect for the universal.

Case study 2: The twofold truth of labour

Like the gift, labour can be understood in its *objectively* twofold truth only if one performs the *second reversal* needed in order to break with the scholastic error of failing to include in the theory the 'subjective' truth with which it was necessary to break, in a first para-doxal reversal, in order to construct the object of analysis. The objectification that was necessary to constitute wage labour in its objective truth has masked the fact which, as Marx himself indicates, only becomes the objective truth in certain exceptional labour situations:[29] the investment in labour, and therefore miscognition of the objective truth of labour as exploitation, which leads people to find an intrinsic profit in labour, irreducible to simple monetary income, is part of the real conditions of the performance of labour, and of exploitation.

The logic of the (theoretical) move to the limiting case disguises the fact that these conditions are very rarely realized and that the situation in which the worker expects only his wage from his labour is often experienced, at least in some historical contexts (for example, in Algeria in the 1960s), as profoundly abnormal. The experience of labour lies between two extremes, forced labour, which is determined only by external constraint, and scholastic labour, the limiting case which is the quasi-ludic activity of the artist or writer. The further someone moves from the former, the less they work directly for money and the more the 'interest' of work, the inherent gratification of the fact of performing the work, increases – as does the interest linked to the symbolic profits associated with the name of the occupation or the occupational status and the quality of the working relations which often go hand in hand with the intrinsic interest of the labour. (It is because work in itself provides a profit that the loss of employment entails a symbolic mutilation which can be attributed as much to the loss of the *raisons d'être* associated with work and the world of

---

[29] The equalization of differences in rates of profit presupposes the mobility of the labour force which itself presupposes, among other things: 'indifference of the labourer to the nature [*Inhalt*] of his labour; the greatest possible reduction of labour in all spheres of production to simple labour; the elimination of all vocational prejudices among labourers' (K. Marx, *Capital*, vol. 3, part 2, ch. 10 (London: Lawrence and Wishart, 1974), p. 196).

work as to the loss of the wage.) Workers may contribute to their own exploitation through the very effort they make to appropriate their work, which *binds* them to it through the freedoms – often minute and almost always 'functional' – that are left to them, and under the effect of the competition born of the differences – relative to unskilled workers, immigrants, the young, women – that are constitutive of the occupational space functioning as a field.[30] This is especially true when the dispositions that Marx calls 'vocational prejudices' ('professional conscience', 'respect for the tools of production', etc), which are acquired in certain conditions (occupational heredity, in particular) find the conditions for their actualization in certain characteristics of the work itself, such as competition in the occupational space, with, for example, bonuses or symbolic privileges, or the granting of some room for manoeuvre in the organization of tasks, which enables the worker to create areas of freedom and to invest in his labour all the additional commitment not provided for in the employment contract and which the 'work to rule' precisely aims to refuse and withdraw.

It can be assumed that the subjective truth is that much further removed from the objective truth when the worker has greater control over his own labour (thus, in the case of subcontracting craftsmen or small farmers supplying agribusiness, it may take the form of self-exploitation); and also when the place of work (office, department or company) functions more as a competitive space generating stakes irreducible to their strictly economic dimension and capable of producing investments that bear no relation to the economic profits received in return (with for example the new forms of exploitation of the holders of cultural capital in industrial research, advertising, the media, etc., along with all the forms of payment in symbolic profits, at little economic cost, since a productivity bonus can act as much by its distinctive effect as by its economic value).

Finally, the effect of these structural factors obviously depends on the workers' dispositions: the propensity to invest in work and to misrecognize its objective truth no doubt rises with the degree to which collective expectations inscribed in the job description correspond more fully to the dispositions of its occupant (for example, in the case of junior civil servants with supervisory functions, commitment to the institution, rigour, etc.). Thus, what is apparently most 'subjective' and personal' is an integral part of the reality that analysis

---

[30] *A contrario*, the consequences of the absence of all the social conditions of the experience of work as valorized and valorizing can also be observed (cf. L. Duroy, 'Embauché dans une usine', *Actes de la Recherche en Sciences Sociales*, 115 (Dec. 1996), pp. 38–47).

has to account for in each case in models capable of integrating the representations of the agents, which, sometimes realistic, often fictitious, sometimes fantastical, but always partial, are always partially effective.

In the most constraining work situations, such as production-line work, investment in labour tends to vary inversely with the external constraint in the labour. It follows that, in many work situations, the *margin of freedom* left to the worker (the degree of vagueness in the job description which gives some scope for manoeuvre) is a central stake: it introduces the risk of non-work or even sabotage, going slow, etc.; but it opens the possibility of investment in work or self-exploitation. This depends, to a large extent, on how it is perceived, appreciated and understood (and therefore on schemes of perception, and in particular on occupational, and trade union, traditions, and also on memory of the conditions in which it was acquired or won, and on the previous situation). Paradoxically, it is because it is perceived as a conquest (for example, the freedom to smoke a cigarette, to move around, etc.) or even a privilege (granted to the longest serving or the most skilled) that it can help to mask the overall constraint which gives it its whole value. The minor privilege that people cling to makes them forget all the rest (thus, in asylums, the small perks of the oldest inmates make them forget the asylum and join in the process of 'asylumization', as described by Goffman, a role similar to that of small individual or collective conquests in the process of 'factory-ization'). The strategies of the dominant can rely on what might be called the principle of Socrates' shackles, which consists in alternating the hardening of constraint and tension and partial relaxation, which makes the return to the previous state appear as a privilege, the lesser evil as a good (and which places the old-timers, and union officials, the guardians of the memory of these alternations and their effects, in a difficult position, generating position-takings which may sometimes appear conservative).[31]

Thus the scope for manoeuvre that agents win for themselves (and which theories of 'resistance' are quick to celebrate, in their concern to rehabilitate, as proof of inventiveness) may be the condition of their contribution to their own exploitation. It is on this principle that modern management theory, while taking care to keep control of the instruments of profit, leaves workers the freedom to organize their own work, thus helping to increase their well-being but also to

---

[31] The same principle applies at the level of the collective of the employees of a company, with threats of redundancies (30,000 jobs have to go) which make the real lay-offs (perhaps 5,000 jobs) seem like a favour or a victory.

displace their interest from the external profit of labour (the wage) to the intrinsic profit. The new techniques of company management, and especially what is known as 'participatory management', can be understood as an effort to make methodical and systematic use of all the possibilities that the ambiguity of labour objectively offers to employers' strategies. Unlike, for example, the bureaucratic charisma which enables an administrative manager to obtain a form of excess work and self-exploitation, the new strategies of manipulation – 'job enrichment', encouragement of innovation and communication of innovation, 'quality circles', permanent evaluation, self-evaluation – which aim to encourage investment in work are consciously devised and explicitly set out on the basis of scientific studies, either general or applied to the particular company.

But the illusion that one might sometimes have of the realization, at least in some places, of the utopia of total control by the worker over his own work should not lead one to forget the hidden conditions of the symbolic violence exerted by the new forms of management. While it may exclude recourse to the most brutal and most visible constraints of the old modes of control, this gentle violence continues to be based on a power relation which resurfaces in the threat of redundancy and in fear, more or less deliberately maintained, linked to the precariousness of the position occupied. Hence a contradiction, with whose effects managerial staff have long been familiar, between the imperatives of symbolic violence, which require a whole effort to disguise and transfigure the objective truth of the labour of domination, and the structural conditions of its exercise. This contradiction is all the greater when the recourse to redundancies as a technique of commercial and financial adjustment tends to expose the structural violence of the situation.

6

Social Being, Time and the Sense of Existence

~∿~

The scholastic situation implies, by definition, a particularly free relationship to what is normally called time, since, as a suspending of urgency, the pressure of 'things to do', of business and busyness, it inclines us to consider 'time' as a thing with which we have a relation of externality, that of a subject facing an object. This vision is reinforced by the habits of ordinary language, which make time something that one has, that one gains or wastes, lacks or has on one's hands, etc. Like the body-as-thing of the Cartesian idealist vision, time-as-thing, the time of clock-makers and scientists, is the product of a scholastic point of view which has found its expression in a metaphysics of time and history which considers history either as a pregiven reality, a thing in-itself, previous and external to practice, or as the (empty) *a priori* framework for every historical process. We can break with this point of view by reconstructing the point of view of the acting agent, of practice as 'temporalization', thereby revealing that practice is not *in* time but *makes* time (human time, as opposed to biological or astronomical time).

One cannot constitute a still non-present reality as a present centre of interest, 'presentiate' it as Husserl says, without 'depresentiating' what has just been actualized, sending it back into the non-actual, as an unperceived background, in the margins that one has had dealings with and will again have dealings with.[1] As a consequence, to take an

---

[1] E. Husserl, *Ideas: General Introduction to Pure Phenomenology* (London: Allen and Unwin, 1931), esp. pp. 101ff.

interest, to constitute some reality or other as a *centre of interest*, is to set in motion the process of 'presentiation–depresentiation', 'actualization–deactualization', 'interest–disinterest', in other words to 'temporalize' oneself, to *make* time, in a relationship to the directly perceived present which has nothing in common with a project. In opposition to the indifference which apprehends the world as devoid of interest and importance, the *illusio* (or interest in the game) is what gives 'sense' (both meaning and direction) to existence by leading one to invest in a game and in its forth-coming [*son à venir*], in the *lusiones*,[2] the chances, that it offers to those who are caught up in the game and who expect something from it (which gives a foundation to the belief that it is sufficient to define the *illusio* as illusion, and to suspend interest, and the forward rush, into 'diversion', that it determines, in order to suspend time).

And to be able to capture the truth of the ordinary experience of pre-occupation and immersion in the forth-coming in which time passes unnoticed, one also has to question the intellectualist view of temporal experience which excludes any other relation to the future than the conscious project, aiming at ends and possibles that are posited as such. This typically scholastic representation is based, as ever, on the substitution of a reflexive vision for the practical vision. Husserl did indeed clearly establish that the *project* as a conscious aiming at the future in its reality as a contingent future must not be conflated with *protention*, a prereflexive aiming at a forth-coming which offers itself as quasi-present in the visible, like the hidden faces of a cube, that is, with the same belief status (the same doxic modality) as what is directly perceived; and that it is only when it is retrieved in scholastic reflection that it can appear, retrospectively, as a project, which it is not in practice (all the paradoxes concerning contingent futures spring from the fact that practice is being asked questions of truth – what will be true or false tomorrow must be true or false today – which arise for the observer but which, except in crisis situations, when the process of 'actualization–deactualization' is suspended, remain unknown to the agent whose sense of the game is immediately adjusted to the forth-coming of the game.).[3]

The imminent forth-coming is present, immediately visible, as a present property of things, to the point of excluding the possibility that it will not come about, a possibility which exists theoretically so

---

[2] *Lusiones* is, with *casus*, *alea*, *sors* and *fortuna*, one of the words used by Huyghens to designate chances (cf. I. Hacking, *The Emergence of Probability: A Philosophical Study of Early Ideas about Probability, Induction and Statistical Inference* (Cambridge: Cambridge University Press, 1975).

[3] Cf. J. Vuillemin, *Nécessité ou contingence, l'aporie de Diode et les systèmes philosophiques* (Paris: Éditions de Minuit, 1988).

long as it has not come about. This is particularly clear in the case of emotion, fear for example, which, as is testified by the reactions of the body, especially its internal secretions, similar to those that would be provoked by the situation that is anticipated, sees the forth-coming – the threatening dog, the onrushing car – as something already-there, irremediable ('I'm done for', 'I'm a goner').[4] But, beyond these extreme situations in which, being really put at stake by the world, the body is snatched by the forth-coming of the world, what we aim at in ordinary action is not a contingent future: the good player is the one who, as in Pascal's example, 'places' the ball better or who places himself not where the ball is but where it is about to land. In either case, the forth-coming in relation to which he positions himself is not a possible which may happen or not happen but something which is already there in the configuration of the game and in the present positions and postures of team-mates and opponents.

The presence of the forth-coming

Thus, the experience of time is engendered in the relationship between habitus and the social world, between the dispositions to be and to do and the regularities of a natural and social cosmos (or a field). It arises, more precisely, in the relationship between the practical expectations or hopes which are constitutive of an *illusio* as investment in a social game, and the tendencies immanent to this game, the probabilities of fulfilment that they offer to these expectations, or, more precisely, the structure of the mathematical probabilities, *lusiones*, that is characteristic of the game in question. Practical anticipation of a forth-coming inscribed in the immediate present, protention, pre-occupation, is the most common form of the experience of time, a paradoxical experience, like that of the self-evidence of the familiar world, since time does not offer itself in it to be felt and passes in a sense unnoticed (someone who has been engrossed in an activity will say 'I didn't notice time passing').

Time (or at least what we call time) is really experienced only when the quasi-automatic coincidence between expectations and chances, *illusio* and *lusiones*, expectations and the world which is there to fulfil them, is broken. We then feel directly the breaking of the tacit collusion between the course of the world – astronomical

---

[4] Because he treats it not as protention, an anticipation endowed with the doxic modality of perception, but as a project aimed at a contingent future, Sartre cannot ground the seriousness of an emotion such as fear, which is thus reduced to a form of 'bad faith'.

movements (such as the cycle of the seasons) or biological processes (such as ageing), or social processes (such as family life cycles or bureaucratic careers), over which we have less than full power or no power at all – and the internal movements which relate to them (*illusio*). It is the discrepancy between what is anticipated and the logic of the game in relation to which this anticipation was formed, between a 'subjective' disposition (which does not mean an internal or mental one) and an objective tendency, which gives rise to relations to time such as waiting or impatience – the situation in which, as Pascal says, 'we anticipate the future as too slow in coming, as if in order to hasten its course' – regret or nostalgia – the feeling experienced when the object whose presence is desired is no longer there, or threatens to disappear, and 'we recall the past, to stop its too rapid flight'[5] – boredom or 'discontent' in the sense used by Hegel (as read by Eric Weil), a dissatisfaction with the present that implies the negation of the present and the propensity to work towards its supersession.

(Immersion in the forth-coming as a presence to the future which is not experienced as such contrasts with some forms of the experience of 'free time' – particularly prized by overworked executives – such as the one which consists in living the temporary *skholè* of holidays as an existence liberated from time because liberated from *illusio*, from pre-occupation, through the suspension of insertion into the field and therefore in the competition (there is much talk of 'clearing the deck' and 'cooling out') and, when the case arises, by insertion into universes without competition, such as the family and some holiday 'clubs', fictitious social universes, often experienced as 'liberated' and 'liberating' because they bring together strangers who have no stakes in common, who are stripped of their social investments – and not only of their clothes and their hierarchical attributes, as the journalistic vision would have it. In fact, unless a special effort is made, 'free time' does not readily escape from the logic of investment in 'things to do', which even when it does not go as far as the explicit concern to 'succeed in one's holidays', according to the precepts of the women's magazines, prolongs the competition for the accumulation of symbolic capital in various forms: suntan, souvenirs or anecdotes, photos or films, monuments, museums, landscapes, places to visit or explore or simply to 'do' – 'we've done Greece . . .' – by implementing the imperative suggestions of the tourist guides.)

What is aimed at by the pre-occupation of practical sense, an anticipated presence to what it aims at, is a forth-coming already present

---

[5] Pascal, *Pensées*, 172.

in the immediate present and not constituted as future. The project, by contrast, or premeditation, posits the end as such, that is, as one end chosen among all others and coloured by the same modality, that of the contingent future, which may happen or not happen. If one accepts Hegel's demonstration in which the design, the project, the *Vorsatz*, presupposes representation, *Vorstellung*, and intention, *Absicht*, which itself presupposes abstraction, the separation of subject and object, it is clear that one is indeed in the order of the conscious and the reflected, of action conscious of itself in its objective reality as the actualization of a possible.[6]

The present is the set of those things to which one is present, in other words, in which one is interested (as opposed to indifferent, or absent). It therefore cannot be reduced to a momentary instant (which only appears, it seems to me, in the critical moments when the forth-coming does not come, but is suspended, in question, objectively or subjectively): it encompasses the practical anticipations and retrospections that are inscribed as objective potentialities or traces in the immediate given. Habitus is that presence of the past in the present which makes possible the presence in the present of the forth-coming. It follows from this first that, having within itself its own logic (*lex*) and its own dynamic (*vis*), it is not mechanically subjected to an external causality, and that it gives a freedom with respect to direct and immediate determination by the present circumstances (in contrast to what is asserted by mechanistic instantaneism). The autonomy with respect to the immediate event, a trigger rather than a determinant, that is given by habitus (and which becomes manifest when a fortuitous and insignificant stimulus, such as the 'heather-mixture stocking' in *To the Lighthouse*, provokes a disproportionate reaction[7]) is correlative with the dependence on the past that it introduces and which orients one towards a certain forth-coming: habitus combines in a single aim a past and a forth-coming neither of which is posited as such. The already-present forth-coming can be read in the present only on the basis of a past that is itself never aimed at as such (habitus as incorporated acquisition being a presence of the past – or to the past – and not memory of the past).

The capacity to anticipate and to see in advance that is acquired in and through practice and familiarization with a field is nothing like a knowledge that can be mobilized at will by means of an act of memory.

[6] G. W. F. Hegel, *Philosophy of Right*, tr. T. M. Knox (Oxford: Clarendon Press, 1942).

[7] V. Woolf, *To the Lighthouse* (London: Hogarth Press, 1927), and E. Auerbach, *Mimesis: The Representation of Reality in Western Literature* (Princeton: Princeton University Press, 1953), pp. 525ff.

It is only manifested in concrete situations and is linked as if by a relation of *mutual prompting* to the occasion which calls it forth and which it causes to exist as an opportunity to be seized (whereas someone else would let it pass, unnoticed). Interest takes the form of an encounter with the objectivity of things 'full of interest'. 'We are', says Pascal, 'full of things which take us out of ourselves. Our instinct makes us feel that we must seek our happiness outside ourselves. Our passions impel us outside, even when no objects present themselves to excite them. External objects tempt us of themselves, and call to us, even when we are not thinking of them. And thus philosophers have said in vain: "Retire within yourselves, you will find your good there." We do not believe them, and those who believe them are the most empty and the most foolish.'[8] The things to do, things to be done (*pragmata*) which are the correlate of practical knowledge, are defined in the relationship between the structure of the hopes or expectations constitutive of a habitus and the structure of probabilities which is constitutive of a social space. This means that the objective probabilities are determinant only for an agent endowed with the sense of the game in the form of the capacity to anticipate the forth-coming of the game. (This anticipation relies on a practical precategorization based on the implementation of the schemes of habitus which, arising from experience of the regularities of existence, structure the contingencies of life in terms of previous experience and make it possible to anticipate in practice the probable futures previously classified as good or bad, bringing satisfactions or frustrations. This practical sense of the forth-coming has nothing in common with a rational calculation of chances – as shown by the discrepancies between an explicit appreciation of probabilities and practical anticipation, which is both more precise and more rapid, as is shown by the well-known observations of Amos Tversky and Daniel Kahneman, or the experience, familiar to all of us, of the unexpected feeling that occurs when a lift, instead of going straight down to the ground floor, stops at the first floor, where someone has called it, showing us that we have an embodied measurement of the usual duration of the ride, a measurement which cannot be precisely expressed in seconds, although it is very accurate, since the gap between the first floor and the ground floor is only a couple of seconds.)

The sense of the game is that sense of the forth-coming of the game, of what is to be done ('it was the only thing to do' or 'he did what was needed') in order to bring about the forth-coming state of the game that is visible there for a habitus predisposed to anticipate

[8] Pascal, *Pensées*, 464.

it, the sense of the history of the game, which is only acquired through experience of the game – which means that the imminence and pre-eminence of the forth-coming presuppose a disposition which is the product of the past. Strategies oriented by the sense of the game are practical anticipations of the immanent tendencies of the field, never stated in the form of explicit forecasts, still less in the form of norms or rules of behaviour – especially in fields in which the most effective strategies are the ones which appear as the most disinterested. The game, which both provokes and presupposes investment in the game, interest in the game, produces the forth-coming for someone who has something to expect from the game. Conversely, investment or interest, which presupposes possession of a habitus and a capital capable of providing it with at least a minimum of profits, is what brings people into the game, and into the time that is specific to it, that is to say, the forth-coming and the urgencies that it offers. It is proportionate to capital as profit potential – disappearing when the chances of appropriation fall below a certain threshold.

(Like the future, the past is the product of investment in the present, that is, in the game and in the stakes that are constitutive of the game. People are not as surprised as they should be by the fact that a cultural object of the past – a monument, piece of furniture, a text, a painting, etc. – can be not only conserved in its material substance, like fossils, ruins or 'archives' forgotten in attics, but rescued from symbolic death, from the state of a *dead letter*, and kept alive, that is to say, in the ambiguous status which defines the historical object, which is at once out of use, detached from its original use, its original field – like tools, machines or religious implements converted into museum pieces – and yet continuously used and reactivated as an object of contemplation or speculation (in both senses), dissertation or meditation. We can give Heidegger credit for having raised this problem in the analysis of what causes the 'antiquities' conserved in a museum to be 'past'. But he encounters the question of whether these objects are historic as 'objects of a historiographic interest of archaeology and ethnology' only to dismiss it with one of those inversions of which he is the master, enabling him always to situate himself outside 'naive anthropology': it is not the present interest of historians in history that makes the historical object, it is the historicity of *Dasein*, the proper object of existential analysis, which makes historicity and historical interest. In fact, as is recalled by the Kabyle belief that a man's chances of surviving disappearance depend on the number and quality of the descendants that he has produced and who will be able to cite his name and so resuscitate him, the principle of the selective survival of the past lies in the present. Technical or

cultural objects can achieve the status of ancient works, deserving to
be conserved and durably admired, only in so far as they become the
object of competition for the monopoly of the material or symbolic
appropriation, interpretation, 'reading', performance, that is regarded
as legitimate at a given time. Thus, inherited writings – whether they
be esoteric texts which only owe their survival to the conflicts of
specialists, or great religious or political prophetic works capable of
mobilizing groups by modifying their schemes of perception and therefore their practices, in the name of the *belief* they are granted – are
never the real causes or the pure pretexts of the conflicts they arouse,
although people always proceed as if the whole value of the stake
had its principle not in the game, but in the intrinsic properties of the
stake.)

So it is in and by practice, through the practical implication that it
implies, that social agents temporalize themselves. But they can 'make'
time only in so far as they are endowed with habitus adjusted to the
field, that is, to the sense of the game (or of investment), understood
as a capacity to anticipate, in the practical mode, forth-comings [*des
à venir*] that present themselves in the very structure of the game; or,
in other words, in so far as they have been constituted in such a way
that they are disposed to see objective potentialities in the present
structure which force themselves upon them as things to be done.
Time is indeed, as Kant maintained, the product of an act of construction, but it is the work not of the thinking consciousness but of
the dispositions and practice.

'The order of successions'

Investment is associated with uncertainty, but a limited and, in a
sense, regulated uncertainty (which explains the pertinence of the
analogy with games). In order for the particular relationship between
subjective expectations and objective chances which defines investment, interest or *illusio* to be set up, the objective chances have to be
situated between absolute necessity and absolute impossibility; the
agent has to have chances of winning which are neither nil (losing on
every throw) nor total (winning on every throw). In other words,
nothing must be absolutely sure, but not everything must be possible.
There has to be some degree of indeterminacy, contingency in the
game, some 'play', but also a certain necessity in the contingency,
and therefore the possibility of knowledge, a form of reasonable anticipation, the one provided by custom, or, failing that, the 'doctrine of
chances' which Pascal tries to work out and which, as he says, makes

it possible to 'work for the uncertain'.[9] (And indeed, the social order is situated between two limits: on the one hand, radical determinism, logicist or physicalist, leaving no room for the 'uncertain', on the other, total indetermination, the credo – denounced by Hegel as the 'atheism of the moral world'[10] – of those who, in the name of the Cartesian distinction between the physical and the mental, deny the social world the necessity they grant to the natural world – like Donald Davidson, to take but one example, who asserts that there can be 'strict' laws and 'precise' predictions, based on a 'serious' determinism, only in the physical domain.[11])

It is only in the relationship with the immanent tendencies of a social universe, and the probabilities inscribed in its regularities or in the mechanisms ensuring the stability of the distributions and the principles of redistribution, and therefore of the chances of profit on the various markets, that dispositions (preferences, tastes) can be constituted that are both not indifferent to the game and capable of making differences in it, and that these dispositions can engender hope or despair, expectation or impatience, and all the other states of mind through which we experience time. More precisely, it is because it is the product of a durable confrontation with a social world presenting indisputable regularities that habitus can ensure a minimal adaptation to the probable course of this world, through 'reasonable' anticipations, roughly adjusted (outside of any calculation) to the objective chances and tending to contribute to the circular reinforcement of these regularities (thereby giving the appearances of a foundation to models, especially economic ones, based on the hypothesis of rational action[12]).

The social world is not a game of chance, a discontinuous series of perfectly independent events, like the spins of a roulette wheel (whose attraction, as Dostoevsky suggests in *The Gambler*, is explained by the fact that it can enable a person to move in an instant from the lowest to the highest rung of the social ladder). Those who talk of equality of opportunity forget that social games – the economic game, but also the cultural games (the religious field, the juridical field, the

---

[9] Pascal, *Pensées*, 234.

[10] Hegel, *Philosophy of Right*.

[11] D. Davidson, *Essays on Actions and Events* (Oxford: Oxford University Press, 1980).

[12] This is one of the cases which most clearly illustrate the logic whereby social mechanisms, far from revealing themselves, disguise themselves as illusions of intentionality, rationality or even free choice. The scholastic illusion leads one to record in a naive description social realities as they appear to a gaze that is itself caught, without realizing it, in those mechanisms.

philosophical field, etc.) are not 'fair games'. Without being, strictly speaking, rigged, the competition resembles a handicap race that has lasted for generations or games in which each player has the positive or negative score of all those who have preceded him, that is, the cumulated scores of all his ancestors. And they should rather be compared to games in which the players progressively accumulate positive or negative profits, and therefore a more or less great capital, which, together with the tendencies (to prudence, daring, etc.) inherent in their habitus and partly linked to the volume of their capital, orient their playing strategies.

The social world has a history and, for this reason, it is the site of an internal dynamic, independent of the consciousness and will of the players, a kind of *conatus* linked to the existence of mechanisms which tend to reproduce the structure of the objective probabilities or, more precisely, the structure of the distribution of capital and of the corresponding chances of profit. To speak of a tendency or a *conatus* is to say that, like Popper, one regards the values taken by probability functions as measures of the strength of the propensity of the corresponding events to produce themselves – what Leibniz called their *pretentio ad existendum*. That is why, to designate the temporal logic of this social cosmos, one could speak of the 'order of successions': thanks to the double meaning of the word 'succession', Leibniz's definition of time also evokes the logic of social reproduction, the regularities and rules of the transmission of powers and privileges which is the condition of the permanence of the social order as a regular distribution of *lusiones*, of probabilities or objective expectations.

What determines this redundancy of the social world and, by limiting the space of possibles, makes it livable, capable of being practically foreseen through the practical induction of habitus? On the one hand, there are the tendencies immanent in agents in the form of habitus that are (mostly) coherent and (relatively) constant (over time) and (more or less precisely) orchestrated, which tend (statistically) to reconstitute the structures of which they are the product; and on the other hand there are the tendencies immanent in the social universes, particularly in the fields, which are the product of mechanisms independent of consciousnesses and wills, or of rules or codes explicitly designed to ensure the conservation of the established order (precapitalist societies depend mainly on habitus for their reproduction whereas capitalist societies depend principally on objective mechanisms, such as those which tend to guarantee the reproduction of economic capital and cultural capital, to which should be added all the forms of organizational constraints – one thinks of the postman discussed by

Schutz[13] – and codifications of practices, customs, conventions, law, some of which are expressly designed, as Weber observes, to ensure predictability and calculability.

The relationship between expectations and chances

I have so far argued as if the two dimensions constitutive of temporal experience – subjective expectations and the objective chances, or more precisely the actual or potential power over the immanent tendencies of the social world which governs the chances attached to an agent (or his or her position) – were identical for all; as if, in other words, all agents had both the same chances of material and symbolic profit (and were therefore, in a sense, dealing with the same economic and social world) and the same dispositions to invest. But agents have powers (defined by the volume and structure of their capital) which are very unequal. As for their expectations and aspirations, these are also very unequally distributed (despite some cases of mismatch with the capacities for satisfaction), by virtue of the law that, through the dispositions of habitus (themselves adjusted, most of the time, to agents' positions) expectations tend universally to be roughly adapted to the objective chances.

This tendential law of human behaviours, whereby the subjective hope of profit tends to be adjusted to the objective probability of profit, governs the propensity to invest (money, work, time, emotion, etc.) in the various fields. So it is that the propensity of families and children to invest in education (which is itself one of the major factors of educational success) depends on the degree to which they depend on the educational system for the reproduction of their capital and their social position, and on the chances of success for these investments in view of the volume of the cultural capital they possess – these two factors combining to determine the considerable differences in attitudes towards schooling and in success at school (those for example which separate the child of a university teacher from the child of a manual worker, or even the child of a primary teacher from the child of a small shopkeeper).

One is always surprised to see how much people's wills adjust to their possibilities, their desires to the capacity to satisfy them; and to discover that, contrary to all received ideas, *pleonexia*, the desire always to have more, as Plato called it, is the exception (and can,

---

[13] A. Schutz, *Collected Papers*, vol. 2 (The Hague, Boston, London: Martinus Wijhoff, 1962), p. 45.

moreover, be understood, as will be seen, in terms of the fundamental law). This is true even in societies where, with the generalization of schooling, generating a structural *déclassement* linked to the
devaluation of educational qualifications, and the generalization of
insecurity of employment, the mismatch between expectations and
chances becomes more frequent. Whenever the dispositions that produce them are themselves the product of conditions identical or similar to those in which they are implemented, the strategies that agents
use to defend their actual or potential position in social space and,
more generally, their image of themselves – always mediated by others
– are objectively adjusted to these conditions – which does not mean
that they necessarily correspond to the interests of their authors. For
example, the realistic, even resigned or fatalistic, dispositions which
lead members of the dominated classes to put up with objective
conditions that would be judged intolerable or revolting by agents
otherwise disposed can have the appearances of purposiveness only if
it is forgotten that, by a paradoxical counterfinality of adaptation to
reality, they help to reproduce the conditions of oppression.

Thus power (that is, capital, social energy) governs the potentialities
objectively offered to each player, her possibilities and impossibilities,
her degrees of empowerment, of power-to-be, and at the same time
her desire for power, which, being fundamentally realistic, is roughly
adjusted to the agent's actual empowerment. Early and lasting insertion into a condition defined by a particular degree of power tends,
through experience of the possibilities offered or denied by that condition, to institute durably in the body dispositions-to-be which are
(tendentially) proportioned to these potentialities. Habitus is this
'can-be' which tends to produce practices objectively adjusted to the
possibilities, in particular by orienting the perception and evaluation
of the possibilities inscribed in the present situation.

To understand the realism of this adjustment, one has to take
account of the fact that the automatic effects of the conditionings
imposed by the conditions of existence are added to by the directly
educative interventions of the family, the peer group and the agents
of the educational system (assessments, advice, injunctions, recom-
mendations), which expressly aim to favour the adjustment of aspirations to objective chances, needs to possibilities, the anticipation and
acceptance of the limits, both visible and invisible, explicit and tacit.
By discouraging aspirations oriented to unattainable goals, which are
thereby defined as illegitimate pretensions, these calls to order tend to
underline or anticipate the sanctions of necessity and to orientate
aspirations towards more realistic goals, more compatible with the
chances inscribed in the position occupied. The principle of all moral

education is thus set out: become what you are (and what you have to be) socially, do what you have to do, what is incumbent upon you – this is Plato's *ta autou prattein* – an 'ought to be' which may require a supersession of self ('noblesse oblige') or recall one to the limits of what is reasonable ('that's not for you').

Rites of institution, in which the social manipulation of aspirations is set out in full view because it is less masked than elsewhere by the functions of technical learning, are simply the limiting case of all the actions of suggestion, in the strong sense of the word, that the family tends to exercise. These solemn injunctions confer a collective and public form on an extra-ordinary performative act of institution (of the boy as a boy, for example, in the case of circumcision) which condenses into a discontinuous act of great social intensity all the continuous, infinitesimal and often unnoticed actions that every group exerts on its new members: I am thinking in particular of all the demands and taboos – those, for example, that are implied in all acts of nomination (terms of reference or terms of address) – which, whether implicit, insinuated or simply inscribed in the practical state in interactions, are addressed to the child and help to shape his representation of his (generic or individual) capacity to act, his value and social being.

Digression: Still more scholastic abstractions

It is only through an abstraction tending to prevent real understanding of the mechanisms involved that one can speak, as Weber does, of 'typical' or 'average' chances (which nonetheless has the merit of making explicit a number of the postulates that economic theory implicitly applies, especially when it posits that investments tend to be adjusted to the interest rates expected or really obtained in the previous period). To hypothesize that there is a relation of intelligible causality between the generic chances 'existing objectively on average' and 'subjective expectations'[14] is to presuppose, first, that one can set aside the differences between agents and the principles which determine them and, secondly, that agents act 'rationally' or 'judiciously', that is, by referring to what is 'objectively valid'[15] or as if they

[14] Cf. M. Weber, 'The logic of historical explanation', in *Max Weber: Selections in Translation*, ed. W. G. Runciman (Cambridge: Cambridge University Press, 1978), pp. 111–31.
[15] Ibid.

had known 'all the circumstances and all the intentions of those involved',[16] like the scientist, alone able to construct by calculation – and generally only after the event – the system of objective chances on which an action performed in full knowledge of the situation would have to align itself.

Weber's definition of rational action as the 'rational response' of an interchangeable, indeterminate agent to 'potential opportunities' – such as the average rates of profit offered by the various markets – seems to me to be a typical example of scholastic lack of realism. How can it be denied that agents are practically never in a position to gather all the information about the situation that a rational decision would require and that they are in any case very unequally endowed in this respect? To escape this objection, it is not sufficient to tinker with the inadequate paradigm by speaking, as Herbert Simon does, of 'bounded rationality', limited by the uncertain and imperfect nature of the available information and the limits of the calculating capacity of the human mind (again in general . . .), and by redefining the aim of maximizing profit as a quest for 'acceptable minima'.

Nor can one stop at the theory of 'rational anticipations', which, even if it seems at first sight closer to the facts because it posits the correspondence between anticipations and probabilities, remains unreal and abstract. Ignoring the fact that expectations and chances are unequally distributed and that this distribution corresponds to the unequal distribution of capital in its various forms, it unwittingly universalizes the particular case of the scientist, sufficiently removed from necessity to be able to confront rationally an economic world characterized by a high degree of correspondence between economic structures and dispositions. Similarly, although it is apparently very close to the theory of habitus as the product of conditionings predisposing the agent to react to conventional and conditional stimuli, the Bayesian theory of decision,[17] according to which probability can be interpreted as an individual 'rational degree of belief', attributes no lasting effect to 'conditionalization' (the assimilation of new information in the structure of belief).[18] It presupposes that the rational degrees of belief – subjective probabilities – attributed to different events change continuously (which is true) and completely (which is

---

[16] M. Weber, 'The nature of social action', in *Selections in Translation*, p. 9.

[17] Cf. P. Suppes, *La Logique du probable* (Paris: Flammarion, 1981). (Thomas Bayes, 1701–1761, was the author of 'Essay towards solving a problem in the doctrine of chances' (1763). *Trans.*)

[18] Cf. E. Ellis, *Rational Decision and Causality* (Cambridge: Cambridge University Press, 1982).

never entirely true) on the basis of new data. And while it is acknowledged that action depends on information and that this may not be
complete, that rational action encounters its limits in the limits of the
information available and that only well-informed rational action
deserves to be called 'prudential action', the fact remains that rational
action, understood as the action which makes the best consequences
the most probable ones, is conceived as the product of a *decision*
based on a *deliberation*, and therefore on examination of the possible
consequences of choosing the different possible courses of action and
on evaluation of the merits of the different courses of action in terms
of their consequences.

As ever, when faced with such constructions, one can only wonder
what status they should be given: is this a normative theory (how
should one decide?) or a descriptive theory (how do agents decide?).
Is it a rule in the sense of a regularity (it regularly happens that . . .)
or a rule in the sense of a norm (the rule is that . . .)? And to escape
from this, it is not sufficient to invoke the unconscious or a mysterious intuition: 'A commitment to coherence does not involve the agent
in abandoning his inarticulate skills of judgement and self-knowledge
in favour of conscious manipulation of a formal apparatus. . . . At its
best deliberation fits Dewey's description: "The laws of mechanics
underlie the skill of the cyclist who, at his best, is unconscious of
them; and just so, the logic of decision underlies the skill of the moral
agent who, at his best, is not conscious of it." '[19] Such explanations,
like an appeal to a 'dormitive power', explain nothing. But above all,
whereas, when he explicitly used the language of 'average chances',
Max Weber at least had the merit of tacitly taking account of the
inequality of chances, which he placed at the centre of his theory
of stratification, the typically scholastic theory of rational decision-
making ignores the inequalities of economic and cultural capital and
the inequalities which result from them, in the objective probabilities,
in beliefs and in the available information. In fact, strategies are not
abstract responses to an abstract situation, such as a state of the
labour market or an average rate of profit: they are defined in relation to promptings, inscribed in the objective world, in the form of
positive or negative indices which are not addressed to just anyone
but which only 'speak' (as opposed to what 'says nothing to them')
to agents characterized by possession of a certain capital and a certain habitus.

---

[19] R. C. Jeffrey, 'Ethics and the logic of decision', *Journal of Philosophy*, 62 (1965),
pp. 528–39 (quoting John Dewey, *Human Nature and Conduct* (New York: Random
House, 1930), p. 194).

A social experiment on time and power

Thus, social scientists regularly forget the economic and social conditions which make possible the ordinary order of practices, in particular those of the social world. Now, there exists, in the social world, a category, that of the subproletarians, which highlights these conditions by showing what happens when life is turned into a 'game of chance' (*qmar*), as an unemployed Algerian put it, and when the limited desire for power which is habitus in a sense capitulates before the more or less long-lasting experience of powerlessness. Just as, as psychologists have observed, the annihilation of chances associated with crisis situations leads to the collapse of psychological defences, so here it leads to a kind of generalized and lasting disorganization of behaviour and thought linked to the disappearance of any coherent vision of the future. Thus, better than any 'imaginary variations', this analyser requires one to break with the self-evidences of the ordinary order by bringing to light the presuppositions tacitly engaged in the view of the world (which are common to phenomenological analysis and the theorizations of rational action theory or Bayesianism.[20]

The often disorganized and even incoherent behaviours, constantly contradicted by their discourse, of these people without a future, living at the mercy of what each day brings and condemned to oscillate between fantasy and surrender, between flight into the imaginary and fatalistic surrender to the verdicts of the given, are evidence that, below a certain threshold of objective chances, the strategic disposition itself, which presupposes practical reference to a forth-coming, sometimes a very remote one, as in the case of family planning, cannot be constituted. The real ambition to control the future (and, *a fortiori*, the project of conceiving and rationally pursuing what the theory of rational anticipations calls 'subjective expected utility') varies with the real power to control that future, which means first of all having a grasp on the present itself. It follows that, far from contradicting the law of correspondence between structures and habitus, or between positions and dispositions, the dream-like ambitions and millenarian hopes that the most deprived sometimes express still testify that, in contrast to this imaginary demand, real demand has its basis and therefore also its limits in real power. When listening to subproletarians – unemployed Algerians in the 1960s or adolescents living without prospects on desolate housing estates in the 1990s – one discovers how the powerlessness that, by destroying potentialities,

[20] See above, p. 219, note 17. *Trans.*

prevents investment in social stakes engenders illusions. The link between the present and the future seems to be broken, as is shown by the projects they entertain, completely detached from the present and immediately belied by it: sending a daughter to university when it turns out that she has already abandoned school, or setting up a leisure centre in the Far East, when there is no money for travelling anywhere . . .[21]

In losing their work, the unemployed have also lost the countless tokens of a socially known and recognized *function*, in other words the whole set of goals posited in advance, independently of any conscious project, in the form of demands and commitments – 'important' meetings, cheques to post, invoices to draw up – and the whole forth-coming already given in the immediate present, in the form of deadlines, dates and timetables to be observed – buses to take, rates to maintain, targets to meet . . . Deprived of this objective universe of incitements and indications which orientate and stimulate action and, through it, social life, they can only experience the free time that is left to them as dead time, purposeless and meaningless. If time seems to be annihilated, this is because employment is the support, if not the source, of most interests, expectations, demands, hopes and investments in the present, and also in the future or the past that it implies, in short one of the major foundations of *illusio* in the sense of involvement in the game of life, in the present, the primordial investment which – as traditional wisdom has always taught, in identifying detachment from time with detachment from the world – creates time and indeed *is* time itself.

Excluded from the game, dispossessed of the vital illusion of having a function or a mission, of having to be or do something, these people may, in order to escape from the non-time of a life in which nothing happens and where there is nothing to expect, and in order to feel they exist, resort to activities which, like the French *tiercé*, or *totocalcio, jogo de bicho* or all the other lotteries or gambling systems of all the *bidonvilles* and *favelas* of the world, offer an escape from the negated time of a life without justification or possible investment, by recreating the temporal vector and reintroducing expectation, for a moment, until the end of the game or Sunday night, in other words finalized time, which is in itself a source of satisfaction. And, to try to escape from the sense, so well expressed by the Algerian

[21] P. Bourdieu, *Travail et travailleurs en Algérie* (Paris and The Hague: Mouton, 1964), pp. 352–62; *La Misère du monde* (Paris: Éditions de Minuit, 1993), pp. 607–11, tr. in Pierre Bourdieu, 'Those were the days', in *The Weight of the World* (Cambridge: Polity Press, 1999).

subproletarians, of being the plaything of external constraints ('I'm like a scrap of peel on water'), and to break out from a fatalistic submission to the forces of the world, the younger of them especially may also use acts of violence which in themselves count for more than, or as much as, the profits they procure, or death-defying games with cars or motor-bikes, as a desperate way of existing in the eyes of others, for others, of achieving a recognized form of social existence, or, quite simply, of making something happen rather than nothing.

Thus, the limiting-case experience of those who, like the subproletarians, are excluded from the ordinary (economic) world has the virtues of a kind of radical doubt: it forces one to raise the question of the economic and social conditions which make possible access to time as something so self-evident as to pass unnoticed. It is indeed certain that the scholastic experience which in its very principle involves a very particular relation to time, based on a fundamental freedom with respect to the ordinary logic of action, in no way aids understanding of different experiences of the world and of time, or understanding of itself, especially as regards temporality.

The extreme dispossession of the subproletarian – whether of working age or still in that ill-defined zone between schooling and unemployment or underemployment in which many working-class adolescents are kept, often for a rather long time – brings to light the self-evidence of the relationship between time and power, by showing that the practical relation to the forth-coming, in which the experience of time is generated, depends on power and the objective chances it opens. It can be confirmed statistically that investment in the forth-coming of the game presupposes a basic minimum of chances in the game, and therefore power over the game, over the present of the game; and that the aptitude to adjust behaviour in relation to the future is closely dependent on the effective chances of controlling the future that are inscribed in the present conditions. In short, adaptation to the tacit demands of the economic cosmos is only accessible to those who possess a certain minimum of economic and cultural capital, that is, a certain degree of power over the mechanisms that have to be mastered. It is all the more necessary to make this point because, in addition to the effect of the scholastic condition, which, like gravity, affects everything we think without becoming visible, there is the specific effect of public time. Being defined in mathematical or physical terms, this astronomical time is naturalized, dehistoricized, desocialized, becoming something external which flows 'of itself and by its nature', as Newton put it, and which thus helps to conceal the links between power and the possible under the appearances of the consensus that it helps to produce.

The plurality of times

In fact, really to break with the universalistic illusion fostered by analysis of essence (to which I have had to make some concessions in describing the temporal experience that I have contrasted with the intellectualist view of rational decision), one would need to describe the different ways of temporalizing oneself, relating them to their economic and social conditions of possibility. The empty time that has to be 'killed' is opposed to the full (or well-filled) time of the 'busy' person who, as we say, does not notice time passing – whereas, paradoxically, powerlessness, which breaks the relation of immersion in the imminent, makes one conscious of the passage of time, as when waiting. But it is equally opposed to *skholè*, time used freely for freely chosen, gratuitous ends which, for the intellectual or the artist, for example, may be those of work, but work that is freed, in its rhythm, moment and duration, from every external constraint and especially from the constraint imposed through direct monetary sanction. It was when the artist's life came to be invented, as a bohemian life, close to the life of the apprentice or student, that this loosely structured temporality was developed, which reverses night and day, without schedules or urgency (except what may be self-imposed), a relation to time embodied in the poetic disposition as a pure openness to the world which is in reality based on distance from the world and from all the mediocre concerns of the ordinary existence of ordinary people. And one could show, similarly, how the temporal assurances that are constitutive of the notion of career – a kind of Leibnizian essence containing the principle of the unfolding of a whole existence without drama and even without events – can favour the quite paradoxical experience of time that is authorized by university life, with, in particular, the blurring of the ordinary division between work and leisure: an exceptional experience, which can be set in relation to one of the most constant effects of the scholastic illusion, the bracketing of time – itself correlative with the tendency to transform the privation linked to exclusion from the world of practice into a cognitive privilege, with the myth of the 'impartial spectator', or the 'outsider' according to Simmel, who are exclusive beneficiaries of access to the point of view on points of view which opens perspectives on the game as a game.

Compared to these quasi-free times, or the negated time of subproletarians, experiences as different as those of the factory worker, the café waiter or the overworked executive have something in common: as well as some general conditions, already mentioned, such as the existence of constant tendencies of the economic and social order

in which one is inserted and on which one can count, there are particular conditions, such as the fact of having stable employment and
of occupying a social position implying an assured future, possibly a
career in the sense of a predictable trajectory. This set of assurances
and guarantees, which are hidden from view by their very effects, are
the necessary condition for the constitution of the stable, orderly
relation to the future which underlies so-called 'reasonable' behaviours, including those aiming at a more or less radical transformation
of the established order. Possession of the necessary minimum of
assurances concerning the present and the future, which are inscribed
in the fact of having a permanent job and the associated security, is
what provides such agents with the dispositions needed to confront
the future actively, either by entering into the game with aspirations
roughly adjusted to their chances, or even by trying to control it, on
an individual level, with a life plan, or on a collective level with a
reformist or revolutionary project, fundamentally different from an
explosion of millenarian revolt.[22]

When powers are unequally distributed, the economic and social
world presents itself not as a universe of possibles equally accessible
to every possible subject – posts to be occupied, courses to be taken,
markets to be won, goods to be consumed, properties to be exchanged
– but rather as a signposted universe, full of injunctions and pro-
hibitions, signs of appropriation and exclusion, obligatory routes or
impassable barriers, and, in a word, profoundly differentiated, especially according to the degree to which it offers stable chances, capable
of favouring and fulfilling stable expectations. Capital in its various
forms is a set of pre-emptive rights over the future; it guarantees
some people the monopoly of some possibles although they are officially guaranteed to all (such as the right to education). The exclusive
rights consecrated by law are only the visible, explicitly guaranteed
form of this set of appropriated chances and pre-empted possibles,
which are thereby converted, for others, into *de jure* exclusions or *de
facto* impossibilities, through which present power relations are projected into the future, orienting present dispositions in return.

Thus, even if the description of temporal experience as immediate
investment in the forth-coming of the world is true for all those who,
unlike the subproletarians, are busy in the world because they have
business in the world, who engage with the forth-coming [*l'à venir*]

---

[22] I will not repeat here the analysis I have made of the difference, in all areas of
practice and especially in the relation to politics, between those who can be called
subproletarians (casual workers, the unemployed) and workers with stable employment (cf. P. Bourdieu, *Travail et travailleurs en Algérie*, and *Algeria 1960* (Cambridge: Cambridge University Press, 1979)).

because they have a future [*un avenir*] in it, it remains clear that it is specified according to the form and degree of the urgency with which the necessities of the world impose themselves. Power over the objective chances governs aspirations, and therefore the relation to the future. The more power one has over the world, the more one has aspirations that are adjusted to their chances of realization, and also stable and little affected by symbolic manipulation. Below a certain level, on the other hand, aspirations burgeon, detached from reality and sometimes a little crazy, as if, when nothing was possible, everything became possible, as if all discourses about the future – prophecies, divinations, predictions, millenarian announcements – had no other purpose than to fill what is no doubt one of the most painful of wants: the lack of a future.

In contrast to subproletarians, who, since their time is not worth anything, have a deficit of goods and an excess of time, overworked executives have an excess of goods and an extraordinary lack of time. The former have time to give away, and they often 'squander' it in the tinkering, inventive to the point of absurdity, that they indulge in so as to prolong the life of objects or to produce the ingenious substitutes for manufactured goods that can be seen in the streets or in the markets of many poor countries. The latter, by contrast, are, paradoxically, always short of time, condemned to live permanently in the *askholia*, the hurry, which Plato opposed to philosophical *skholè*, and overwhelmed by goods and services which exceed their capacity to consume them and which they 'squander', in particular by economizing on the effort of maintenance and repair. If this is the case, it is because they have so many and such profitable opportunities to invest, by virtue of the economic and symbolic value of their time (and of themselves) in the various markets, that they acquire a practical sense of the rarity of time which orients all their experience.

The rarity of a person's time, and therefore the value set on his or her time, and more especially on the time he or she *gives*, which is the most precious, because most personal, gift – no one can do it in one's place, and to give one's time is a truly 'personal' act – is a fundamental dimension of the social value of that person. This value is constantly underlined on the one hand through solicitations, expectations and requests, and on the other hand through what is received in return, such as, of course, the price set on labour time, but also symbolic services such as marks of *eager attentiveness* [*empressement*], the form of deference reserved for 'important' people, who are known to be in a hurry [*pressés*] and to regard their time as precious.

The effects of the increase in the rarity and value of time which accompanies the rise in the price of labour (itself linked to the growth of productivity) are intensified by one of the direct effects of the resulting increase in profits, namely the increased possibilities offered to consumption (of goods and services) which also takes time, reaching its limit in the biological impossibility of consuming everything. The paradox of the overwork of the privileged thus finds its explanation: the more economic and cultural capital increases, the greater the chances of succeeding in the social games and, consequently, the more the propensity to invest time and energy in this also increases, and the harder it becomes to contain all the possibilities of material or symbolic production or consumption within the limits of a biologically non-extensible time.

This model also provides a very simple explanation of a number of social changes which conservative philosophies attribute to various forms of moral decline, such as the disappearance of the 'Heideggerian' lifestyle of the old peasantry, with their 'hand-crafted' products and their measured use of speech, or the withering away of a whole system of social exchanges based on the art of giving time – to children, old people, neighbours, workmates, friends, etc. – rather than goods or even, when it is simpler and more expeditious, money.[23] The effort devoted to the upkeep of enchanted relationships, between equals or even between unequals, because it presupposes a considerable expenditure of time – the expense needed to bind and 'hold' someone durably, with feelings of affection, recognition, gratitude, fraternity, etc. – can only decline as the price of time rises, throughout the society or in a particular category (and as more economical ways develop of creating durable relationships, such as economic constraint or contracts). And those who speak of a 'return to individualism' as if this were an inevitability, a fashion or an elective and universal break with a detestable 'collectivism' might look to the rise in available resources to find the source of the progressive decline in a number of practical and traditional solidarities and cooperative or collective arrangements for the sharing of goods or services which is seen to occur (other things being equal) as the resources (especially monetary ones) of individuals and groups increase.

Time and power

Power can be exerted on the objective tendencies of the social world, those which are measured by objective probabilities, and, consequently, on subjective aspirations or expectations. It is often forgotten, because it is so self-evident, that temporal power is a power to perpetuate or transform the distributions of the various forms of capital by

[23] V. Zelizer, *The Meaning of Money* (New York: Basic Books, 1994).

maintaining or transforming the principles of redistribution. A world founded on stable principles of redistribution is a predictable world that one can count on, even in its risks. By contrast, absolute arbitrariness is the power to make the world arbitrary, mad (with for example the racist violence of Nazism, the limiting case of which is the concentration camp, where everything becomes possible); total unpredictability creates a context favouring every form of manipulation of aspirations (such as rumours), and the total disconcerting of anticipations that it induces favours strategies of despair (such as terrorism) which deviate, by excess or shortfall, from the reasonable behaviours of the ordinary order.

Absolute power is the power to make oneself unpredictable and deny other people any reasonable anticipation, to place them in total uncertainty by offering no scope to their capacity to predict. This power, an extreme that is never reached except in the theological imagination, with the unjust omnipotence of a wicked God, frees its possessor from the experience of time as powerlessness. The all-powerful is he who does not wait but who makes others wait.

Waiting is one of the privileged ways of experiencing the effect of power, and the link between time and power – and one would need to catalogue, and analyse, all the behaviours associated with the exercise of power over other people's time both on the side of the powerful (adjourning, deferring, delaying, raising false hopes, or, conversely, rushing, taking by surprise) and on the side of the 'patient', as they say in the medical universe, one of the sites par excellence of anxious, powerless waiting. Waiting implies submission: the interested aiming at something greatly desired durably – that is to say, for the whole duration of the expectancy – modifies the behaviour of the person who 'hangs', as we say, on the awaited decision. It follows that the art of 'taking one's time', of 'letting time take its time', as Cervantes puts it, of making people wait, of delaying without destroying hope, of adjourning without totally disappointing, which would have the effect of killing the waiting itself, is an integral part of the exercise of power – especially in the case of powers which, like academic power, depend significantly on the belief of the 'patient' and which work on and through aspirations, on and through time, by controlling time and the rate of fulfilment of expectations ('he has time', 'he's young' or 'too young', or 'he can wait', is sometimes an academic verdict left to speak for itself): an art of 'turning down' without 'turning off', of keeping people 'motivated' without driving them to despair.[24]

[24] Cf. P. Bourdieu, *Homo Academicus* (Cambridge: Polity Press, 1988), pp. 87–105.

Kafka's *The Trial* can be read as the model of a social universe dominated by such an absolute and unpredictable power, capable of inducing extreme anxiety by condemning its victim to very strong investment combined with very great insecurity. Despite its extraordinary appearance, the social world described in that novel could be simply the limiting case of a number of ordinary states of the ordinary social world or of particular situations within this world, such as that of some stigmatized groups – Jews in the time and place of Kafka, blacks in the American ghettos, or the most helpless immigrants in many countries – or some social islands that are subjected to the absolute arbitrariness of a chief, big or small, and which are to be found, more often than one might think, in private and even public corporations. (Joachim Unseld's analysis,[25] which shows that the publisher, whose verdict is needed to enable a book to be published, that is to exist publicly, occupies within the process of literary production a position analogous to that of the judge, encourages one also to see *The Trial* as a very realistic model of the fields of cultural production, governed by powers which, like those of the university world, are based on a hold over other people's time.)

K. has been slandered. At first, he carries on as if nothing had happened; then he begins to worry, and he takes a lawyer. He enters into the game, and therefore into time, into waiting and anxiety. This game is characterized by a very high degree of unpredictability: nothing at all can be relied on. The tacit contract of continuity, self-constancy, the same one which, in Cartesian theology, is guaranteed by the truthful God, is suspended. There is neither security nor objective assurance, therefore no subjective assurance, nothing to entrust oneself to. Anything can be expected; the worst is never ruled out. It is no accident that the institution ordinarily mandated to limit arbitrariness, the court, is here the site par excellence of an arbitrariness which proclaims itself as such and does not even pretend to be anything else. For example, it complains that others are late when it itself is always late, flouting the principle that a rule also applies to the person who lays it down, the tacit foundation of any universal norm. In short, it makes arbitrariness, and therefore randomness, a principle of the order of things.

Absolute power has no rules, or rather its rule is to have no rules – or, worse, to change the rules after each move, or whenever it pleases, according to its interests: heads I win, tails you lose. In contrast to the bank, the site of reasonable and effective activity, whose procedures

[25] J. Unseld, *Franz Kafka, ein Schriftstellerleben: die Geschichte seiner Veroffentlichungen* (Munich: C. Hanser, 1982).

are methodically organized in relation to clearly defined ends, the court functions in a totally random way, as regards both its procedures and its effects: it convenes whenever it likes and does whatever it wants; like the members of the bank, its members have only generic names, but in their case, the use of their names is taboo, and when K. asks Titorelli the name of the judge he is painting, he replies that he is 'not authorized to say'.

Faced with this instituted disorder, what can K. do as, having been at first fairly indifferent, he gradually becomes caught up in the game and discovers its extreme uncertainty? The lawyer, like most of the other characters, is someone who, on the grounds of his supposed mastery of the game, manipulates K.'s hopes and expectations, soothing him with vague hopes and tormenting him with vague threats. (Reduced in this way to schematic form, the lawyer appears as the paradigm of a very large class of agents who, like the long-standing inmates and staff of all total institutions – boarding schools, prisons, asylums, barracks, factories, concentration camps – or, more generally, all the informed intermediaries who, in the name of a supposed familiarity with a powerful and worrying institution – school, hospital, bureaucracy, etc. – can exert a hold and an influence proportionate to the anxiety felt by the 'patient', blowing hot and cold, alternately worrying and reassuring, and so intensifying the investment in the game and the incorporation of the immanent structures of the game.)

In the extreme situations where uncertainty and investment are simultaneously maximized, because, as in a despotic regime or a concentration camp, there are no longer any limits to arbitrariness and unpredictability, all the ultimate stakes, including life and death, are brought into play at every moment: everyone is exposed without defence (like K., or like the members of the subproletariat) to the most brutal forms of manipulation of their fears and expectations. The power to act on time, through the power to modify the objective chances (for example, with measures that may cancel out or reduce the chances of a whole category of persons such as a currency devaluation, or the imposition of a quota, or age limits – or any other decision aimed at transforming 'socially expected durations', as Merton calls them[26]), makes possible (and probable) a strategic exercise of power based on the direct manipulation of aspirations.

Outside of situations of absolute power, the games with time which can be played wherever there is power (between the publisher who

---

[26] R. Merton, 'Socially expected durations: a case study of concept formation in sociology', in W. Powell and R. Robbins (eds), *Consensus and Conflict* (New York: Free Press, 1984), pp. 262–83.

delays a decision on a manuscript and the author, between the thesis supervisor who delays a decision on the date of examination and the student, between the office manager and subordinates desperate for promotion, etc.) can only be set up with the (extorted) complicity of the victim and his investment in the game. A person can be durably 'held' (so that he can be made to wait, hope, etc.) only to the extent that he is invested in the game so that the complicity of his dispositions can in a sense be counted on.

Back to the relationship between expectations and chances

The 'causality of the probable' which tends to favour the adjustment of expectations to chances is no doubt one of the most powerful factors of conservation of the established order. On the one hand, it ensures the unconditional submission of the dominated to the established order that is implied in the doxic relation to the world, an immediate adherence which puts the most intolerable conditions of existence (from the point of view of a habitus constituted in other conditions) beyond questioning and challenge. On the other hand, it favours the acquisition of dispositions which, being adjusted to disadvantaged, declining positions, threatened with disappearance or overtaken by events, leave agents ill-prepared to face the demands of the social order, especially inasmuch as they encourage various forms of self-exploitation (I am thinking in particular of the sacrifices undertaken by the clerical workers or junior executives who have taken on enormous debts so as to become home-owners).[27]

The dominated are always more resigned than the populist mystique believes and even than might be suggested by simple observation of their conditions of existence – and above all by the organized expression of their demands, mediated by political and trade union spokespersons. Having adapted to the demands of the world which has made them what they are, they take for granted the greater part of their existence. Moreover, because even the harshest established order provides some advantages of order that are not lightly sacrificed, indignation, revolt and transgressions (in starting a strike, for example) are always difficult and painful and almost always extremely costly, both materially and psychologically.

And this is true, despite appearances, even of adolescents, who might be thought to be radically at odds with the social order, to

---

[27] Cf. P. Bourdieu et al., 'L'économie de la maison', *Actes de la Recherche en Sciences Sociales*, no. 81–2 (Mar. 1990).

judge from their attitude to their 'elders', whether at home, at school or in the factory.[28] Thus, while he rightly emphasizes the acts of resistance, often anarchic and close to delinquency, with which working-class adolescents fight against schooling, and also against their 'elders', and through them against working-class traditions and values, Paul Willis (whose work has been enrolled on the side of 'resistance', as the term opposed to 'reproduction', in one of those pairs of opposites beloved of scholastic thought) also describes the rigidity of this harsh world, dedicated to the cult of toughness and virility (women only exist there through men, and recognize their own subordination).[29] He shows clearly how this cult of male strength, the extreme form of which is the exaltation of 'lads' (another focus of populist mythology, especially as regards language), is based on the affirmation of a solid, stable, constant world, collectively guaranteed – by the gang or the group – and, above all, profoundly rooted in its own self-evidences and aggressive towards anything different. As is shown by a profoundly rigid mode of speech, which refuses abstraction in favour of the concrete and of common sense, emotionally supported and punctuated by striking images, *ad hominem* appeals and dramatizing expletives, and also by a whole ritual – stereotyped terms of address, nicknames, mock fights, nudging, etc. – this world-view is profoundly conformist, especially on points as essential as everything concerned with social hierarchies, and not only between the sexes. (And one could draw quite similar conclusions from studies – notably those by Loïc Wacquant[30] – of blacks in the American ghettos.) Revolt, when it is expressed, stops short at the limits of the immediate universe and, failing to go beyond insubordination, bravado in the face of authority or insults, it targets persons rather than structures.[31]

In order not to naturalize dispositions, one has to relate these durable ways of being (I am thinking for example of 'plain speaking' or the – very moving – gruffness of moments of intense emotion) to the conditions of their acquisition. Habitus of necessity operate as a

---

[28] M. Pialoux, 'Jeunes sans avenir et travail intérimaire', *Actes de la Recherche en Sciences Sociales*, no. 26–7 (1979), pp. 19–47.

[29] P. E. Willis, *Profane Culture* (London: Routledge and Kegan Paul, 1978) and *Learning to Labour: How Working Class Kids Get Working Class Jobs* (Aldershot: Ashgate, 1977).

[30] Cf. L. Wacquant, 'The Zone: le métier de "hustler" dans le ghetto noir américain', *Actes de la Recherche en Sciences Sociales*, no. 93 (June 1992), pp. 50–61 (see also 'Inside "The Zone": the social art of the hustler in the American ghetto', in Bourdieu et al., *The Weight of the World*).

[31] Among the subproletarians of Algeria, I observed the same inclination to denounce or condemn persons rather than institutions or mechanisms.

defence mechanism against necessity, which tends, paradoxically, to escape the rigours of necessity by anticipating it and so contributing to its efficacy. Being the product of a learning process imposed by the sanctions or injunctions of a social order acting also as a moral order, these profoundly realist dispositions (close sometimes to fatalism) tend to reduce the dissonances between expectations and outcomes by performing a more or less total closure of horizons. Resignation is indeed the commonest effect of that form of 'learning by doing' which is the teaching performed by the order of things itself, in the unmediated encounter with social nature (particularly in the form of the sanctions of the educational market and the labour market), next to which the intentional actions of domestication performed by all the 'ideological State apparatuses' are of little weight.

And the populist illusion which is nowadays nourished by a simplistic rhetoric of 'resistance' tends to conceal one of the most tragic effects of the condition of the dominated – the inclination to violence that is engendered by early and constant exposure to violence. There is a *law of the conservation of violence*, and all medical, sociological and psychological research shows that ill-treatment in childhood (in particular, beatings by parents) is significantly linked to increased chances of using violence against others in turn (often one's own companions in misfortune), through crime, sexual abuse and other forms of aggression, and also on oneself, especially through alcoholism and drug addiction. That is why, if we really want to reduce these forms of visible and visibly reprehensible violence, there is no other way than to reduce the overall quantity of violence which is neither noticed nor punished, the violence exerted every day in families, factories, workshops, banks, offices, police stations, prisons, even hospitals and schools, and which is, in the last analysis, the product of the 'inert violence' of economic structures and social mechanisms relayed by the active violence of people. The effects of symbolic violence, in particular that exerted against stigmatized populations, do not tend, as the lovers of humanist pastorals seem to believe, always to favour the emergence of successful realizations of the human ideal – even if, to stand up against the degradation imposed by degrading conditions, agents always find some defences, individual or collective, momentary or durable, being durably inscribed in habitus, such as irony, humour or what Alf Lüdtke calls *Eigensinn*, 'stubborn obstinacy', and so many other misunderstood forms of resistance.[32] (This is what makes it so difficult to talk about the dominated in an

---

[32] A. Lüdtke, 'Ouvriers, *Eigensinn* et politique dans l'Allemagne du XXe siècle', *Actes de la Recherche en Sciences Sociales*, no. 113 (June 1996), pp. 91–101.

accurate and realistic way without seeming either to crush them or exalt them, especially in the eyes of all the do-gooders who will be led by a disappointment or a surprise proportionate to their ignorance to see condemnations or celebrations in informed attempts to describe things as they are.)

A margin of freedom

But it would be wrong to conclude that the circle of expectations and chances cannot be broken. On the one hand, the generalization of access to education – and the consequent structural discrepancy between the qualifications attained, and therefore the positions hoped for, and the jobs actually obtained – and of occupational insecurity tends to multiply the situations of mismatch, which generate tensions and frustrations.[33] There will be no return to those social universes in which the quasi-perfect coincidence between objective tendencies and subjective expectations made the experience of the world a continuous interlocking of confirmed expectations. The lack of a future, previously reserved for the 'wretched of the earth', is an increasingly widespread, even modal experience. But there is also the relative autonomy of the symbolic order, which, in all circumstances and especially in periods in which expectations and chances fall out of line, can leave a margin of freedom for political action aimed at reopening the space of possibles. Symbolic power, which can manipulate hopes and expectations, especially through a more or less inspired and uplifting performative evocation of the future – prophesy, forecast or prediction – can introduce a degree of play into the correspondence between expectations and chances and open up a space of freedom through the more or less voluntarist positing of more or less improbable possibles – utopia, project, programme or plan – which the pure logic of probabilities would lead one to regard as practically excluded.

The force of the process of incorporation which tends to constitute habitus as an *esse in futuro*, a durable principle of durable investments, reinforced by the explicit and express interventions of pedagogic action, is no doubt such that even the most subversive symbolic actions, if they are not to condemn themselves to failure, must reckon with dispositions, and with the limitations these impose on innovative

---

[33] Cf. P. Bourdieu, *Distinction* (Cambridge: Harvard University Press, 1984), pp. 99–168.

imagination and action. They can succeed only to the extent that – acting as symbolic triggers capable of legitimating and ratifying senses of unease and diffused discontents, socially instituted desires that are more or less confused, by making them explicit and public – they manage to reactivate dispositions which previous processes of inculcation have deposited in people's bodies.

But to observe that symbolic power can only operate to the extent that the conditions of its efficacy are inscribed in the very structures that it seeks to conserve or to transform is not to deny it all independence with respect to these structures. By bringing diffuse experiences to the full existence of 'publication' and consequent officialization, this power of expression and manifestation intervenes in that uncertain site of social existence where practice is converted into signs, symbols, discourses, and it introduces a margin of freedom between the objective chances, or the implicit dispositions that are tacitly adjusted to them, and *explicit aspirations*, people's representations and manifestations.

This is a site of twofold uncertainty: *a parte objecti*, on the side of the world, whose meaning, because it remains open, like the future on which it depends, lends itself to several interpretations; and *a parte subjecti*, on the side of the agents, whose sense of the game can express itself or be expressed in various ways or recognize itself in various expressions. This margin of freedom is the basis of the autonomy of struggles over the sense of the social world, its meaning and orientation, its present and its future, one of the major stakes in symbolic struggles. The belief that this or that future, either desired or feared, is possible, probable or inevitable can, in some historical conditions, mobilize a group around it and so help to favour or prevent the coming of that future.

Whereas heresy (the word itself, containing the idea of choice, implies this) and all forms of critical prophesy tend to open up the future, orthodoxy, the discourse of the maintenance of the symbolic order, works, as is clearly seen in the periods of restoration which follow crises, in a sense to stop time, or history, by closing down the range of possibles so as to try to induce the belief that 'the chips are down' for ever, and, passing off a performative as a constative, by announcing the end of history, a reassuring inversion of all millenarian utopias. (This kind of fatalism may take the form of a sociologism which constitutes sociological laws as quasi-natural iron laws or an essentialist pessimism based on belief in an immutable human nature.)

These symbolic actions merely redouble all the operations, often entrusted to rituals, which aim to inscribe the future in people's bodies, in the form of habitus. We know that a central place is everywhere given to the rites of institution through which groups, or more precisely, (corporate) bodies aim to imprint, very early in life and for the whole of life, an irrevocable pact of immediate subscription to their demands, in the bodies of those whom they institute, often for life, as recognized members. These rites, which, for the most part, merely reinforce the automatic action of the structures, almost always play on the relation to time and seek to create the aspiration to be integrated by making the candidate wait and hope for it. In addition, by solemnly investing him with a right and a dignity, they incite the beneficiary of this exceptional treatment (even in the sometimes extreme suffering it entails) to place all his psychological energy in this dignity, right or power, or to show himself worthy of the dignity conferred by the investiture ('noblesse oblige'). In other words, they guarantee a durable social status (*dignitas*) in exchange for the durable commitment – symbolized by the rituals of *inceptio*, incorporation (in all senses of the word) – to assume in a worthy fashion the explicit and often implicit obligations of that status (the best guarantee of which is of course the appropriate habitus, the very one which the operations of co-option are designed to detect).

But the dependence of all effective symbolic action on pre-existing dispositions is also visible in the discourses or actions of subversion, which, like provocations and all forms of iconoclasm,[34] have the function and in any case the effect of showing in practice that it is possible to transgress the limits imposed, in particular the most inflexible ones, those which are set in people's minds. This can be the case in so far as, attentive to the real chances of transforming the power relation, they are able to work to raise expectations beyond the objective chances on which they spontaneously tend to be aligned, but without pushing them beyond the threshold where they would become unreal and foolhardy. The symbolic transgression of a social frontier has a liberatory effect in its own right because it enacts the unthinkable. But it is itself possible, and symbolically effective, instead of being simply rejected as a scandal which rebounds on its author, only if certain objective conditions are fulfilled. In order for an utterance or action (iconoclasm, terrorism, etc.) aimed at challenging the objective structures to have some chance of being recognized as legitimate (if not reasonable) and to be seen as exemplary, the structures that are contested must themselves be in a state of uncertainty and crisis that favours uncertainty about them and an awakening of critical consciousness of their arbitrariness and fragility.

---

[34] Cf. O. Christin, *Une Révolution symbolique. L'iconoclasme huguenot et la reconstruction catholique* (Paris: Éditions de Minuit, 1991).

The question of justification

We must go back to K. His uncertainty about the future is simply another form of uncertainty about what he is, his social being, his 'identity', as one would say nowadays. Dispossessed of the power to give sense, in both senses, to his life, to state the meaning and direction of his existence, he is condemned to live in a time orientated by others, an alienated time. This is, very exactly, the fate of all the dominated, who are obliged to wait for everything to come from others, from the holders of power over the game and over the objective and subjective prospect of gain that it can offer, being therefore masters at playing on the anxiety that inevitably arises from the tension between the intensity of the expectancy and the improbability of its being satisfied.

But what truly is the stake in this game, if not the question of *raison d'être*, the justification, not of human existence in its universality, but of a particular, singular existence, which finds itself called into question in its social being – through the initial slander, a kind of original sin without an origin, like the racist stigma? It is the question of the *legitimacy* of an existence, an individual's right to *feel justified in existing as he or she exists*; and this question is inseparably eschatological and sociological.

No one can really proclaim, either to others or, above all, to himself, that 'he dispenses with all justification'. And if God is dead, who can be asked to provide this justification? It has to be sought in the judgement of others, this major principle of uncertainty and insecurity, but also, and without contradiction, of certainty, assurance, consecration. No author – except perhaps Proust, but in a less tragic register – has better evoked than Kafka the confrontation of irreconcilable points of view, particular judgements aspiring to universality, the endless clash of suspicion and denial, backbiting and praise, slander and rehabilitation, a terrible parlour game in which the verdict of the social world is hammered out as the inexorable product of the multifarious judgement of others.

In this 'truth game' of which *The Trial* offers the model, Joseph K., innocent but slandered, struggles to reach the point of view on points of view, the highest court, the last instance. One remembers the moment where Block explains to him that the lawyer who is defending them both is wrong to call himself one of the 'great advocates': 'Anyone can naturally call himself great if it pleases him, but in this case it is the custom of the court which decides.' And the question of the *verdict*, the judgement solemnly pronounced by an authority capable of saying of each what he or she truly is, returns at the end of the novel, in K.'s last questionings: 'Where was the judge that he had never seen? Where was the high court that he had never reached?'

What game is more vital, more total, than the symbolic struggle of all against all in which what is at stake is the power of *naming*, or categorization, in which everyone stakes his being, his value, the idea he has of himself? It may be objected that nothing forces people to enter the race, that one has to join in the game in order to have some chance of being caught up in it. As can be seen from K.'s relationship with each of his informants, the lawyer, the painter, the merchant and the priest, who are also intercessors, and who try to exercise power over him by making him believe that they have power and by using their presumed connections to encourage him to carry on when he threatens to give up, the mechanism can only work in the relationship between an expectation, an anxiety, and the objective uncertainty of the desired or feared future. As if his main function were not to defend K. but to drive him to *invest* in his trial, the lawyer endeavours to 'soothe him with vague hopes and torment him with vague fears'. If hope or fear, associated with objective and subjective uncertainty as to the outcome of the game, are the precondition for commitment to the game, then Block is the ideal client for the judicial institution: 'A person can't start a sentence without you looking at them as if they were about to pronounce your final verdict.' He is so attuned to the game that he anticipates the sanctions of the judge. The absolute recognition that he gives it is the basis of the absolute power that the institution has over him. Likewise, K. is in the grip of the apparatus of justice only in so far as he *takes an interest* in his trial, actually cares about it. When he withdraws the task of defending him from his lawyer, he frustrates the strategies through which the latter sought to encourage his investment in the game and his dependence upon him.

But while it is right to recall that the court derives its power from the recognition it is given, there is no question of suggesting that one can escape from the games in which symbolic life and death are at stake. As in *The Trial*, where the slander is present from the first phase, the most categorical categoremes are there, from the beginning, from entry into life, which – and Kafka, a Jew in Prague, knew this well – starts with an assignment of identity designating a category, a class, an ethnic group, a sex or, for racist eyes, a 'race'. The social world is essentialist, and one has that much less chance of escaping the manipulation of aspirations and subjective expectations when one is symbolically more deprived, less consecrated or more stigmatized, and therefore less well placed in the competition for the 'esteem of men', as Pascal put it, and condemned to uncertainty as to one's present and future social being, which vary with one's power or impotence. With investment in a game and the recognition that can come from cooperative competition with others, the social world offers humans that which they most totally lack: a justification for existing.

Indeed, is it possible to understand the almost universal seduction of the symbolic baubles – decorations, medals, palms or ribbons – and the acts of consecration they mark or perpetuate, or even the most ordinary supports of investment in the social game – mandates or missions, ministries or magistracies – without taking note of an anthropological datum which our habits of thought tend to consign to the metaphysical, namely the contingency of human existence, and above all its finitude, of which Pascal observes that, although it is the only certain thing in life, we do everything we can to forget it, by flinging ourselves into diversion or fleeing into 'society': 'We are fools to depend upon the society of our fellow-men. Wretched as we are, powerless as we are, they will not aid us; we shall die alone. We should therefore act as if we were alone, and in that case should we build fine houses, etc.? We should seek the truth without hesitation; and, if we refuse it, we show that we value the esteem of men more than the search for truth.'[35]

So, without indulging in the existential exaltation of '*Sein-zum-Tode*', one can establish a necessary link between three indisputable and inseparable anthropological facts: man is and knows he is mortal, the thought that he is going to die is unbearable or impossible for him, and, condemned to death, an end (in the sense of *termination*) which cannot be taken as an end (in the sense of a *goal*), since it represents, as Heidegger put it, 'the possibility of impossibility', he is a being without a reason for being, haunted by the need for justification, legitimation, recognition. And, as Pascal suggests, in this quest for justifications for existing, what he calls 'the world', or 'society', is the only recourse other than God.[36]

One understands, armed with this equivalence, that what Pascal describes as the 'wretchedness of man without God', that is, without a reason for being, is sociologically attested in the form of the truly metaphysical wretchedness of men and women who have no social *raison d'être*, abandoned to the insignificance of an existence without necessity, abandoned to its absurdity. And one also understands,

---

[35] Pascal, *Pensées*, 211.
[36] That is why, speaking as a moralist, he describes worldly consolations or consecrations as a fallacious refuge against abandonment and solitude and as a ruse of bad faith to avoid a resolute confrontation with the human condition.

a contrario, the quasi-divine power of rescuing people from contingency and gratuitousness that is possessed, whether one likes it or
not, by the social world, and which is exercised in particular through
the institution of the State: as the central bank of symbolic capital,
the State is able to confer that form of capital whose particularity is
that it contains its own justification.

Symbolic capital

Through the social games it offers, the social world provides something more and other than the apparent stakes: the chase, Pascal reminds us, counts as much as, if not more than, the quarry, and there
is a happiness in activity which exceeds the visible profits – wage,
prize or reward – and which consists in the fact of emerging from
indifference (or depression), being occupied, projected towards goals,
and feeling oneself objectively, and therefore subjectively, endowed
with a social mission. To be expected, solicited, overwhelmed with
obligations and commitments is not only to be snatched from solitude
or insignificance, but also to experience, in the most continuous and
concrete way, the feeling of counting for others, being *important* for
them, and therefore in oneself, and finding in the permanent plebiscite
of testimonies of interest – requests, expectation, invitations – a kind
of continuous justification for existing.

But, to bring to light, perhaps less negatively and more convinc-
ingly, the effect of consecration, capable of rescuing one from the
sense of the insignificance and contingency of an existence without
necessity, one could, rereading Durkheim's *Suicide*[37] – in which he
pursues his scientist faith to the point of excluding the question of
the *raison d'être* of an act which raises, in the highest degree, the
question of reasons for existing – observe that the propensity to commit suicide varies inversely with recognized social importance and
that the more that agents are endowed with a consecrated social
identity, that of husband, parent, etc., the more they are protected
against a questioning of the sense of their existence (that is, the married more than the single, the married with children more than the
married without children, etc.). The social world gives what is rarest,
recognition, consideration, in other words, quite simply, reasons for
being. It is capable of giving meaning to life, and to death itself, by
consecrating it as the supreme sacrifice.

---

[37] É. Durkheim, *Suicide: A Study in Sociology* (London: Routledge and Kegan Paul,
1952).

One of the most unequal of all distributions, and probably, in any case, the most cruel, is the distribution of symbolic capital, that is, of social importance and of reasons for living. And it is known, for example, that even the treatment and care that hospital institutions and agents give to the dying are varied, more unconsciously than consciously, according to their social importance.[38] In the hierarchy of worth and unworthiness, which can never be perfectly super-imposed on the hierarchy of wealth and powers, the nobleman, in his traditional variant, or in his modern form – what I call the State nobility – is opposed to the stigmatized pariah who, like the Jew in Kafka's time, or, now, the black in the ghetto or the Arab or Turk in the working-class suburbs of European cities, bears the curse of a negative symbolic capital. All the manifestations of social recognition which make up symbolic capital, all the forms of perceived being which make up a social being that is known, 'visible', famous, ad-mired, invited, loved, etc. are so many manifestations of the grace (*charisma*) which saves those it touches from the distress of an exist-ence without justification and which gives them not only a 'theodicy of their own privilege', as Max Weber said of religion – which is in itself not negligible – but also a theodicy of their existence.

Conversely, there is no worse dispossession, no worse privation, perhaps, than that of the losers in the symbolic struggle for recogni-tion, for access to a socially recognized social being, in a word, to humanity. This struggle is not reducible to a Goffmanian battle to present a favourable representation of oneself: it is competition for a power that can only be won from others competing for the same power, a power over others that derives its existence from others, from their perception and appreciation (so that one does not have to choose between Hobbes' *homo homini lupus* and Spinoza's *homo homini Deus*), and therefore a power over a desire for power and over the object of this desire. Although it is the product of subjective acts of donation of meaning (not necessarily implying consciousness and representation), this symbolic power, charm, seduction, charisma, appears endowed with an objective reality, as if determining the gazes which produce it (like *fides* as described by Émile Benveniste or charisma as analysed by Max Weber, himself a victim of the effects of fetishization both of the transcendence arising from the aggrega-tion of gazes and above all of the concordance of objective structures and incorporated structures).

---

[38] Cf. B. G. Glaser and A. Strauss, *Awareness of Dying* (Chicago: Aldine, 1965), and *Time for Dying* (Chicago: Aldine, 1968).

Every kind of capital (economic, cultural, social) tends (to different degrees) to function as symbolic capital (so that it might be better to speak, in rigorous terms, of the *symbolic effects of capital*) when it obtains an explicit or practical recognition, that of a habitus structured according to the very structures of the space in which it has been engendered. In other words, symbolic capital (male honour in Mediterranean societies, the honourability of the *notable* or the Chinese mandarin, the prestige of the celebrated writer, etc.) is not a particular kind of capital but what every kind of capital becomes when it is misrecognized as capital, that is, as force, a power or capacity for (actual or potential) exploitation, and therefore recognized as legitimate. More precisely, capital exists and acts as symbolic capital (securing profits – as observed, for example in the maxim 'honesty is the best policy') in its relationship with a habitus predisposed to perceive it as a sign, and as a sign of importance, that is, to know and recognize it on the basis of cognitive structures able and inclined to grant it recognition because they are attuned to what it is. Produced by the transfiguration of a power relation into a sense relation, symbolic capital rescues agents from insignificance, the absence of importance and of meaning.

To be known and recognized also means possessing the power to recognize, to consecrate, to state, with success, what merits being known and recognized, and, more generally to say what is, or rather what is to be thought about what is, through a performative act of speech (or prediction) capable of making what is spoken of conform to what is spoken of it (a power of which the bureaucratic variant is the legal act and the charismatic variant is the prophetic pronouncement). Rites of institution, acts of symbolic investiture intended to justify the consecrated being in being what it is, existing as it exists, literally *make* the person to whom they are applied by raising him or her from illegal exercise, the delirious fiction of the imposter (the limiting case of which is the madman who thinks he is Napoleon) or the arbitrary imposition of the usurper. This it does by declaring publicly that he is indeed what he claims to be, that he is legitimated to be what he claims, that he is entitled to enter into the function, fiction or imposture which, being proclaimed before the eyes of all as deserving to be universally recognized, becomes a 'legitimate imposture', in Austin's phrase,[39] in other words *misrecognized*, denied as an imposture by all, not least by the imposter himself.

In solemnly imposing the name or title which defines him in an inaugural ceremony of enthronement – the *inceptio* of a medieval

[39] J. L. Austin, *How to Do Things with Words* (Oxford: Clarendon Press, 1975).

master, the ordination of a priest, the dubbing of a knight, the crowning of a king, an inaugural lecture, the opening session of a court, etc., or, in a quite different order of things, circumcision or marriage – these acts of performative magic both enable and require the recipient to become what he is, that is, what he has to be, to enter, body and soul, into his function, in other words into his *social fiction*, to take on the social image or essence that is conferred on him in the form of names, titles, degrees, posts or honours, and to incarnate it as a legal person, the ordinary or extraordinary member of a group, which he also helps to make exist by giving it an exemplary incarnation.

Despite its apparent impersonality, the rite of institution is always highly personal. It must be performed in person, in the presence of the person (barring an extraordinary exception, attendance at a consecration ceremony cannot be delegated), and the person who is installed in the dignity, of which it is said that it cannot die (*dignitas non moritur*), to signify that it will survive the body of its holder, must indeed assume it in his whole being, that is, with his body, in fear and trembling, in preparatory suffering or painful test. He must be personally invested in his investiture, that is, engage his devotion, his belief, his body, give them as pledges, and manifest, in all his conduct and his speech – this is the function of the ritual words of recognition – his faith in the office and in the group which awards it and which confers this great *assurance* only on condition that it is fully assured in return. This guaranteed identity requires its recipient to give in return guarantees of identity ('noblesse oblige'), of conformity to the social being which the social definition is supposed to produce and which must be maintained by an individual and collective work of representation aimed at making the group exist as a group, at producing it by making it known and recognized.

In other words, the rite of investiture is there to reassure the recipient as to his existence as a full member of the group, his legitimacy, but also to reassure the group as to its own existence as a consecrated group, capable of consecrating, and as to the reality of the social fictions – names, titles, honours – which it produces and reproduces and which the recipient causes to exist by consenting to receive them. The representation, through which the group *produces itself*, can only fall to agents who, being called upon to symbolize the group that they represent in the theatrical sense but also in the legal sense, as proxies endowed with *procuratio ad omnia facienda*, must be committed bodily and give the guarantee of a habitus naively invested in an unconditional belief. (By contrast, a reflexive disposition, particularly towards the ritual of investiture and what it institutes, would constitute a threat to the successful circulation of symbolic power and authority, or even a kind of misappropriation of symbolic capital to the benefit of an irresponsible and alarming subjectivity.)[40] As biological persons, plenipotentiaries, proxies, delegates and spokespersons are subject to sickness and passion, and mortal. As representatives, they partake of the eternity and ubiquity of the group which they help to make exist as permanent, omnipresent and transcendent, and which they temporarily incarnate, giving it voice through their mouths and representing it in their bodies, converted into symbols and emblems to rally around.

As Eric Santner shows with reference to the case, made famous by Freud's analysis, of President Daniel Paul Schreber, who fell into a paranoid delirium when appointed in June 1893 as *Senatspräsident*, chairman of the third chamber of the Supreme Court of Appeal, the possibility, or threat, of crisis is always present, potentially, in inaugural moments when the arbitrariness of the institution may become apparent.[41] If this is so, it is because the appropriation of the function by the nominee is also appropriation of the nominee by the function: the nominee enters into possession of his function only if he consents to be possessed bodily by it, as is asked of him in the rite of investiture, which, by imposing the adoption of particular clothing – often a uniform – a particular language, itself standardized and stylized, like a uniform, and an appropriate body *hexis*, aims to fasten him durably to an impersonal manner of being and to manifest by this quasi-anonymization that he accepts the – sometimes exorbitant – sacrifice of his private person. It is no doubt because this appropriation by the heritage, the precondition of the right to inherit, is sensed in advance (or suddenly discovered, in the arbitrariness of the beginning) that it cannot be taken for granted. And the rites of institution are there, concentrating all the actions and words – countless, imperceptible and invisible, because they are often infinitesimal – which tend to recall each person to order, to the social being that the social order assigns to him or her ('she's your sister', 'you are the first-born'), that of a man or a woman, eldest son or younger son, and so to ensure the maintenance of the symbolic order by regulating the circulation of symbolic capital between the generations, first within the family and then within institutions of all kinds. By giving himself 'body and soul' to his function and, through it, to the *corporate body* which entrusts it – *universitas, collegium, societas*, as the canonists put it – the legitimate successor, whether dignitary or functionary, helps to

---

[40] Cf. P. Bourdieu, *Leçon sur la leçon* (Paris: Éditions de Minuit, 1982).
[41] E. L. Santner, *My Own Private Germany: Daniel Paul Schreber's Secret History of Modernity* (Princeton: Princeton University Press, 1996).

ensure the eternity of the function which pre-exists him and will outlive him, and of the mystic body which he incarnates and of which he partakes, partaking thereby of its eternity.

Rites of institution give an enlarged and particularly visible image of the effect of the institution, an arbitrary being which has the power to rescue from arbitrariness, to confer the supreme *raison d'être*, the one constituted by the affirmation that a contingent being, vulnerable to sickness, infirmity and death, is worthy of the dignity, transcendent and immortal, like the social order, that he is given. And acts of nomination, from the most trivial acts of bureaucracy, like the issuing of an identity card, or a sickness or disablement certificate, to the most solemn, which consecrate nobilities, lead, in a kind of infinite regress, to that realization of God on earth, the State, which guarantees, in the last resort, the infinite series of acts of authority certifying by delegation the validity of the certificates of legitimate existence (as a sick or handicapped person, an *agrégé* or a priest). And sociology thus leads to a kind of theology of the last instance: invested, like Kafka's court, with an absolute power of truth-telling and creative perception, the State, like the divine *intuitus originarius* according to Kant, brings into existence by naming and distinguishing. Durkheim was, it can be seen, not so naive as is claimed when he said, as Kafka might have, that 'society is God'.

Subject Index

action and agency: attribution 148–9; bodily knowledge 138–42; collective action theory 156; discordant and improvised behaviours 159–63; habitus and dexterity 142–6; rational action theory 138–40, 156

action and agents: espousing the role 153–5; practical strategies 151

aesthetics: popular culture 75–6; universalism 73–7

agency *see* action and agency

Algeria 42, 70, 202; powerless subproletarians 221–3

anamnesis 24; history of philosophy 47; origins 115–18

anti-Semitism 72

art: aesthetic universalism 73–7; born of constraint 115, 116; evolution of symbolic process 20–1; habitus 100; labour 202; legitimation of power 105; point of view 22

attribution theory 148–9

auctor 47, 53

Augustine, Saint: credited with *cogito* 62

authenticity: philosopher's role 25–8

autobiography: 'ego history' 33–4

belief: deliberate 11–12

bodily knowledge 128–31; collectivization of individuals 155–9; discordant and improvised behaviours 159–63; emotions of submission 169–70, 180; espousing the role 153–5; habitus and dexterity of action 142–6; learning reasonable action 138–42; mind–body dualism 133; performing action 144; practical comprehension of the world 135–7, 142; practical sense of place 182–5; scholastic representation of action 137–8; situation in a place 131–4; social space 134–5; symbolic power of law 168–72; twofold naturalization 179–82

Name Index

CPSIA information can be obtained
at www.ICGtesting.com
Printed in the USA
LVHW111554141118
597116LV00002B/378/P

9 780804 733328